Winding It Back

Winding It Back

Teaching to Individual Differences in Music Classroom and Ensemble Settings

Edited by Alice M. Hammel,
Roberta Y. Hickox,
and
Ryan M. Hourigan

OXFORD
UNIVERSITY PRESS

OXFORD
UNIVERSITY PRESS

Oxford University Press is a department of the University of Oxford. It furthers
the University's objective of excellence in research, scholarship, and education
by publishing worldwide. Oxford is a registered trade mark of Oxford University
Press in the UK and certain other countries.

Published in the United States of America by Oxford University Press
198 Madison Avenue, New York, NY 10016, United States of America.

Library of Congress Cataloging-in-Publication Data
Names: Hammel, Alice, editor. | Hickox, Roberta Y., editor. | Hourigan, Ryan M., editor.
Title: Winding it back: teaching to individual differences in music classroom and ensemble
settings / edited by Alice M. Hammel, Roberta Y. Hickox, and Ryan M. Hourigan.
Description: Oxford; New York: Oxford University Press, [2016] | Includes bibliographical
references and index.
Identifiers: LCCN 2015027226| ISBN 9780190201616 (alk. paper) | ISBN 9780190201623
(alk. paper) | ISBN 9780190201630 (alk. paper) | ISBN 9780190201647 (alk. paper) |
ISBN 9780190201654 (alk. paper)
Subjects: LCSH: Music—Instruction and study. | Inclusive education.
Classification: LCC MT1 .W823 2016 | DDC 780.71—dc23LC record available at
http://lccn.loc.gov/2015027226

CONTENTS

ORGANIZATION OF CHAPTERS

This book addresses the concept of winding instruction to address the individual learning needs of all students. The application of its contents covers a wide span of ages, classroom settings, and diversity of students and is organized as follows:

Chapter 1: establishes a framework for the concept of winding and introduces the reader to the three teaching principles that link the various topics

Chapter 2: explores winding back, side, and forward with young children in an early childhood setting to promote musical, cognitive, and social development

Chapter 3: continues the concept of winding in the primary general music classroom in the skill areas of singing, movement, playing instruments, and melodic and rhythmic reading and writing

Chapter 4: utilizes winding of creative movement concepts for students of all ages and classroom settings

Chapter 5: surveys the topic of melody, continuing from the skills mastered in the primary grades, and provides an instructional sequence through which to apply winding techniques

Chapter 6: investigates the topic of rhythm, continuing from the skills mastered in the primary grades, and offers an instructional framework through which to implement winding techniques

Chapter 7: offers multiple access points for vocal creativity as a means of personal expression and a precursor to more formalized improvisation

Chapter 8: presents winding techniques as a means of leveling the playing field for older students from a variety of musical backgrounds and for those in choral ensemble settings

Chapter 9: suggests winding techniques to enhance student understanding of extensions of tonal knowledge in the study of scales,
intervals, partwork, and harmony

Chapter 10: examines the role of winding in instrumental settings
through moving, chanting, and singing

We hope you find the concept of winding easily applicable to your own
teaching situation; useful with students of all ages, musical backgrounds,
and classroom settings; and beneficial in honoring the learning differences
of students of all levels of ability.

Alice M. Hammel, Roberta Y. Hickox, and Ryan M. Hourigan
Collaborative Editors

Bruce R. Hammel
Companion Website Editor

ABOUT THE COMPANION WEBSITE

www.oup.com/us/windingitback

Username: Music2
Password: Book4416

Oxford has created a password-protected website to accompany *Winding It Back*. Material that cannot be made available in a book, namely, supplemental material for each chapter, video demonstrations, and all the songs referenced in the book, is provided here. The reader is encouraged to consult this resource in conjunction with each chapter. Examples available online are indicated in the text with Oxford's symbol ⊙.

Winding It Back

CHAPTER 1

Winding It Back

A Framework for Inclusive Music Education

ALICE M. HAMMEL, *James Madison University*
RYAN M. HOURIGAN, *Ball State University*

T'ASINA

T'asina had just begun her third year of teaching. Her middle school choral room was cheerfully decorated with inspiring posters, and her folder cabinet was clean and free of clutter. Her principal had asked if her choir could perform for a Veteran's Day ceremony in November, and she had already chosen the octavos she wanted to program for this event. The first few weeks of school flew by with meetings, student paperwork and permission forms, and the busy nature of the start of each year. By the end of September, T'asina began to worry about her upcoming performance. Many of her students this year seemed unprepared to read music, pay attention during rehearsals, and consistently sing on pitch. This seemed to happen each year as students from self-contained classrooms, those who were just beginning to learn English, and students who were unable to behave appropriately in other classes were included in her choir. T'asina began to think that her teaching goals and objectives were unattainable for some of her students. How could she possibly prepare them for the concert, find out which students needed extra help with singing and note reading, and create ways to improve her classroom management skills? She knew how to teach music, had excellent musicianship skills, and had graduated with honors in music education from her university. What was going wrong?

There are many reasons educators enter the teaching profession. Some feel called to the field as a mission or service, while others enter to achieve a relatively secure occupation status. Regardless of the path, each teacher becomes responsible for the preparation, presentation, and practice of the chosen subject matter for his or her students. Ultimately, all educators are held accountable for the effectiveness of their instruction and the success of all students. In reality, these assumptions can become cumbersome, unwieldy, and difficult to achieve, especially when attempting to meet the needs of all students.

Measures chosen to demonstrate progress through time may change with the advent of each new educational reform season. Moreover, the expectation that teachers will be successful with every student can become relatively unreasonable because success depends on the preparation that teacher has received, the diverse learners that inhabit his or her classroom, and the overarching administrative culture within a school system. Music educators must be prepared for ever-changing tides in school reform *and* demographics within their classrooms. This can only come with a solid pedagogical and theoretical framework for teaching music.

WINDING IT BACK: A FRAMEWORK FOR PEDAGOGY

The literature has many examples of theoretical perspectives that guide teachers toward an inclusive and individualized philosophy of teaching music. However, many teachers who choose to implement inclusive and individualized education practices have found that these resources provide limited assistance for long-term curricular creation, especially for ensuring equal access for all music students, including those with learning differences. The concept of a stellar single lesson and a binder full of great individual lessons is not as effective as a long-term scope and sequence designed to prepare and assess each music student in a holistic and developmentally appropriate manner.

In designing this project, we formulated an underlying framework for *winding it back* based on three research-informed best-practice principles.

Principle 1: Honoring the Individual Learning Needs of All Students

Students with learning differences often feel removed from instruction at both cognitive and social levels. Researchers in self-determination theory often describe this phenomenon as crucial to understanding student learning. Ryan and Deci (2000) state: "Human beings can be proactive and engaged or, alternatively, passive and alienated, largely as a function of the social conditions in which they develop and function" (p. 68). In music, much of our self-worth is determined by success. And our motivation to engage the subject (music) is determined by our self-worth. Therefore, the philosophy behind this text is to be constantly aware of a student's self-esteem and to provide as many opportunities for success as possible, honoring that all music learning is important. The final goal is to determine ways to encourage self-motivation and incremental goal setting based on the previous success of the individual. This self-motivation, we believe, cultivates self-worth and the future success of not only the individual but also groups of students.

The added benefit is that with each success, music educators feel more confident and able to teach students who learn differently and at a different pace. Research has shown this to be crucial to both pre-service and in-service music educators (Hammel and Gerrity, 2012; Hourigan, 2009).

Principle 2: Multiple Access Points and Learning Levels

Winding it back pedagogy provides multiple access points for all students at a variety of learning levels. Principle 2 has been widely influenced by *Universal Design for Learning* (Meyer, Rose, and Gordon, 2014). Universal design for learning (UDL) proposes that for students to be successful, they must be offered multiple means of engagement, representation, action, and expression. Within winding it back pedagogy, we offer one more step (in music): multiple points of access across a varied set of learning levels.

This is a different concept from other theoretical constructs such as UDL (Meyer et al., 2014), *spiral curriculum* (Bruner, 1960/1977), and *conditions of learning* (Gagne and Medsker, 1996). Twenty-first-century music educators must teach to a wide variety of learning readiness levels within one classroom. One key difference of this text is that instead of focusing on chronological age or developmental level, the authors are designing curricula based on *individual* differences of *all* students and providing accessibility within a diverse inclusive music classroom. If a child has no access to a music education or cannot function within existing parameters, music educators need tools to change focus and to provide students with another access point to engage them in music.

Multiple means of access requires music educators to ensure that every-one is engaged within a music lesson and that it flows across learning levels and access points. For example, one group of students may be performing a rhythm they composed while other students who are still learning the difference between steady beat and rhythm are performing an ostinato to accompany the rhythm compositions of their peers. However, all students are engaged and participating according to their needs, experience, and requisite skills and understanding.

Principle 3: Adequate Conditions for Simultaneous Learning

Winding it back pedagogy provides adequate conditions for *all* students to learn. Research has shown that students with special needs require the following conditions to be in place for music learning to occur: (1) clear instruction and repetition, (2) student choice and self-advocacy within a positive atmosphere, (3) increased response time, and (4) a positive behav-ior plan (Gerrity, Hourigan, and Horton, 2013). These conditions can also be facilitated through one-on-one support from either a peer or a para-professional, when possible. It is essential for music educators to have the competencies necessary to provide these inclusive pedagogical concepts (Hammel, 2001). We believe this resource will begin to provide the tools appropriate for attainment of these competencies.

All contributing authors to this text are or have been public school music educators. We understand that even when outside influences (e.g., admin-istrators, school conditions) challenge the application of learning condi-tions suggested previously, it is our responsibility to continue to advocate for the active honoring of the individual differences of all students, a daily plan to provide multiple access points and learning levels that are appropri-ate for all students, and adequate conditions for simultaneous learning in modern music classrooms and ensembles.

WINDING IT BACK: THE PEDAGOGY IN PRACTICE

Winding it back—to adjust expectations and skill level requirements to an earlier observable competency in a learning sequence. The expecta-tion is modified to meet the current performance level of the student on that particular objective.

Before winding a skill back, it is essential to carefully sequence that skill from the most elemental observable musical competency forward to the current goal. When a student struggles with the current goal, a teacher moves to preceding skills to find the step, or earlier objective, that can be performed by the student. When that place in the sequence is found, the teacher may then work to assist the student to achieve the subsequent step.

LENA

Lena is in fourth-grade general music class. She sings very well and can decode and derive all grade-level rhythms and melodies. Lena struggles with the glockenspiel and recorder because her visual-spatial skills are weaker than most of her classmates. Mr. Wisenberg, her music teacher, is introducing low E and D on the recorder. He knows Lena will need to have some of the expectations wound back. He sees that Lena is able to play B, A, G, and sometimes F well. During class, he asks Lena to choose D or E and to rest when the other note is being played. Lena chooses D and audiates the Es that are in the music. During the next class, Mr. Wisenberg asks Lena to switch and play E and audiate D. Soon, Lena is able to switch between the notes when a rest is placed between them. Mr. Wisenberg hopes that by the end of fourth grade, Lena will be able to combine D and E with other notes on the recorder.

Winding it forward—to adjust expectations and skill-level require-ments to a competency that would normally be observed later in a learning sequence. The expectation is modified to meet the current per-formance level of a student on that particular objective. This modifica-tion is made to maintain an environment that challenges all students, regardless of current level of competency.

Students may be months or years ahead of their peers in both cognitive and musical skills. By expanding an objective, or topic area, to allow a stu-dent to demonstrate his or her true achievement level, we are providing a framework for success for that student. An ability to accelerate, compact, or otherwise individualize instruction for a student who needs to learn at a later point in a sequence is at the center of the winding-forward para-digm (Heward, 2009). Figure 1.1 describes a student in need of modifica-tions that wind forward curricula to meet the current learning level.

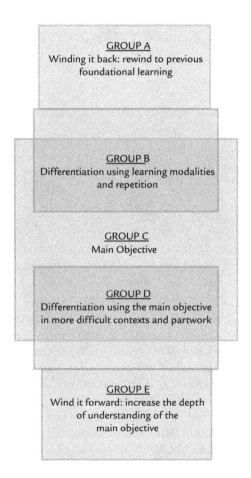

GROUP A
Winding it back: rewind to previous
foundational learning

GROUP B
Differentiation using learning modalities
and repetition

GROUP C
Main Objective

GROUP D
Differentiation using the main objective
in more difficult contexts and partwork

GROUP E
Wind it forward: increase the depth
of understanding of the
main objective

Figure 1.1

TALLY

Tally is in the same fourth-grade general music class as Lena. Her musical achievement skill level is high, and she is often bored by the slow pace Mr. Wisenberg takes when teaching recorders and barred instruments to the class. Mr. Wisenberg is aware of this and has begun winding content forward for Tally. During the current recorder unit, Mr. Wisenberg offers Tally the option of improvising in Dorian rather than providing a response to the call from Mr. Wisenberg's recorder. When he plays a melody and rhythm, the other students are challenged to play either the same or a different melody and rhythm. Tally finds herself immersed in creating new Dorian patterns while monitoring her use of appropriate modal harmonic and cadential functions.

HOW WINDING IT BACK SUPPORTS LABEL-FREE CLASSROOMS AND ENSEMBLES

Winding curricula back and forward is necessary when teaching in heterogeneous and inclusive music classrooms and ensembles, as well as in self-contained classrooms where each student has an Individualized Education Program (IEP). By creating detailed sequences that move incrementally through skill development, teachers are able to quickly adjust their teaching to meet the needs of all students. They are also able to demonstrate progress through time and the ways in which specific goals are achieved by students, even if some are in different places in the same skill sequence.

In previous texts, we have consistently spoken of the importance of a label-free environment in education (Hammel and Hourigan, 2011, 2013). Our philosophy is that a focus on teaching and learning, rather than on etiology, general characteristics, and the inherent generalities of labels, promotes an individualized and person-centered approach to teaching. This label-free philosophy allows teachers to consider the individual needs of *every* child and to provide an individualized education for each student, rather than solely for students with specialized plans (e.g., IEPs and Section 504 Plans) and other standard aids and services offered only to those who meet qualifying diagnoses under the Individuals with Disabilities Education Act (IDEA) or the Americans with Disabilities Act (ADA).

When every student is both challenged and supported in the learning environment, there is no need for labels. Students and teachers experience learning with a growth mindset that creates an appropriate pace for—and assessment of—learning for all within a classroom of diverse learners. This environment can be created by winding goals forward and backward and by assessing students according to their needs and current achievement levels. Students are often not even aware that expectations are not the same for everyone because all learning experiences are individualized for all students.

Every student will need to have a concept wound back or forward at some time in his or her educational experience. For example, a student who has a high music aptitude may glide through elementary general music without ever needing a concept to be wound back. He may also often need to have aural concepts wound forward because he needs an extra challenge in the music classroom. That same student, however, may struggle in high school band as the smaller note heads and staves and more complicated melodic and rhythmic writing can provide a huge challenge once the difficulty level exceeds his ability to decode all his French horn parts aurally.

A second example is a student who transfers into a very high-level choral program. She has never been asked to read notation and struggles with the reading demands required to perform the literature at her new school. By winding back reading concepts for her, she can begin to read music. This scaffolding process will allow her to learn at her own pace while performing repertoire with her musical peers.

An awareness of this individualized approach often improves the inclusive atmosphere. As a result, each day students experience the strengths and relative challenges of one another as they support and are supported by their peers in a music setting. By meeting the needs (strengths and/or challenges) of each student, all have the opportunity to succeed, fail, try again, and perhaps conquer their own goals. They also become aware of the same opportunities in those around them—regardless of the pace or level.

Furthermore, through use of this pedagogy, students have the opportunity to gain confidence, become self-motivated, and meet academic musical goals. Research has shown that students who learn differently often experience failure. In fact, when experiencing failure, students can often question their intelligence and their ability to solve the next problem they face (Dweck, 2000, p. 8). By winding back our pedagogy, teachers provide opportunities for students at all levels to engage in the content and attain their goals.

REFLECTIVE TEACHING AND LEARNING: THE FINAL STEP OF WINDING IT BACK

In *Educating the Reflective Practitioner,* Donald Schon (1987) speaks about the importance of reflective practice at all levels of education. He states: "We think and try out new actions intended to explore the newly observed phenomena, test our tentative understandings of them, or affirm the moves we have invented to change things for the better" (p. 28). As a result of this process, our procedural and theoretical knowledge is expanded. This foundational premise of the text can be considered in two ways: reflection on action and reflection in action.

Reflection on action is seen as a result of the "on the spot" experiments and experiences that music educators face. Questions may arise after the fact such as: Did this work? Why did or didn't this work? How would I do this again if given the opportunity? These questions and further experiments lead to adjusting the practice for the next day. Schon states: "We may reflect *on* action, thinking back on what we have done in order to discover how our knowing-in-action may have contributed to the unexpected outcome" (p. 26). This constant adjustment leads to the refining of one's craft and the evolution of expertise.

Reflection in action occurs when something out of the ordinary occurs during practice (in the moment). This allows a music educator to question the assumptions of previous knowledge and to reflect and decide on what "got us into this fix or opportunity" (p. 28). Related to winding it back, music educators take risks based on the principles mentioned previously, reflect on these risks, and assess whether or not the sequence is currently appropriate for a specific student. If not, necessary adjustments to the pedagogy are made to meet the needs of all students. Active participation in this reflective practice will increase the applicability and appropriateness of the winding pedagogy for specific students in classrooms and ensembles.

When reflecting on or in action, an inclusive music educator must ask: Am I honoring the individual needs of the student (principle 1)? Am I providing multiple access points in my instruction (principle 2)? And am I providing adequate conditions for simultaneous learning (principle 3)? This constant cognitive and behavioral process, we believe, contributes to thoughtful inclusive classrooms that are adapted to the individual learning needs of *all* students.

CHOICES MADE TO CREATE THIS RESOURCE

In creating this framework, we wanted to provide a resource for undergraduate and graduate students, preservice and in-service music educators, and teacher educators. There are several key factors to consider when presenting a framework for many stakeholders. We have now set the stage for winding it back and winding it forward. We present this paradigm in an effort to advance our craft and consider winding to be critical when preparing, teaching, and assessing all students throughout their music education. If our profession does not consider the disparate needs of individual students and know precisely where their understanding ends, how are we to confirm that we are providing an appropriate music education for all?

Undergraduate Preparation

During undergraduate coursework, music educators are prepared in ways similar to general and special educators. The same coursework, summative standardized testing, licensing guidelines, and ongoing expectations for further professional development that are in place for general and special educators also exist for music educators. One fundamental difference in undergraduate music education preparation is that sequencing of musical objectives, strands of skills, and elements of creativity may not *always* be as carefully presented and taught as in other areas of education. In addition, individualization of instruction is not always demonstrated in congruence with pedagogy.

There are an incredible variety of musical goals and objectives and diverse philosophies regarding the relative importance of various musical elements, specific sequences, instructional delivery methods, and varying outcomes expected throughout prekindergarten through twelfth-grade music instruction. Because of this, music majors sometimes graduate with education degrees yet have not had experience carefully sequencing objectives to ensure that each student's needs are properly met. Conway and Hodgman (2006) state: "Music education students must constantly grapple with the potential differences between what is presented in music education courses and what actually happens in school music programs" (p. 8). However, many students either are not provided with or do not seek authentic experiences in the field. Often music teacher educators provide field experiences but do not encourage sets of lessons that are sequential while also meeting the needs of individual learning differences. Research has shown that this is essential in successful undergraduate preparation (Hourigan, 2009; VanWeelden and Whipple, 2005).

In music education, essential skills, techniques, sets of experiences, repertoires, and organizational principles are taught in various ways. Future music teachers learn what to expect in a variety of classroom and ensemble situations. Grade- and ensemble-level expectations are taught along with repertoire and standard literature for various groups of students within a preservice curriculum. In the process, music educators often begin to think of third-grade general music as a group of third-grade students. The limiting factor in this philosophy is that the teacher will expect to teach one block of students who are all expected to learn the same materials at the same time in the same way, rather than to address the needs of each of the sixteen to twenty-five individual children in his or her classroom.

While this approach may meet the needs of most students, there are others who will not keep pace with their companions. There are also students who have already mastered the scope and sequence for the entire third-grade music curriculum before the first day of school. These students are clearly at risk in music classes and ensembles because *their* needs are not being met either. We can insert any grade level and class or ensemble setting into this scenario and begin to understand why the ability to wind our instruction forward and back can potentially lead to not only a greater number of students having their musical needs met but also more meaningful and individualized instruction for all students.

Experienced Music Educators

The same holds true for in-service music educators. Music educators who seek to become certified in various areas of pedagogy (e.g., Kodály, Orff, Music Learning Theory, etc.) often do not receive instruction regarding modification of instruction for individual learning levels. Each pedagogical and philosophical area has discrete skill levels and sequences; however, no specific instruction is offered to raise competencies in the individualization of instruction for students who learn differently or at a different pace.

Research has shown that courses may have been offered; however, most music educators receive coursework related to students who learn differently from sources outside their discipline (Colwell and Thompson, 2000). Nevertheless, when provided adequate professional development regarding individual learning needs, in-service music educators gain the skills and confidence to address the needs of each music student (Hammel and Gerrity, 2012).

Differentiation of content is a concept applied unevenly as many methods maintain focus on meeting a central objective or an overarching theme, repertoire choice, or general education goal rather than meeting the musical needs of each individual student. It is not the fault of any particular content, method, or repertoire choice, but rather the necessity for a paradigm that values the individual achievement of each student over the glossy linear goal for a class or an ensemble.

Students with Special Needs

All students learn more when instruction is individualized for them. Banks et al. (2005) state: "Of course diversity is the nature of the human species, and students are and always have been different from each other in a variety of ways" (p. 233). Some students are able to learn with the addition of adaptations and accommodations to the class or ensemble environment. Hammel and Hourigan (2011) describe four primary teaching considerations accordingly: size, color, pacing, and modality (auditory, visual, and kinesthetic). Through use of these four considerations, many students who learn differently will be able to meet the original music objective set by the music educator for students who are considered neurotypical or who are at roughly the same place in their musical development.

Some students, however, will not be able to meet the stated objective for the class or ensemble, and for these students, use of the four primary teaching considerations will not be enough to allow them to learn at their own pace, or to progress at all. For these students, modified objectives are necessary. These objectives require winding back the original objective until the very first, or most elemental, skill is found. When winding an objective either forward or backward, incremental steps are essential because many students, including students with special needs, may demonstrate progress on an incremental level.

Students who have already mastered the objective set for the class or ensemble may also require modified objectives to meet their needs. When teaching students who require more advanced objectives, incremental winding is an effective tool to move forward in a sequence or to set a new goal for them to meet. By winding content and expectations forward for students, music educators are more likely to also meet the needs of students who are not challenged in classes and ensembles when only *one* neurotypical objective is presented for *all* students.

Teacher Success and Retention

The challenges described previously can contribute to the overall retention of good teachers in the field. Even music educators with the best intentions can become overwhelmed by inclusion and find themselves without the tools necessary to sequence instruction for students with learning differences. Therefore, it is important for all music educators, preservice and in-service, to have a guide for pedagogy for *all* students.

This book is intended to include all areas of music education. Music educators who study this process of individualization can immediately put applications to use. Teacher educators can use theoretical frameworks and pedagogical examples directly in music methods classrooms. We hope that by providing not only a theoretical construct for inclusive music education but also actual examples for application, music educators and music teacher educators will feel more confident in providing inclusive pedagogy. Most important, we hope this will assist in retaining music educators who provide inclusive and individualized music education experiences for all students.

This text will reinforce several of our philosophical tenets. In addition to the person-centered and label-free focus, we also frequently demonstrate that all students need the highest possible quality in their music education instruction. Because of this, *Winding It Back* will show sequential and incremental progression in as many music education settings as possible, from early childhood through high school graduation. The idea of winding is used in some prekindergarten through twelfth-grade music classrooms and ensembles by teachers who have experienced this in Kodály, Orff, and Music Learning Theory postgraduate work; however, to date, few secondary music education teachers are employing this philosophy in classrooms and ensembles.

It is important to note that some chapters are written or cowritten by long-time, experienced, very successful music educators in the field. The pedagogy described is based on successful teaching and learning with many students with a variety of learning needs. The educators chosen to write for this text do not espouse any singular or dual educational theory. Their intent is to provide theory to practice pedagogy necessary to individualize music instruction. Therefore, teaching ideas are not meant to be loyal to any specific method or pedagogy. For example, you may see rhythm syllables that are often included in Kodály music classrooms in the same discussion as melodic patterns from Music Learning Theory. This is done to show true, authentic teaching practices that place the highest importance on exemplary teaching rather than on a method or theory. We consider this one of the great strengths of this text and know it will be useful to all audiences to provide as many varied examples as possible.

Many texts are written by university faculty or by authors who do not currently teach in prekindergarten through twelfth-grade public and private school music situations. It is foundational to us that the voices of those currently teaching be added to the chorus of those who often write. Because of this, our collaborative team of authors spans all areas of music education, from early childhood through graduate school. We also chose to use collaborative authors rather than contributing authors. All authors have cross-referenced other chapters and have collaborated, when appropriate, with other chapter authors. Furthermore, all authors have collaborated in using the basic framework of winding it back to provide quality pedagogy for instruction.

CONCLUSION

This book was strategically written by some of the best in-service music educators, teacher educators, and researchers in the field. Each chapter was vetted by the authors, and contributions were made to chapters by authors who were not necessarily slated to contribute in certain sections to maximize examples of best practice, theory, and pedagogical application.

The aim of this text is to provide a research-driven best-practice framework that is inclusive for *all* students regardless of ability or disability. In addition, this text provides insight into sequenced practice at multiple access levels with examples embedded within the text, appendix, and a robust companion website. We include strategies at all levels, including preschool through secondary instruction. Finally, we hope this book becomes a practical reference for embracing students where they are and providing them with a solid foundation for a lifetime of music making.

REFERENCES

Banks, J., Cochran-Smith, M., Moll, L., Richert, A., Zeichner, K., & LePage, P. (2005). Teaching diverse learners. In L. Darling Hammond & J. Bransford (Eds.), *Preparing teachers for a changing world* (pp. 232–274). San Francisco, CA: Jossey-Bass.

Bruner, J. S. (1960/1977). *The process of education.* Cambridge, MA: Harvard University Press.

Colwell, C. M., & Thompson, L. K. (2000). "Inclusion" of information on mainstreaming in undergraduate music education curricula. *Journal of Music Therapy, 37,* 205–221.

Conway, C. M., & Hodgman, T. M. (2006). *Handbook for the beginning music teacher.* Chicago, IL: GIA Publications.

Dweck, C. S. (2000). *Self-theories: Their role in motivation, personality, and development.* Philadelphia, PA: Psychology Press.

Dweck, C. (2006). *Mindset: The new psychology of success.* New York, NY: Ballantine.

Gagne, R. M., & Medsker, K. L. (1996). *The conditions of learning training applications.* Fort Worth, TX: Harcourt Brace Publishing

Gerrity, K., Hourigan, R., & Horton, P. (2013). Conditions that facilitate music learning among students with special needs: A mixed methods inquiry. *Journal of Research in Music Education, 61*(2), 144–159.

Hammel, A. M. (2001). Preparation for teaching special learners: Twenty years of practice. *Journal of Music Teacher Education, 11*(1), 5–11.

Hammel, A. M., & Gerrity, K. W. (2012). The effect of instruction on teacher perceptions of competence when including students with special needs in music classrooms. *Update: Applications of Research in Music Education, 23*(6), 6–13.

Hammel, A. M., & Hourigan, R. M. (2011). *Teaching music to students with special needs: A label-free approach.* New York, NY: Oxford University Press.

Hammel, A. M., & Hourigan, R. M. (2013). *Teaching music to students with autism.* New York, NY: Oxford University Press.

Heward, W. L. (2009). *Exceptional children: An introduction to special education* (9th ed.). Jersey City, NJ: Pearson.

Hourigan, R. (2009). Preservice music teachers' perceptions of fieldwork experiences in a special needs classroom. *Journal of Research in Music Education, 57,* 152–168. doi:10.1177/0022429409335880

Meyer, A., Rose, D. H., & Gordon, D. (2014). *Universal design for learning.* Wakefield, MA: CAST Publishing.

Ryan, R. M., & Deci, E. L. (2000). Self-determination theory and the facilitation of intrinsic motivation, social development, and well-being. *American Psychologist, 55*(1), 68–78.

Schon, D. A. (1987). *Educating the reflective practitioner.* San Francisco, CA: Jossey-Bass.

VanWeelden, K., & Whipple, J. (2005). The effects of field experience on music education majors' perceptions of music instruction for secondary students with special needs. *Journal of Music Teacher Education, 14*(2), 62–70. doi:10.1177/10570837050140020109

CHAPTER 2

Early Childhood Music

Setting the Tone for Inclusive Music Learning

HERBERT D. MARSHALL,
Baldwin Wallace University Conservatory of Music

CHAPTER OVERVIEW

This chapter focuses on teaching and learning for children from birth to age six, including any learners who are new to music and learners who function best in Piaget's first two stages: sensorimotor and pre-operational. I will focus on the following topics:

- Philosophical questions and pedagogical points of view: *What are our roles as musical mentors for young children? How will we best facilitate musical learning for each child?*
- Strategies and techniques that promote musical, cognitive, and social development for each child
- Indicators of children learning or struggling so that the educator can make adaptations, adjustments, and corrections to his or her instruction to help more children experience success learning music

The *winding* in this chapter will include *winding it back* to use developmentally appropriate techniques that help children succeed; *winding it to the side* to provide a different, but developmentally equivalent, opportunity to engage; and *winding it forward* for those times when a musical activity captures a child's attention and he or she clamors for more, to the point of satiation.

Young children demonstrate a wide range of responses to music and movement stimuli. In group instruction, the instructor is responsible for shaping the learning environment and modeling music and movement. The learners' responses, however, will also have a significant impact on the environment, music, and movement in the room. Each learner's responses will likely differ from other learners' responses, and often, each learner will offer different responses from one meeting to the next. Further, while this diversity may be overwhelming in itself, what young learners show us may be just the tip of the iceberg of what is occurring in their musical brains, their audiation. The following vignette offers a glimpse into this learning environment.

SHAKER SONG

A group of three-year-olds is participating in an activity song with shaker eggs. In modeling this activity, the instructor helps learners explore space—taking up as much space as possible, and then constricting into a small space—and encourages them to move their middles, their center of gravity. The song is jazzy, mostly neutral vocables, in Mixolydian mode and duple, but lightly swung (notation shown in Musical Example 2.1). There is a strong cadence at the end, with a fermata on "and" (sung on the dominant) coming to rest on "stop!" (sung on the tonic). During these final pitches, the instructor models a large "X" shape (think Leonardo da Vinci's drawing *Vetruvian Man*) on the dominant (singing "and"), then contracts as if just catching a football in the belly on tonic (singing "stop!"). In a class of ten toddlers and their caregivers, many are engaged in this activity, each in his or her own way. Eve is standing by her mom, smiling, moving the shaker egg a bit, but mostly observing. Opal is moving her middle like a pro while mouthing the words; she doesn't make much difference between her "big space" and "little space," but approximates what others are doing. Benny moves his middle, shakes the egg, and mouths the words to the song. Near the end, he strikes a superhero-type pose and loudly sings "and stop!" Aaron's mop of dirty blonde hair bounces as he shimmies and sings with reckless abandon. He is matching the beat of the song well but only the contour, not the exact pitches, of the melody. When the instructor takes a big breath before "and," Aaron beats her to the pitch, nailing the dominant confidently and cadencing to tonic while first making a huge "X" with his body, then scrunching into a ball.

Musical Example 2.1 "A Shake."

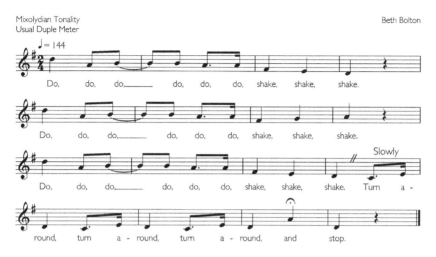

A Shake

Mixolydian Tonality
Usual Duple Meter

Beth Bolton

Copyright © Beth Bolton Music, 2015

PRINCIPLES OF MUSIC AND MOVEMENT INSTRUCTION FOR YOUNG CHILDREN

As more researchers focus on development and learning in young children, practitioners have an opportunity to examine different theories and approaches that explain how children learn and provide schema for sequential development. An excellent summary of several important theories is found in Persellin's chapter in Flohr's *The Musical Lives of Young Children* (2005). Find one or more researchers or theories that speak to you as an educator and fit your philosophies and goals. A good developmental theory will help the music educator see where he or she fits in the big picture of child development and provide a framework on which to build a personal curriculum. If your approach is new for your institution or community, it is helpful to have solid research and pedagogy supporting why you do what you do. My approach is drawn primarily from Gordon (2013), with ample borrowing from other scholars and pedagogues. Whatever scholarship you choose to guide you, the following principles will align with many different approaches and help keep a focus on *playful* learning that is primarily *unstructured* and *informal*.

Childlike Play

Researchers and practitioners from Johann Pestalozzi to Fred Rogers to Alison Gopnik, Andrew Meltzoff, and Patricia Kuhl posit that play is essential in the development of children. *Play* is the *work* of childhood, and through a childlike sense of wonder and experimentation, children strive to construct their understanding of the world around them. Thus, the natural approach for children is to use their bodies and senses to playfully interact with their environment, including their aural environment, to explore what interests them and all the ways possible to manipulate what they hear, see, taste, and feel.

Johann Heinrich Pestalozzi, a Swiss-born education pioneer (1746–1827), demonstrated the value of social reform and experiential learning, including play, in education. Pestalozzi, in an early nineteenth-century letter to a former student, advised the student that a well-rounded education must include not only physical education but also experiential learning for all the senses.

> It cannot be difficult for a mother to introduce a number of them [teaching exercises], calculated to develop and perfect the eye and the ear, into the amusement of her children. For it is desirable that everything of that kind should be treated as an amusement, rather than as anything else. The greatest liberty must prevail, and the whole must be done with a certain cheerfulness, without which all these exercises, as gymnastics themselves, would become dull, pedantic, and ridiculous. (Pestalozzi, 1982, p. 92)

Thus, the concept of a playful, amusing, cheerful learning environment is not new. Somehow, perhaps because educators are professionals and employed, we have adopted the attitude that our teaching has to have the appearance of *work*. A learner-centered approach, however, leads me to assert that teaching and learning with young children should resemble play.

Each child perceives his or her world differently, has different interests, and finds different ways to explore his or her environment through play. The instructor strives to create an environment where possibilities for play exist and he or she facilitates learners' play. Everything that can be perceived can be a plaything: a song, a hand drum, a scarf, a toe, a chant, a trampoline, a marker, a book, a word, a facial expression, and so forth. Sometimes the instructor may be the instigator, by playing with the jingles on a tambourine rather than the head. Other times the instructor may be the validator, by observing that a child is making upward sirenlike glides with his or her voice and imitating those glides to indicate that (1) the instructor heard and understood how the child was exploring his or her voice, and (2) the instructor wants to try to explore like that as well.

There is no right or wrong play, beyond the limits of safety for the children and equipment. Thus, the validation is merely a way to communicate nonverbally that the instructor understands the learner and wants to follow his or her lead. If the child is absorbed in his or her own behavior and not attending to the instructor, this direct imitation often elicits a response that indicates the learner recognizes the instructor has just joined his or her game. In the siren glide example noted earlier, this may mean using a visual accompaniment to the glide, like a scarf, within the field of vision of the learner. Another technique is to time the instructor's glides so that they are coming in between the learner's glides—in the pause for a breath—so the learner hears the direct imitation. The willingness of the instructor to initiate or join in the play is an essential element of establishing a playful and accepting learning environment. Communication via imitation and facial expression eliminates language as a barrier, thus making the interaction inclusive for children who are not communicating with spoken language or those whose preferred language is not the same as the instructor's.

Unstructured Guidance

The degree to which you teach in planned, sequential steps might be seen as points along a continuum from *unstructured* to *structured* (see Figure 2.1). The activity in the opening vignette is closer to the *structured* end of the continuum because the instructor is directly leading the activity, but when during the class the activity occurs and how many repetitions are done are mostly the result of feedback received from the learners. Working with young children in the playlike manner described previously requires flexibility, which necessitates a less structured approach to instruction. In fact, "instruction" may be too structured of a term, so "coaching" or "guidance" may be more apt. This may feel awkward and even frightening for those taught to plan and execute lessons in a programmed, sequential manner. Young children, however, rarely approach the world in that sort of style. They tend to follow their curiosity, mood, and energy level as they explore their world. Young learners may stay with a manipulative puzzle for an hour, examining every color, shape, and texture, or they may give it a half-hearted attempt, turn it upside down, and head for the pots and pans.

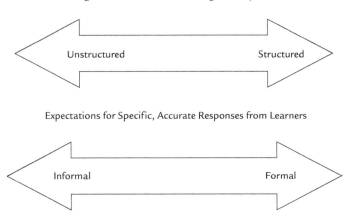

Figure 2.1 Continua describing principal elements of instruction.

Thus, a discovery learning approach seems a better fit for how children learn. This approach may be attributed to many sources, including historic educational scholars such as Dewey, Montessori, and Bruner. Hammer (1997) notes that

> discovery learning has taken on a range of meanings, but most often it refers to a form of curriculum in which students are exposed to particular questions and experiences in such a way that they "discover" for themselves the intended concepts. The student's inquiry is usually "guided" by the teacher and the materials. (p. 489)

In our music and movement classes, the materials include all manipulatives and instruments, as well as the songs, chants, and movements themselves.

Informal Guidance

Like structure, the degree to which the instructor expects or attempts to elicit specific, accurate responses can be seen as points along a continuum from *informal* to *formal* (see Figure 2.1). The activity in the opening vignette is closer to the *informal* end of the continuum because the instructor is hoping only for engagement, not accuracy. Because there is movement, singing, and rhythm involved, the instructor is observing all these elements to note the learners' development. In the early stages of music and movement development, there is a long process of acclimation in which the learners are listening to and observing music and movement, guided by the instructor. Just as parents cannot predict the order of words a child will learn or the length a child will crawl, the music educator cannot predict when a child will keep a steady beat or echo a tonal pattern. In these formative stages, we are investing time and energy in a diverse set of experiences that the learner will attend to and organize in his or her own way. Spending precious moments of class time attempting to elicit a specific response comes at the expense of exposing learners to more music and movement and allowing more time for experimentation.

Certainly, a teacher may have a general goal in mind or a predictable next step based on prior learning and responses. These may be based on research that provides a general guide to typical vocal development (Rutkowski and Trollinger, 2005; Welch, Sergeant, and White, 1995/1996) or beat competency (Rainbow, 1981). But rigid benchmarks like *Students will demonstrate a steady beat in duple by thirty-six months* and *Students will match the contour of "Let Us Chase the Squirrel" by forty-two months* are developmentally inappropriate. Fixed learning goals appear during more advanced learning (see subsequent chapters in this book). For learners from birth to age six, we are primarily laying the foundation for more formal and structured learning that will occur when developmentally appropriate.

One of the epiphanies that drove me into early childhood and higher education was the parallel between learning music and learning language and the focus on music, movement, and cognitive development in young children noted by researchers such as Bolton (1996) and Gordon (2013). Learning music like we learn language aligns well with established schema of Piaget, Bruner, and Bloom, as well as the work of psychologist Robert Gagné and psycholinguist Frank Smith.

In *The Book of Learning and Forgetting*, Smith (1998) writes about the formation of identity in young children and the crucial role played by those who surround children. He explains that if a child is raised among a group of readers, then that child is inducted into the "reading club" and probably becomes a reader. By extension, if your music class can become a "music club" of caregivers and children, the children will probably form an identity as a musical person. Smith states that

> infants are not born knowing the person they are, no matter how unique they might seem to us. Their identity is something to be learned, and they learn it from their observation of the people around them, the company they keep, in the clubs they join, from the people they take for granted they are like. And in the process of learning who they are, they learn about language and about many other things as well. (p. 17)

Thus, as an instructor, I accept the role of (1) creating a community of music makers, (2) serving as a music and movement model guiding this community primarily through unstructured and informal means, and (3) maintaining a spirit of childlike play as we explore, absorb, and respond to music and movement. I am not fluent enough, however, to simply *wing it* for forty-five minutes. I need to prepare a set of flexible, strategic frameworks that provide me with a starting point and multiple pathways for my teaching. These frameworks provide a guide for how to wind backward and wind forward. Like Lego pieces, the frameworks provide me with a launching pad, but the points of connection and expansion are only limited by my imagination—and how many Lego sets I acquire.

STRATEGIC FRAMEWORKS

In this section, I will focus on the organizational frameworks that govern how I plan instruction, how I choose repertoire, how I design music and movement experiences, and my general approach to instruction. The key frameworks include play, movement, diverse musical repertoire, and creativity.

Play, Curiosity, and Experimentation

If you observe children at play, you will notice two common themes: repetition and variation. They find something about which they are curious, manipulate it in some way, and repeat that manipulation to satiation—as if conducting an experiment to determine if the last outcome was chance or follows some rule of nature. Their other natural impulse seems to be to hypothesize *what if I change this one thing. . . .* They alter one variable, curious to learn how that change may alter the outcome. As the instructor, your challenge is to wind it back, to the side, or forward until you find a song, activity, or manipulative that incites this curious exploration. "It isn't just that babies can explore and explain their world; they seem driven to do so, even at the risk of life and limb and maternal conniption fits" (Gopnik, Meltzkoff, and Kuhl, 1999, p. 162).

Harnessing this drive is like harnessing solar- or hydro-power: it takes time to set up the correct conditions, but once engaged, you have a limitless flow of energy. Children want to hear a tune or chant over and over again, until they master it. Then they want to play with it: take turns singing/chanting phrases, add instruments, add movement, or create a variation.[1]

Laban Elements of Movement

Music educators are still discovering the work of Rudolf Laban (1879–1958). He was a contemporary of Dalcroze (1865–1950), but, unlike the

Swiss pedagogue, was always firmly grounded in movement, not in music. Today, musicians apply his work to early childhood music (Valerio, Seaman, Yap, Santucci, and Tu, 1998), instrumental music (Conway, Marshall, and Hartz, 2014), and conducting (Billingham, 2009). While Laban made many contributions to dance, movement education, and therapy, his effort elements of flow, weight, space, and time apply most to teaching young children. These elements, each expressed as a continuum, are the basic terms used to describe and analyze movement. By using these elements, educators plan experiences that guide young learners to coordinate their movements in response to music. Using this terminology, the educator may structure movement experiences that help learners explore new skills or refine others. Because Laban codified his terms thoroughly enough to develop a system of dance notation ("Labanotation"), his description and analyses are precise enough to be used by educators to describe and assess children's movements. Many early childhood practitioners use schema from Weikart, Gilbert, or Dalcroze in the same way. In this chapter, I will focus on Laban terminology, but I believe you will find similar terms and parallel applications in the work of several other movement theorists and researchers (see chapters 3, 4, and 10).

Figure 2.2[2] provides an example of integrated music and movement in a playful, imaginative context. The activity is primarily informal and unstructured, with many chances to explore and experiment. There is something about the relaxed, swung feel of "Down by the Station," the onomatopoeia sounds, and trains in general that appeal to young children. To accommodate a variety of learners, I will suggest ways to wind back the activity to help some children be more successful, as well as ways to wind to the side and forward to vary the activity in response to learners' needs.

Songs With or Without Words

Can it be a song if it contains a pitched melody but no definable words, just vocables or nonsense syllables? A quick glance at our Western musical heritage demonstrates that Debussy, Fauré, Holst, Mendelssohn, Ravel, Spohr, and Vaughn Williams all wrote solo voice or choral music for voices on vowels. We expect instrumentalists to absorb musical skills largely without the aid of sung text. Therefore, I conclude that songs without definable text, whether you call them *songs* or *tunes* or *melodies*, are legitimate musical content for early childhood music curricula, depending on the goals of those curricula.

If your goal is to pass along cultural icons from our musical heritage, then you will use primarily songs with words. If your goal is to improve vocabulary and grammar, then surely you will use songs that target

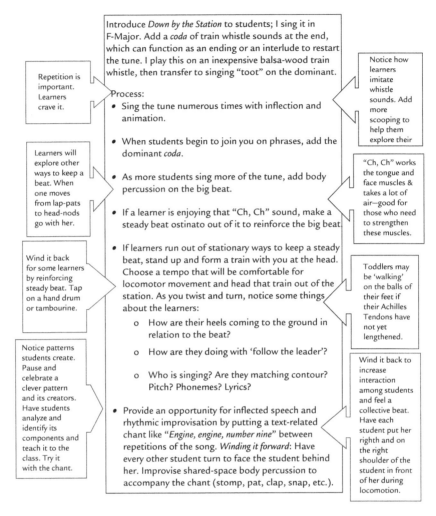

Figure 2.2 "Down by the Station" activity.

specific, developmentally appropriate vocabulary. If your goal is to teach concepts such as addition or subtraction, colors, names, animals, body parts, motions, and so forth, then you will teach a repertoire of activity and indication songs that include these concepts. These and many other goals are perfectly sound curricular goals for young people, and songs with words are well suited to help accomplish these goals. The primary purpose of these goals, however, is to teach nonmusical goals using music. Children will be learning music vicariously as they learn to count, spell, or identify colors, but musical fundamentals are not at the core of the lesson.

Researchers such as Gardner (2011) and Gordon (2011) have theorized that musical intelligence is unique with its own aptitude that develops, and can be measured, independently of other intelligences such as linguistic, spatial, and mathematical. It follows that, because of the way our complex neurological networks function, if we isolate musical intelligence by playing with songs and chants without words, we may help young learners focus their attention and learning on primarily musical ingredients: pitch, tonality, rhythm, meter, harmony, timbre, and so forth. It is possible that children whose language aptitudes are higher than their music aptitudes may fixate on the language of the song rather than the musical ingredients of the song. Research by Marshall (2002) suggests that children are able to learn and retain musical information from songs without words, as well as songs with words. Therefore, when the curricular goals for young learners are primarily musical goals, it may be advantageous to include repertoire that specifically targets musical intelligence, such as songs, chants, and recorded music without words.

CHILDREN WITH COMMUNICATION CHALLENGES

When children are second-language learners, speech delayed, or simply not using language with the same fluency as their peers, a heavily language-based music class can be frustrating. Conversely, a child with communication challenges and musical interest may find it extremely liberating to participate in a music class that is focused on musical intelligence and not language skills. I have seen this look of relief on the faces of these learners, and it has made me an even stronger believer in songs without words. Further, when language is removed, a learner with communication challenges may be able to provide an appropriate or accurate musical response (like echoing a pattern or improvising to the steady beat). Perhaps this will be a confidence-building moment for a child who is not successful in other subjects. For very young learners, winding it back may mean singing on vocables, which allows the instructor to use specific phonemes and syllables to improve articulation. Bilabial sounds, like "boo" and "ma," are done with the lips, allowing the learner to see and imitate them. Alveolar sounds, like "too" and "daw," are more explosive and help strengthen the tongue. As children hear and explore linguistic sounds in a musical context, it is possible that they will transfer these skills to regular speech. "It is imperative that music educators focus on language components when considering ways to deliver instruction to students with communication and language differences" (Hammel and Hourigan, 2011, p. 82). By consulting with parents and specialists and employing a wide array of musical repertoire, the music instructor can support the learner's language development while still attending to his or her musical development.

Diverse Tonalities and Meters

If we are to provide a musical diet for children that piques their curiosity and grows their musical intelligence, then we must provide an imaginative and diverse diet. Herein lies the art of good teaching, because young children like repetition and what is familiar, but what makes them think and solve puzzles is new stimuli. Consider the numbers zero through nine. These are the basic building blocks that will lead to decades of quantitative study. After children explore numbers on their fingers and toes, and use manipulatives to see the difference between three jelly beans and eight jelly beans, they will begin exploring different functions (addition, subtraction, etc.) to learn ever more sophisticated mathematical concepts, all using that original set of natural numbers that were first explored on fingers and toes.

Similarly, the Western music system includes just seven diatonic pitches in a scale, expanding to twelve chromatic pitches, and a small variety of common, elemental rhythmic patterns. So much of the music marketed to young children (and their parents) is a steady diet of major tonality and duple meter. Even if you alter the accompaniment from simple folk-style chords to more contemporary harmonies, the prime material—melody—is still the same. That is analogous to using numbers to count only from one to ten in the same order and in the same direction, every time. In that scenario, children remain unaware of the diverse palette of sounds found in the musical world. Further, children exposed to only one flavor of music have less reason to compare and contrast or search for patterns in music—basic processes for building intelligence in any discipline.

I am advocating *do*-based major and *la*-based minor in moveable *do*. An advantage to this is that when you begin labeling with solfège, the learners hear modes as distinct entities, each with its own characteristic sound and "home base" or resting tone. Thus, major is the result of seven pitches orbiting *do* as the tonal center, Mixolydian is the result of seven pitches orbiting *sol* as the tonal center, and so forth.

When you expose children to music of different tonalities, you are using the same diatonic building blocks, but instead of *do* being the resting tone, now *la* may be the resting tone.

While the diatonic pitches maintain their relationships to each other, their relationship to the resting tone changes and children experience pitch and melody in a different way. Children might liken it to our solar system. If a different planet assumed the mass and properties of our sun, then the other planets' orbits would adjust to orbit a new center: same planets, new relationships.

Similarly, when we alter the subdivision of big beats from duple to triple (2/4 to 6/8) or provide music with unequal big beats (such as 5/8 or 7/8), we significantly alter the proportions of the music and its relationship to learners' typically dichotomous arms and legs. In Western music, we often start children on a duple regimen, which helps them begin to coordinate their two arms and legs to move to the music (such as Musical Example 2.3: "Ally Bally"). If we music educators never move past this starting point, we never allow learners to problem-solve where to put the strong beat or how to move to beats of uneven length. We do not limit young children to single-digit natural numbers, one-syllable words, or primary colors. We know that their world is going to be more diverse than that, and we want to lay a foundation for lifelong learning. Similarly, a foundation for lifelong learning in music includes music in diverse tonalities, meters, harmonies, timbres, and so forth.

Patterns in Music

Well-known and widely used approaches to music education such as Kodály, Orff-Schulwerk, and Music Learning Theory use some form of pattern system to build a foundation of musical understanding (Shamrock, Trinka, and Valerio, n.d.). While there are variations in tonal solfège and rhythm syllables, and how the patterns are constructed, this common strategy provides building blocks that learners will use later to perform, analyze, improvise, and compose music. Like individual letters in the alphabet, individual sounds in music do not convey much meaning (Gordon, 2011). It is the combinations and context of sounds that are the building blocks of music. Syllables and words make up the foundation for fluency in language just as short tonal and rhythm patterns make up the foundation for fluency in music.

Patterns may be (1) excerpted from the song or chant, (2) ostinati that provide an appropriate accompaniment for the song or chant, or (3) patterns *not* present in the song or chant but which help the learner experience a more complete example of the tonality or meter of the piece. Making an analogy with language, you might think of a class being read a story—*Goldilocks and the Three Bears*.

A language instructor employing strategy (1) may

- read the story aloud, then
- pause to repeat key vocabulary words from the story, then
- ask the class to listen to the story again, paying special attention to those words.

A language instructor employing strategy (2) may

- put vocabulary or comprehension questions on the board and instruct students to use the questions to help them focus on the vocabulary and meaning of the story (*boys and girls, we know that in this story "too" is a modifier that means "more than I wanted." Listen for that word "too" and think to yourself "colder than she wanted" or "harder than she wanted"*), then
- read the story aloud while students listen and answer questions.

A language instructor employing strategy (3) may

- read the story aloud, then
- ask extension or inferential questions about the story, such as the following:
  - They were having porridge for breakfast; what's something similar we would eat today?
  - Can you think of other stories we know with three characters like the bears who are similar but each have something unique about them?
  - How might the end to the story change if we changed a fact from the beginning? What if Goldilocks heard them coming and escaped before they found her? What if the three bears weren't bears but eagles— what would change?

In this analogy, a song is like a story and musical patterns are the music educator's version of a language or the literacy teacher's prompts or comprehension questions. While children read a story, a parent or teacher will ask questions that help guide their reading, take note of important information, summarize major ideas, help identify new words or concepts, and predict what might happen next. Music specialists can use patterns to develop music comprehension and literacy in many similar ways. Musical Example 2.2 contains some of the different types of patterns musicians use to aid comprehension (to provide more familiar examples, all of these will be in major tonality and duple meter, but parallel examples should be used in other tonalities and meters).

Musical Example 2.2   Pattern instruction.

Types of Patterns	Examples
Recurring Patterns in Call-Response Songs (responses stems-down)	
Diatonic Stepwise Tonal Patterns that orient the learner to the tonality	
Rhythm Patterns that orient the learner to the meter	
Intervallic Patterns that orient the learner to the harmonic functions	
Pitch Motives that occur frequently in a song	
Rhythmic Motives that occur frequently in a song (from *BINGO*)	
A Rhythmic Ostinato that can accompany a song or chant (for *The Noble Duke of York*)	
A Pitched and Rhythmic ostinato that accompanies a song (*Frère Jacques*)	

Silence

To the parents and teachers of young children, silence is often the cue that something truly horrible has just occurred or is about to occur and immediate intervention is necessary. Silence is just not natural for young people—any visit to a solemn event in a space with a good acoustic reminds us that children like to fill silences with the sounds of their own voices. Therefore, I think that educators learn not to allow for silence in their lessons. They may feel that a *pause to think* is wasted instruction time or will be labeled "poor pacing" by an administrator. In a less formal, less structured teaching environment, however, silence is an opportunity for learners to audiate what they have just heard, connect it to prior learning, offer commentary on what they have heard (including "more!"), or signal that they are ready to take the lesson in a different direction. The sign for "more" is the only sign language I remember because my preverbal students make that sign and approximate the word "more" when they want me to repeat a song or activity. This communication can only happen when I wind back and pause to allow time for them to make a decision and have a say in how their class might proceed.

Besides being golden, silence provides the learner time to think. Because our musical repertoire is active and stimulating, some children are completely engaged in listening or participating or both. A pause after a song or patterns allows them to respond to what you have offered. To be clear, this is not a pause in which I'm signaling for them to echo what I've just done. This is a pause to respond however they please, or just to think—to allow the chant or song to settle for a moment, like a palate cleanser. The instructor can learn *so much* about how the learners are thinking by allowing these pauses. I may hear a snippet of my song. I may hear a learner predict a pattern I would use with this song. I may hear and see "more." I may hear the beginning of another song—telling me that at least one person is ready for a new activity.

Imitation and echoing are certainly important and function in much the same way as convergent questions: there is one correct response and we are guiding the children toward that correct response. Where we are ultimately heading, however, is critical thinking, which is more likely to be captured by more open-ended or divergent questions. Silence is the most open-ended of all options, implying to the learner "I've shared something with you; now what do you think?" The more the instructor thinks about individualizing instruction and musical cognition, the braver he or she will be in incorporating silence into his or her instruction.

Hocket, Variation, and Improvisation

Here I will pursue the notion of our songs, chants, and activities as playthings. Caregivers famously lament that a young person sometimes ignores an expensive toy, choosing instead to play for hours with the box in which it came. This is a clever, curious child. The box can be a fort, a cave, a tunnel, and a mountain. It can be a hat, a helmet, body armor, or a dress. The child can spend time figuring out the complex folding pattern used to seal an end, pick at the adhesive, flatten the corrugation, and, of course, taste it. And if bubble wrap was included, there is no end to the imaginative uses a child can invent. If we can focus on the learners and not so much on the repertoire, then we can embrace and enjoy the new ways they invent to play with the musical gifts they have been given. The instructor can be a catalyst in this process by setting up conditions favorable for hocket, variations, and improvisation. One of my favorite *playthings* to explore these strategies is the folk song "Ally Bally" (Musical Example 2.3).

Musical Example 2.3 "Ally Bally."

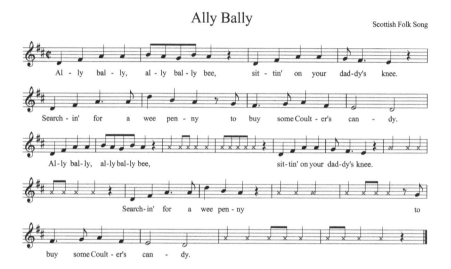

You may remember *hocket* as a term from your first music history course in which two or more voices combine to realize a single melody, each having interlocking pitches that, when combined, form a unified melody. I vary this a bit to alternate phrases with my young people, particularly if part of the song has a repetitive motif or contour. Thus, after the learners have heard numerous repetitions of "Ally Bally" (no words yet), I will draw their attention to the motive *do-mi-sol*, which starts each of the first three phrases.

> I need some help singing my song. Please help me by singing the *do-mi-sol* part
> and I'll sing the rest. Great! Try it again and take a big breath to show me you're
> ready for your parts. Great! (*winding forward if appropriate*) You're doing such a
> great job that now I like your part better than mine. Let's switch and I'll try your
> part and you try mine. Great! But I'm not positive I was doing the *do-mi-sol* part
> as well as you. (*winding forward if they're ready for an audiation step*) This time, I'm
> going to sing that part and then we'll hear the other part silently in our heads,

and you can tell me if I'm doing the first part correctly. How'd I do? Excellent! Let's put it all back together so that everyone can sing everything!

By taking turns and working in teams, I'm allowing them to be more independent and providing time for them to listen, anticipate, prepare, audiate, and learn the component phrases or patterns that make up a song.

Once we know "Ally Bally," I might sing a variation in harmonic minor, or we might saunter around the room to a variation in triple (Musical Example 2.4). This is my version of playing with the tune. I might also make a language variation (parody-ish) and substitute the names of children from the class. A favorite strategy is to give each child three colored objects on the floor, one to represent each pitch of *do-mi-sol* (I use red, yellow, and blue bean bags). We place them in order so that blue represents *do*, red represents *mi*, and yellow represents *sol*. Then, I tap on the bean bags as I sing the three phrases that start with *do-mi-sol*. I go back to the hocket idea and alter the order of *do-mi-sol* for those three phrases. These represent my starter kit to instigate variations. As learners are ready to wind forward, they will invent their own variations. For other learners, it is important that you wind back often to remind them of the original version of the song, to reinforce their audiation.

Musical Example 2.4 Variations on "Ally Bally."

(a)

(b)

When I have established an iconic representation for *do-mi-sol*, we might explore some tonal improvisation. For my learners ages three to six, this has consistently been my most successful first attempt at tonal improvisation. Tapping our bean bags, we sing the *do-mi-sol* pattern (usually in D or whatever key is good for the learner). Then I say, "Be my echo," and I tap and sing a three-pitch tonic pattern in a different order, *mi-sol-do*. After a few of these I say, "You make one up and see if I can sing it." Sometimes a child will tap and not sing, but I believe that he or she is auditing his or her pattern. To check, I'll mess it up and say, "It will help if you sing when you tap so I can hear it," and the child usually will. I have had students go for minutes creating longer and longer patterns trying to stump me with their *do-mi-sol* improvisations (similar to the pitch-memory game Simon). They are playing a game, and I am jumping for joy inside that a child is improvising. Another favorite improvisation strategy, for rhythm this time, is to create rhythm solo breaks between my phrases. I will pause after each of the four "Ally Bally" phrases and fill that time with a rhythmic improvisation—usually in the same style as the song and the same length as the preceding phrase (Musical Example 2.5). This may be done with body percussion, rhythm sticks, hand drums, boomwhackers, barred instruments—whatever you like. Of course, if you are using pitched instruments, you may be more purposeful about the song you choose and how to adjust for pitched improvisation in a developmentally appropriate manner. Once the students understand the game, I have them join me in the improvisation breaks. As I see them get comfortable with this, I wind forward and elicit solos from individuals. Improvisation is the ultimate tool for winding back, sideways, or forward because the learners self-select their responses. If you provide readiness experiences and scaffolding to structure the activity for success, the learners will provide the differentiation because they are (1) making their own choices and (2) sharing a response that indicates what they learn when they teach themselves.

Musical Example 2.5 "Ally Bally" with rhythm solos.

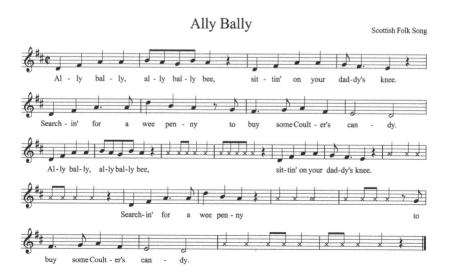

OBSERVATION, ASSESSMENT, AND COMMUNICATION

In this section, I will focus on the criteria, strategies, and rubrics I use to observe and document learning. I observe the learners constantly to monitor their attention, responses, and mood and adjust my teaching accordingly. I assess my students partly to force myself to set defined goals, but also to provide documentation of the learners' progress toward those goals—knowing that I can easily alter the music and movement activities, sequence, and intensity to help focus on particular goals. I communicate with my teaching partners and caregivers so that everyone can be part of each learner's music and movement development and celebrate milestones along that path. Pencil-and-paper testing is inappropriate for most of the learners I am focusing on in this chapter and, in fact, not the best way to document achievement in many of the goals central to an early childhood music curriculum. Many of these learners are not ready, developmentally, to express themselves verbally, and some are not locomotor movers. Thus, winding back for assessment involves a combination of keen sensory perception, some educated inferences, and a shared vocabulary among your constituents (Marshall and Bailey, 2009; Valerio et al., 2006).

Movement

The ways children move reveals much about how they are hearing and processing musical information. Children are natural movers. If you adopt an informal classroom environment, then you are not inhibiting movement; that is, you don't expect children to sit still and face the instructor. Music gets in no matter where children look or how they move. Model appropriate ways to express themselves through movement: flow, weight, space, time, simple body percussion, and folk dance movement. If you are the music specialist in a typical school, yours may be the only classroom where children can act on their impulse to move. How freeing and refreshing that will be for children for whom sitting still is torture. Your musical moments will be the best part of their day! You will need to set parameters on the following based on your situation and tolerance:

- How to move
- Where to move
- When to move

- What props are permitted
- What instruments are permitted
- How much sound may be generated

Any opportunity to express themselves through movement is better than forcing children to adopt stillness when that stillness is not necessary to aid learning. Adopting a movement-friendly attitude to music instruction is one of the most natural and elemental winding back strategies that you can employ.

As children move, they reveal many things about how they are hearing and processing musical stimuli. To wind back for the nonlocomotor learners, you should watch their eyes and breathing. Watch their eyes for facial recognition and focus and to see if they are tracking the gestures and props you are using to animate your songs. Watch their breathing to see if they breathe faster when a song is stimulating to them. Also, some young learners will wait and breathe with you at the ends of phrases, or when you play a game that requires a big breath, like blowing a scarf or making a "raspberry" sound. Taking full breaths and seeing the effects of exhaled breath are essential to good musicianship, and these good habits can start with your youngest learners. Nonlocomotor learners who are on their backs may still be moving their limbs to respond to music. Their limbs will make swimlike movements that will change in speed and intensity during music class. If I sing face to face, a child may grip my finger and squeeze, which I interpret as wanting more musical face time with me. When the grip relaxes, perhaps the child has had enough and needs a break.

For young locomotor learners (crawling, scooching, or walking), much can be demonstrated with the body. They can move to the beat with their head, shoulders, arms, hands, hips, and legs. They can show you the difference between free and bound, gentle and strong, sudden and sustained, and direct and indirect motion. They can trace the contour of a melody, show a *fermata*, and show style with their movement. They can attempt to coordinate their bodies to the steady beat by rocking (on their bottoms); crawling; tapping; patting; head bobbing; blinking; shoulder shrugging; swaying, rocking, or stepping in place; moving hips from side to side; walking; jogging; tip-toeing; galloping; skipping; hopping; jumping; and running. One of my favorite assessment techniques is to put a child on a small (personal-sized) exercise trampoline. While I stand on the floor holding his or her hands, I let the child find a personal tempo while jumping. Winding back to accommodate the child's speed, I adapt a chant or song to this tempo and see if the child can sustain that tempo for a period of time. Eventually,

I will wind forward to see if the child can modulate his or her jumping speed to match other tempi. Jumping on a trampoline reveals much about the child's full-body coordination, but the child seems to perceive it simply as play.

Any time I allow the learner to initiate the musical/movement behavior (as in the trampoline jumping), I am winding back instruction to meet the learner *where he or she is*. In terms of movement experiences, I might then wind sideways to build a larger but developmentally equivalent repertoire of movement. To wind forward, I might take note of the learner's current level of achievement using any appropriate developmental schema (see Figure 2.3). I use this schema to plan movement experiences that will help the learner grow and learn.

1. Acting upon movement directions	2. Describing movement
3. Moving in nonlocomotor ways	4. Moving in locomotor ways
5. Moving with objects	6. Expressing creativity in movement
7. Feeling and expressing steady beat	8. Moving in sequences to a common beat

Figure 2.3   Weikart's key experiences in movement.

We are accustomed to assessing visually from the head and face, but movement assessment requires a different focus (see Figure 2.4). Notice where the motion is initiated, like the shoulders, hips, or wrist, and notice where the movement impacts the environment, like fingertips tapping your leg and feet stepping on the floor. If the child is transitioning between crawling and walking, he or she may still be walking on his or her toes and the balls of his or her feet, and not exchanging much weight when he or she walks (often supporting himself or herself on a railing or with an adult's hand). You will see that these steps lack consistency and coordination, but you can watch the balls of the child's feet to document progress. When the child begins to walk with weight on his or her heels, you will see a more confident, consistent exchange of weight and greater accuracy. Watch the heels. The heels are the best indicators of a child who is actually moving to the beat, because they indicate a child who is coordinating from the inside out and responding to the steady beat using aural perception and whole-body physical response, rather than a child who is patting to the beat and may be timing his or her movements by visual perception with your arm movements.

Movement Goals	Not Observed	Sometimes	Consistently	Movement Goals	Not Observed	Sometimes	Consistently
Eyes track visuals				Patting accurate in Duple			
Limbs move during music				Patting accurate in Triple			
Limbs imitate visual model				Locomotor accurate in Duple			
Takes a breath before a step or a hop				Locomotor accurate in Triple			
Free Flow				Indirect Space			
Bound Flow				Direct Space			
Gentle Weight				Accelerates Time			
Strong weight				Slows Time			

Figure 2.4 Movement goals and observation rubric.

Rhythm, Pulse, and Meter

For me, these are three separate skills, in which

- rhythm is the ability to echo or invent short patterns (two to eight beats),
- pulse is the ability to perceive and demonstrate strong (or big) beats, and
- meter is the ability to perceive and organize big beats (macrobeats) and little beats (microbeats) into a metric pattern—duple, triple, and uneven or complex meters—and demonstrate that meter.

Young learners will be able to demonstrate these in different ways—usually by moving, chanting, or singing, but you may want to use some of these winding back or sideways strategies to elicit responses.

Many children will show pulse by patting first, but some would rather move a scarf. Some children prefer something they can grip, such as a rhythm stick, to show pulse and meter. Social children may show pulse by giving you a high five on a strong beat. Shy children may demonstrate more rhythmic achievement when you let them face a wall and tap on it with a shaker egg or boomwhacker. With time, some children will chant rhythm patterns aloud to the whole class, while others will respond if chanting into a microphone, while still others prefer to whisper a pattern—like a secret—into a caregiver's ear. By using diverse activities and keen observation, the educator can note the learners' preferred modes to respond to pulse, meter, and rhythm responses and build upon them (see Figure 2.5).

I follow a logical order, increasing difficulty within these skills so that I can wind it forward once students have mastered a skill; for example, once some learners have chanted two-beat patterns I include some four-beat patterns, and while students are working on skills in duple meter I am concurrently exploring the ways in which triple meter feels different. For an example of one stage theory (a theory that there is a pattern or order to how children typically develop increasingly sophisticated skills or understandings) with degrees of understanding and parallel music and movement activities, see the *Music Play* curriculum (Valerio et al., 1998).

I may end a song or chant with rhythm patterns for the children to echo. That will tell me if they are building a vocabulary of patterns that leads to fluency in this meter. Next (winding forward), I may present a pattern but ask for a different pattern. This will tell me more about their ability to maintain pulse and metric style. I may just leave a silence (winding back) and see if anyone has anything rhythmic to contribute. By allowing for silences and individual responses, you allow learners to teach you what they know and don't know. If the child's performance is preceded by a good, purposeful breath, then I am even more convinced that he or she is beginning to audiate pulse and meter, and may be building a rhythmic vocabulary (Gordon, 2013, p. 37).

Rhythm Goals	Not Observed	Sometimes	Consistently	Rhythm Goals	Not Observed	Sometimes	Consistently
Hears rhythmic sounds				Performs 2-beat pattern in Duple			
Responds rhythmically				Performs 2-beat pattern in Triple			
Response indicates a sense of pulse				Performs 4-beat pattern in Duple			
Attempts to echo rhythmic pattern				Performs 4-beat pattern in Triple			

Figure 2.5   Rhythm goals and observation rubric

Vocal Exploration, Tonality, and Pitch

From birth, one of the very few elements of their environment that infants can control is sound, specifically, their own voices. Soon, they learn that babbling sounds and giggles produce lots of pleasant reactions from the giant faces looming over them, and angry screams get quick attention. Thus begins an infant's love of exploring sounds with his or her voice, leading to imitating sounds around him or her, and eventually speaking and singing the language and songs from his or her environment. Because of this natural exploration, young children are primed and ready for music instruction. To assess the child's vocal achievement, a music instructor should notice how the child responds to (1) a variety of ways to explore the voice, (2) different tonalities, and (3) various opportunities to match pitch and reproduce pitched patterns and melodies (see Figure 2.6).

Tonal Goals	Not Observed	Sometimes	Consistently	Tonal Goals	Not Observed	Sometimes	Consistently
Hears inflected or pitched sounds				Performs stepwise patterns in Major			
Responds tonally with inflection				Performs stepwise patterns in Minor			
Responds tonally with a discernible pitch				Performs skip/leap patterns in Major			
Breathing is coordinated with responses				Performs skip/leap patterns in Minor			
Attempts to echo tonal pattern				Performs portions of a song			

Figure 2.6   Tonal goals and observation rubric.

Rutkowski and Trollinger (2005) provide a helpful summary of how the young child's vocal mechanism functions and what seems to be typical sequential development in young children. For older children and for a focus on finding and developing the singing voice, Rutkowski (1996) provides an excellent assessment process. To guide children through these important vocal experiences, the instructor needs a varied repertoire of

- vocal exploration activities that include glides, swoops, and sirens in all directions;
- spoken chants that use inflection and imitation, including different kinds of animal sounds and human voices and chants with both vocables and language; and

- songs, both limited range and extended range, of many timbres, tonalities, and meters, that draw learners in and compel them to listen and respond (see chapter 3 regarding the repertoire that follows early childhood and chapter 7 for more discussion of vocal exploration).

Watch the child's breathing. Children sometimes demonstrate that they know and understand the song by breathing with you at phrase endings. Watch the child's lips. Some children watch your face intently and copy your lip movements and facial expressions. I describe some of my students as *reluctant singers*. They enjoy class and move as I move, but they are reluctant to make pitched responses for an excruciatingly long time. Some of them are intent listeners and want to hear only me to learn my rendition precisely. Thus, while they are in class, they will not make any competing vocal sounds. Caregivers, however, report that they sing at home. Other children are perfectionists. They are practicing the songs and chants in their heads and do not venture an attempt at pitched responses until they think they have it all correct in their audiation. If you watch their breathing and lips, these children will give you a glimpse into what is happening in their musical brains and reassure you that the music is getting in and even sticking there. Winding it back here includes letting the learner set the timeline for when (or if) he or she is going to sing in class. Pressure and pleading may make music class unpleasant for the child. Just like the emergence of spoken language, if the child is going to sing, he or she will do so when he or she is ready. Sometimes I can get the class into a state of flow such that these reluctant singers lose themselves and sing along; those are great days!

Eye contact and proximity are crucial factors when monitoring vocal development. If you maintain good eye contact with the children, then you may see some of the breathing and lip signs that indicate achievement and audiation. Further, you may see actual singing that

---

A FEW TECHNIQUES TO ELICIT CHANTED OR SUNG RESPONSES

- Young people have become quite comfortable with microphones, so focusing on a microphone or any microphonelike object (shaker egg, rhythm stick) will sometimes elicit a response.
- Put a hand drum on the side of the child's head so that he or she sings into the inside, near the rim, causing the sound to bounce off the head to the other rim next to his or her ear. This helps the child hear his or her own voice.
- Sing into boomwhackers! We use boomwhackers like telescopes to see others in the class and then sing things to each other. Even with my most stubborn reluctant singers, they will get caught up in the playful nature of this and sing hello through the plastic tube.

is so quiet or well blended that you cannot hear it. That is your cue to saunter around the room to change your proximity to the child. I try to meander throughout the class and reposition myself so that I am next to every child in every class. In this way, I will hear things I may not have heard from across the room. For the reluctant singer, however, eye contact and proximity may be inhibiting factors. If they lose themselves in your class and begin to sing aloud but catch you noticing it, they may clam up immediately. Thus, as in everything we do with children, all these suggestions must be individualized to the learners' idiosyncratic needs and habits.

Seeing Patterns in Student Learning

Good teachers reflect on their teaching. Even in a largely informal and unstructured class, I have general goals for each student over the span of a series of classes. And I have some specific personal assignments: make sure you speak to Evan's mom today; pay attention to Chloe's mood today because she had a little meltdown last week; move next to Chris during drum time to hear his rhythmic ideas; and so forth. Patterns of behavior and achievement will emerge in the classes such that atypical behavior will stand out. I just need to be *present* during the class to pay attention, and then listen to that little voice in my head that is taking inventory of the day's events.

Having specific behaviors that you care about will help focus your attention (see Figures 2.4, 2.5, and 2.6). Having a system of documenting these behaviors is a huge help in seeing patterns in learning. I am fortunate in that I always have an assistant teaching with me; we share the documentation duties. If I am not seeing the rhythmic progress I am hoping for over a few weeks, maybe I need a different activity or an instrumental variation on what we are doing. If there seems to be too much of a lull twenty minutes into class, perhaps I need to reorder the repertoire and balance high- and low-energy activities. We assess to improve instruction. Even when we are not assessing for specific benchmarks, a report card, or a standardized test, what we assess reveals our priorities. What we learn from assessing— seeing emerging patterns and trends—makes us better teachers.

Communicating with Caregivers and Colleagues

You may be providing early childhood music education in a learning center or preschool. If so, this is still a relatively new concept for the general public. You may also be providing early childhood music education in an institution or school. Despite years of progress, we are still working to convince parents and policymakers that what we do matters and is of substance. Basing your curriculum on scholarship; following well-established principles; using best-practice techniques; having specific, understandable, long-term goals; and assessing progress toward these goals are all elements of responsible teaching. But other than you, who will know? Share what you are doing and what you are learning about these children! Teachers tend to be service oriented, so it may seem boastful to broadcast the results of your teaching. Do it anyhow! If you maintain a child-centered focus and share who is struggling and who is succeeding, then you are contributing to the larger mission—the village—raising this child.

After having done this for a while, being older than all my administrators, and having a certain healthy confidence about what I do and what I know, I still make time to communicate with administrators on enrollment, families who return to the class, new ideas, and successes. I invite them to watch me teach. Who doesn't want to leave his or her computer screen and paperwork to come watch preschoolers play with music for a few minutes?

I also communicate with parents. I send them research articles, interesting book titles, and links to places where they can acquire music and equipment. I create a parent-friendly "Observation Report" and provide a summary of what their child has shown us in class (see Figure 2.7). I force myself to use this language with them during the semester (mostly before and after class) to help them learn the jargon, so that they can know what I am listening for and how to listen for it as well. I only see the child a few minutes once a week. The parents and caregivers are our teaching partners who see the children the other 167 hours a week. If you can find a way of teaching that is open and transparent, and provide a little bit of adult-level narration along the way, they will continue your good work at home. Sharing with them what I have been noticing helps them see that there is some organizational framework to the class and that I have been paying attention to each child's music and movement development. Those seem like reasonable expectations to me. In the process of summarizing and communicating observations, I continue to deepen my understanding of this process and build stronger connections among my constituents.

CONCLUSION

While there are many ways to approach early childhood music instruction, there are strategies that seem to promote success for diverse learners and that expose children to a wide array of music experiences. First, the instructor must be a keen observer of learner behaviors and possess a vast repertoire of tonal, rhythmic, and movement activities. Second, the

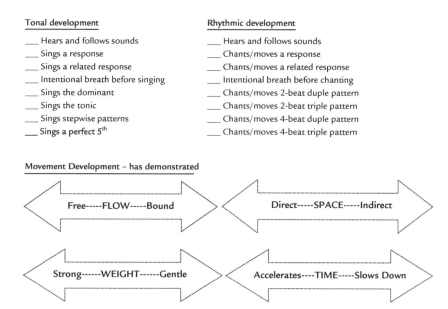

Tonal development

___ Hears and follows sounds
___ Sings a response
___ Sings a related response
___ Intentional breath before singing
___ Sings the dominant
___ Sings the tonic
___ Sings stepwise patterns
___ Sings a perfect 5th

Rhythmic development

___ Hears and follows sounds
___ Chants/moves a response
___ Chants/moves a related response
___ Intentional breath before chanting
___ Chants/moves 2-beat duple pattern
___ Chants/moves 2-beat triple pattern
___ Chants/moves 4-beat duple pattern
___ Chants/moves 4-beat triple pattern

Movement Development – has demonstrated

Free-----FLOW-----Bound   Direct-----SPACE-----Indirect

Strong------WEIGHT------Gentle   Accelerates----TIME-----Slows Down

Figure 2.7 Observation report for parents.

instructor should embody the playful, curious, and experimental spirit of a young person bent on discovery. Third, while the learner may not operate in a sequential or linear manner, the instructor needs to understand a hierarchy of developmentally appropriate steps that will allow for winding back or winding forward to meet the needs of the learner. Finally, observation, assessment, and communication will help the instructor focus on the goal of providing all children with experiences that prepare them for lifelong music and movement learning.

NOTES

1. For other ideas regarding creativity and exploration, see Marshall (2004a, 2004b).
2. For notation to "Down by the Station" and other teaching ideas, see Valerio, Reynolds, Bolton, Taggart, and Gordon (1998).

REFERENCES

Billingham, L. (2009). *The complete conductor's guide to Laban movement theory*. Chicago, IL: GIA.

Bolton, B. (1996). Was that a musical response? Eliciting and evaluating musical behaviors in very young children. *Early Childhood Connections, 2*, 14–17.

Conway, C., Marshall, H., & Hartz, B. (2014). Movement instruction to facilitate beat competency in instrumental music. *Music Educators Journal, 100*(3), 61–66.

Gardner, H. (2011). *Frames of mind: The theory of multiple intelligences* (3rd ed.). New York, NY: Basic Books.

Gopnik, A., Meltzkoff, A., & Kuhl, P. (1999). *The scientist in the crib: Minds, brains, and how children learn.* New York, NY: HarperCollins.

Gordon, E. (2011). *Learning sequences in music: A contemporary music learning theory.* Chicago, IL: GIA.

Gordon, E. (2013). *Music learning theory for newborn and young children.* Chicago, IL: GIA.

Hammel, A., & Hourigan, R. (2011). *Teaching music to students with special needs: A label-free approach.* New York, NY: Oxford.

Hammer, D. (1997). Discovery learning and discovery teaching. *Cognition and Instruction, 15*(4), 485–529.

Marshall, H. (2002). *Effects of song presentation method on pitch accuracy of third grade children* (Doctoral dissertation, Temple University).

Marshall, H. (2004a). Improvisation strategies and resources for general music. *General Music Today, 17*(3), 51–53.

Marshall, H. (2004b). Improvisation strategies and resources, part 2. *General Music Today, 18*(1), 37–39.

Marshall, H., & Bailey, J. (2009). Observing and communicating early childhood music and movement development. *Perspectives, 4*(2), 14–20.

Persellin, D. (2005). Foundations: Theories and approaches. In J. Flohr (Ed.), *The musical lives of young children* (pp. 8–15). Upper Saddle River, NJ: Pearson.

Pestalozzi, H. (1982). Letter to Greaves: Training of eye and ear—Music in education. In M. Mark (Ed.), *Source readings in music education history* (pp. 91–94). New York, NY: Schirmer Books.

Rainbow, E. (1981). A final report on a three-year investigation of the rhythmic abilities of preschool aged children. *Bulletin of the Council for Research in Music Education, 66/67,* 69–73.

Rutkowski, J. (1996). The effectiveness of individual/small-group singing activities of kindergartners' use of singing voice and developmental music aptitude. *Journal of Research in Music Education, 44*(4), 353–368.

Rutkowski, J., & Trollinger, V. (2005). Experiences: Singing. In J. Flohr (Ed.), *The musical lives of young children* (pp. 78–97). Upper Saddle River, NJ: Pearson.

Shamrock, M., Trinka, J., & Valerio, W. (n.d.). *The alliance for active music making.* Retrieved from http://www.allianceamm.org/

Smith, F. (1998). *The book of learning and forgetting.* New York, NY: Teachers College Press.

Valerio, W., Reynolds, A., Bolton, B., Taggart, C., & Gordon, E. (1998). *Music play.* Chicago, IL: GIA.

Valerio, W., Seaman, M., Yap, C., Santucci, P., & Tu, M. (2006). Vocal evidence of toddler music syntax acquisition: A case study. *Bulletin of the Council for Research in Music Education, 170,* 33–45.

Weikart, P. (1997). *Movement plus rhymes, songs, & singing games.* Ypsilanti, MI: High/Scope Press.

Welch, G., Sergeant, D., & White, P. (1995/1996). The singing competencies of five-year-old developing singers. *Bulletin of the Council for Research in Music Education, 127,* 33–45.

CHAPTER 3

Sequential and Flexible Instruction in the Primary Grades

JOY ANDERSON, *Shenandoah Valley Children's Choir and Eastern Mennonite School*

CHAPTER OVERVIEW

This chapter will focus on musical learning in kindergarten through grade two and will discuss the following:

- The goal of mastery for every student and the benefits of sequencing instruction to ensure that all students achieve this mastery
- The ideas of *winding forward and back* based on the three principles outlined in chapter 1
- Several important skills developed in the primary grades, with an example lesson activity to illustrate each:
  - Singing
  - Moving
  - Playing instruments
  - Rhythmic and melodic reading and notating and developing the aural skills on which that reading and notating are based
- Several winding forward and back ideas in the context of these example activities and how those ideas fulfill the three principles
- How careful and ongoing assessment and clear record keeping can benefit efforts to lead all students to mastery

---

Fortunate indeed are children for whom rich, substantive, and sequential music instruction begins in kindergarten, or even earlier. Reynolds and Valerio (2015) state: "Chief among the many valuable outcomes of an early childhood music curriculum: by the time children are eight years old, they organically and consistently live social, playful, music interactions that affirm for them that music not only is a natural part of their play, but also of the world around them" (p. 329). When instruction is begun in early childhood or in the early elementary grades, not only are children given adequate time to build aural, kinesthetic, and visual skills slowly and incrementally, but also important developmental windows of opportunity are wide open at this time. For the music educator, this privilege of "beginning at the beginning" with an entire group of students may seem, initially, to mitigate the need for the amount of differentiation necessary when teaching older students. However, while a group of five-year-old children may not have had as many years as a group of fifteen-year-old students to develop widely divergent experiences and skill levels, these young students certainly present differentiation challenges based on developmental readiness, special needs, and those five entire years of varied experiences.

When a music curriculum is based solidly on developmentally informed sequence foundations, the groundwork is laid for *all* students to develop strong musical skills, even those with learning differences. These foundations, such as introducing experience before symbol, aural skill before visual representation, and concrete experiences before abstract concepts, also allow educators to create important opportunities for continuous and meaningful assessment and the effective differentiation that grows from this assessment. Teachers who foster a flexible sequence of instruction and flexible strategies and tools for assessment ensure that all of their students succeed. But "succeed" how, and at what? Do we envision that all students will demonstrate the same skills at the same time, or that we will hold everyone on each landing, waiting for all students to climb the staircase to join us before proceeding as a group up the next flight of stairs? Or can we find ways to build multiple stairways? Can we find realistic ways to keep track of where each student is in his or her ascent, and can we believe that standing solidly and competently on each landing—or, for that matter, on each step—is as important as reaching the rooftop of each set of skills?

Too often, elementary music educators err in one of two directions: First are teachers who believe elementary music education, especially in primary grades, should consist entirely of experiences, and that mastery is not a desirable or realistic goal. These educators often see the purpose of elementary music as a time to give students many "tastes" of a variety of experiences and to create positive feelings about music class and music in general. For these teachers, mastery of skills and understanding of concepts may be seen as a positive but incidental by-product of the often rich but not necessarily sequenced experiences they provide. In contrast are teachers who believe so strongly in the idea of sequence that their sequential instruction becomes rigid and inflexible—a class checklist that can hold some students back or encourage the educator to accept a superficial level of "mastery" from some students to allow the class to proceed. Neither approach does justice to the great potential for universal mastery of skills and concepts present in a primary grade class.

Certainly, music instruction should begin with, and be based on, *experience*, but we sell our students short if we do not believe them—all of them—capable of mastery. And certainly, a well-designed sequence is an effective means to build skills and assess mastery, but we must be very clear about what we mean by *mastery* at each step in our sequence and at each increment. We must build and be aware of the steps between our steps.

The skills discussed in this chapter are meant to be mastered by students. Students in a classroom whose instruction is based on these ideas should become *experts*. By the end of a year or number of years, they will not all be experts at every step in the sequence, but through the teacher's careful winding forward and winding back, each student will have achieved *expertise* with skills that are appropriate and achievable, and the teacher will know, through flexible and sequence-based assessment, where each student needs to begin working toward the next mastery step. At each step along the way, our three guiding principles, described in chapter 1, will have been addressed:

1. The individual learning needs of all students will have been met.
2. Multiple access points and learning levels will have been offered.
3. Adequate conditions will have been created for simultaneous learning.

Multiple teaching approaches exist that suggest sequences of experiences to lead students to musical mastery. Training in the Kodály approach, Music Learning Theory, and other approaches that emphasize sequential learning can powerfully inform our instruction. Whatever teaching approach or approaches we choose, finding or constructing an effective teaching sequence is crucially important, as it will allow us to lead our students intentionally and incrementally up the most appropriate stairways for each student. Equally important, it will allow us to assess and keep track of each student's progress up those stairways and through those "steps between the steps."

Outlining any specific methodology's instructional sequence for primary grades is far beyond the scope of this chapter. I base my instruction primarily on the Kodály approach, but my teaching is also strongly informed by basic Orff training and by observations of and discussions with colleagues trained in Music Learning Theory and other approaches, and by practical application of their suggestions with my own students. Rather than describing entire rhythmic, melodic, or other sequences, this chapter will provide snapshots of musical experiences within several instructional sequences, illustrating how those specific musical experiences may themselves be sequenced, assessed, and made positive, accessible, and successful for every student.

Comparatives such as louder/softer and higher/lower are often explored in the primary music classroom as a means of reinforcing singing and the study of melody. Exploration of these topics can be found in chapter 3 of the companion website. Additional comparatives that support the study of rhythm such as beat/no beat, faster/slower, big beat/little beat, and marching/swinging can also be found on the companion website.

SINGING

Teaching children to sing is a fundamentally important task for music educators. Houlahan and Tacka (2008) write:

> Every child has the ability to sing; the voice is the most accessible musical instrument. Regardless of social background, race, or musical ability, the voice is the one instrument that is available to all children. Singing has a significant impact on a child's intellectual development. Singing facilitates language development through the performance of beat and rhythm in music. Singing helps children learn and articulate the text of a song; it facilitates memory, as well as the development of vocabulary. (p. 72)

Our most intimate, natural, accessible instrument, the voice also provides a means for aural skill development that ensures the reliance on *hearing* first, because purely mechanical-spatial note playing is not an option when making music with the voice. For in-depth treatment of this important topic, including the ideas mentioned later, please refer to the appendix.

Music classes for young children should incorporate a great deal of singing—and instruction directed toward universal singing *mastery*. Educators who believe that all children (and adults) are capable of masterful singing take responsibility for teaching singing sequentially, incrementally, and intentionally. They delineate (for themselves and the students) clear milestones and goals for success. They foster classroom singing cultures that encourage respectful and positive correction. They provide accurate and musical vocal models, pitch songs in the range that is most age appropriate, and eschew overly complicated or overabundant accompaniments in favor of a cappella singing or simple accompaniments. They do all of these things to ensure their students become the masterful singers they are entitled to become by birthright.

A Basic Singing Sequence

The following sequence and assessment strategies encourage pitch-matching success and allow teachers to troubleshoot and intervene when students are not successful at any step. To be clear, *all* listed activities in the sequence will likely be included *in each lesson*. While vocal exploration is presented here as an earlier stage in the singing sequence, a lesson with only vocal exploration and no singing would not be very musical! The sequential nature of these listed activities lies not in the order in which they are included in a series of lessons, but rather in the order in which students are likely to be successful and the order in which it makes sense to assess them.

1. Vocal Exploration and Discovery of "Head Voice"

Numerous specific vocal exploration ideas are also listed in chapter 7. While these activities encourage students to explore the *full* range of their voices, as well as various tone colors and sounds, one ultimate goal is for students to discover both the feeling and sound of their voices in the *higher* range, with most resonance felt in the head (rather than in the throat or chest). By using vocal sirens, owl hoots, and other sounds, the teacher can turn this skill-building activity into a game. He or she can then ask students to perform the sounds alone or in small groups to assess students' skill in producing a head voice. In the average primary grade class, most students are likely to be successful at finding their head voices fairly quickly. Indeed, many have been making these sounds for years as part of natural play. Vocal exploration should play a part in every primary grade lesson, providing vocal warm-up for all and winding back opportunity to continue work on this skill for those students who have difficulty accessing their head voices.

2. Two-Note Melodies

These consist of echoing and performing "yoo-hoo" and other melodies based on the *sol-mi* tone set. Some controversy exists about the "*sol-mi*" phenomenon and whether the ubiquity of that interval is indeed natural and universal across cultures. Whatever one's opinion may be, it is the experience of many educators, including myself, that the falling minor third interval, pitched wisely, is a good starting place for in-tune singing. Inviting children, individually and as a class, to echo "yoo-hoo!" on a falling minor third, C5-A4: , or slightly lower, has offered a highly successful first pitch-matching experience and assessment.

Introducing this activity in the context of play creates an engaging and safe environment for solo singing and assessment. The "hiding game" offers opportunities for both (Photo 3.1). Invite children to look around the room and imagine good places to hide. When children indicate they have thought of their hiding places, choose one or several students to be "hiders." The class, with eyes closed or hidden, counts to twenty, while the hider or hiders go to their chosen hiding places. When the children open their eyes, the teacher sings "yoo-hoo!" on the *sol-mi* interval (or if several children have hidden at the same time) and the student, having been instructed to "make your voice sound just like mine," responds with "yoo-hoo!" Classmates then "use their ears" to find the hider, using locating words such as "under the piano bench" or "behind the door" to describe the hidden child's location. Even the shyest child feels safe singing alone in this situation, because no one can see him or her and usually he or she cannot see anyone else; the entire class is focused on listening well, and the teacher can perform a formal assessment with the class none the wiser.

"Yoo-hoo" echoes may also be practiced with a toy microphone or in a play acting scenario where the child and teacher stand on chairs ("mountains"!) and echo back and forth (Photo 3.2). Additionally, the *sol-mi* interval may be introduced and pitch matching assessed in the context of "greetings" or "Q&A" (Musical Example 3.1).

Some songs containing only sol-mi exist as well, though most of these songs are probably not true folk songs, but rather rhymes sung in a singsong voice instead of being spoken. These songs (or sing-song rhymes) offer additional opportunities for children to experience and perform this helpful introductory tone set.

Photo 3.1 Hiding game

Photo 3.2 Yoo-hoo game

Musical Example 3.1

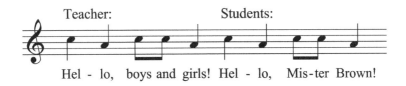

3. Songs Within a Narrow Range

While a steady diet of only *sol-mi* songs would be both tiresome and unmusical—both to sing and to hear—songs containing this interval prominently, along with songs composed of other narrow-range tone sets (such as *mi-re-do, sol-mi-do,* and other ranges of a fifth or less), should form the core repertoire for beginning pitch-matchers. Just as asking children to sing too low can encourage habitual off-pitch singing, so too can a repertoire of songs with ranges and interval leaps that children are not yet capable of singing in tune. Do not trust music publishers to make these determinations! Even publishers who specialize in music for children frequently choose songs to appeal to the adults who will purchase them, rather than making publishing decisions in the best interests of the children who will sing them. See "Choosing song repertoire" on the companion website for chapter 3 for additional information on selection of developmentally appropriate song materials.

Part of the song repertoire for primary grades should include singing games that incorporate solo singing as part of the game. These songs provide additional opportunities for children to hear their own voices alone and to learn to sing solos in ways that are playful and "safe," especially for those who are being included in the classroom and may have self-esteem challenges. These solo opportunities for students also allow the teacher to formatively assess students' skill levels without assessments seeming like "tests." Musical Example 3.2 provides an engaging solo singing game appropriate for primary grade children. An example for older students, "Concentration," may be found in chapter 5 on the companion website.

Musical Example 3.2 Doggie, Doggie, Where's Your Bone?

> One child is chosen to be the "Doggie" and sits on a chair at the front of the room, facing away from the class, with his eyes closed. The bone sits behind the "doggie's" chair. Another student is chosen (silently) to steal the bone and hide it behind her back while the class sings the first part of the song. The "doggie" sings, "Who stole my bone?" as a solo, and the "bone thief" sings, "I stole your bone!" The "doggie" gets three chances to guess who has his bone (aided by his knowledge of the sounds of his classmates' voices.) Singing, he asks each suspect, in turn, "Do you have my bone?" and each suspect sings back either, "No, I don't" or "Yes, I do!" Another doggie is chosen, and the game resumes.

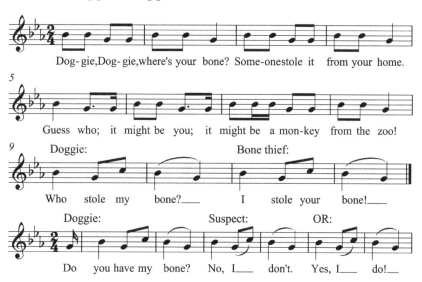

Doggie, Doggie, Where's Your Bone?

Winding It Back

The typical primary grade class includes students at all pitch-matching stages for a number of months and even years. As noted earlier, activities from all sequential stages should be incorporated into each lesson. Because each stage presents opportunities for both solo and whole-class singing, student expertise at each skill level (successfully performing head tones, singing *sol-mi* patterns in tune, and singing narrow-range songs in tune) can be easily assessed, allowing the teacher to focus subsequent experiences and assessments in ways most effective for each student.

As mentioned in the appendix, when a child does not match pitch, the teacher will need to ascertain whether this lack of pitch matching is due to the child not *hearing* the correct pitches or whether the child can actually audiate the pitches but is not yet able to *produce* the correct sounds with the voice. See the appendix for specific ideas about how teachers may make this determination. Obviously, the techniques the teacher uses to help the child learn to match pitch will be different in those two situations. Vocal damage is a possibility that should be explored in some cases when a child demonstrates the ability to audiate correct pitches but cannot yet reproduce them.

Let us examine the following vignette in light of our three guiding principles listed in both chapter 1 and this chapter's introduction.

MS. ROBERTSON

Ms. Robertson's school population is fairly stable, and most of her first-grade music students were with her for kindergarten as well. Ms. Robertson worked diligently on pitch-matching skills throughout that kindergarten year, and she continues to choose songs carefully, so that these first graders continue to learn good singing skills. As a result, fifteen to eighteen students out of each first-grade class of twenty are matching pitch well as they sing songs that are melodically appropriate for their age and development.

Several students are not yet matching pitch in each class. Ms. Robertson begins each class period with vocal exploration activities that also incorporate kinesthetic elements, and with greetings and Q&A experiences (e.g., "What col-or is your shirt? My shirt is purple.") sung on a *sol-mi* interval or other narrow-range melodic pattern, pitched carefully. These experiences function both as warm-up activities for the majority of the class and as continued opportunities for students who are not yet matching pitch to work on those skills. Ms. Robertson makes sure that these students have frequent opportunities to "answer" and use their singing voices, and because she has created a classroom culture in which students feel emotionally safe being corrected, she is able to say, "Erin, you made your voice go higher and lower that time! You were nearly matching my pitches!" or "Kai, you got into your head voice! Now let's work on making your answer sound just like my question!" and make other specific, positive, and constructive comments.

Ms. Robertson also includes frequent singing games that incorporate solo singing, and she strategically matches students with the solos in which they are most likely to be successful. These games also offer opportunities for Ms. Robertson to offer positive, specific, and helpful feedback and for students to hear their own voices alone.

Principle 1: Ms. Robertson's classroom culture honors all students' learning needs by encouraging a culture where making mistakes and being corrected are normal and safe, and where improvement is specifically described and praised.

Principle 2: Her inclusion of solo singing games of varying difficulty levels allows her to choose solo singing opportunities that are most appropriate for each student and to assess each student's improvement and needs in the context of play and music making, creating multiple access points and serving multiple learning levels.

Principle 3: Ms. Robertson's routine of beginning each lesson with vocal exploration encourages all students to warm up and ready their voices for singing. Simultaneously, it allows students who are still working on finding their "head voices" and working on matching pitch to both hear and attempt to produce increasingly wide pitch ranges.

One final note about sequential singing instruction: even in the case of a stable student population, where a majority of students in kindergarten move together to first grade, teachers should "begin at the beginning" each school year. Students who do not sing during the summer or long semester break may lose some progress they have made, and review is important. In highly transient communities, this yearly return to fundamentals (and assessment of fundamentals) is even more crucial.

MOVEMENT AND MUSIC

The great importance of movement in the music curriculum, as well as intentional sequences for creative movement and dance, is covered thoroughly in chapter 4 and the "Teaching Students to Dance" appendix, found on the companion website. This section will not duplicate that information. Rather, the ideas here are designed to give the reader further suggestions for keeping sequences flexible to meet the needs of all students. As with other experiences we provide for students in music classes, we must first ask ourselves, "Why are we teaching this?", "What do we intend our students to learn and gain from this experience?", and "How will we know when they have been successful?" The first question is a crucial one to ask in any instructional situation, but may be especially important regarding the teaching of creative movement and dance in music classes. Elementary music educators are often given woefully inadequate instructional time with students, and to devote time in our once- or twice-weekly (if we're lucky) music periods to an activity that does not seem to contribute directly to strong aural and musical literacy skills or to result in a polished musical performance may seem to represent an enjoyable but otherwise unnecessary use of time. However, the answers to the second question, regarding student learning and skill acquisition, can show that time spent on creative movement and dance can indeed be time well spent.

Creative Movement

Creative movement, most obviously, provides opportunities for individual creativity, in addition to those opportunities provided by rhythmic, melodic, and other types of improvisation. Csíkszentmihályi (1990) states: "The best moments usually occur when a person's body or mind is stretched to its limits in a voluntary effort to accomplish something that is difficult or worthwhile" (p. 3). The absence of "right" and "wrong" answers can be freeing for many students, providing a type of engagement not found in many school activities. This type of engagement, based on "in the moment" choices, can be directly related to the child's ability to achieve "flow," that mental state, sometimes described as being "in the zone," that can increase all kinds of learning and increase the satisfaction of the learner (Csíkszentmihályi, 1990).

Creative movement can also strengthen students' understanding of abstract musical concepts. For students with learning challenges, having a freeing moment without obstacles can often lead to a more pleasurable and productive experience for all involved, including the teacher and students. For a more thorough treatment of creative movement, please see chapter 4. Additional ideas about creative movement in the primary grades can be found in chapter 3 of the companion website.

Dance

Folk dance and other types of social dance provide different but equally important benefits. The types of movement inherent in these dances create opportunities to feel and perform the beat; experience a sense of musical motive and phrase; gain cultural insight; develop musical instincts involving tempo, meter, dynamics, and types of movement; and learn to interact with others in social and musical ways. The experience of community created through folk dancing can inform other interactive music class activities as well. Dancing is frequently a favorite activity in primary grade music classes (Photo 3.3). However, just as creative movement can produce some anxiety for children who like "right" and "wrong" answers, so too can folk dance and

Photo 3.3 Folk dancing

other types of dancing be problematic for some children. The very aspects of dance that make it a valuable activity can also create challenges for some students. For example, dancing successfully requires adequate motor skills, spatial awareness, and sense of timing involving beats and phrases. It can also present interpersonal and sensory issues as dancers are often expected to hold hands, make eye contact, choose partners, and interact in other ways.

How are our three principles applied in the following example?

MS. MIRAGLIOTTA

Ms. Miragliotta has been teaching many, but not all, of her second graders since kindergarten. She has been following an intentional dance sequence, so that most of these students have experienced a variety of folk dance movements and are comfortable with them and with dance in general. Ms. M is teaching "Kings and Queens" from the Amidons' *Sashay the Donut*. The dance includes the following figures in a long-ways set formation:

1. All move (in their own lines, holding hands down the line) forward four beats, then back four beats.
2. Right-hand turn with partners for eight beats.

3. Left-hand turn with partners for eight beats.
4. Gypsy with partners for eight beats (similar to a right-hand turn, but with eye contact instead of hand contact).
5. Head couple sashays down eight beats and back eight beats.
6. Head couple, holding hands, walks regally down to the bottom of the set while all others bow to them as they pass by (sixteen beats).
7. The dance repeats with a new head couple.

Ms. M provides the following opportunities so that all of her students have their needs met, learn from this activity, and are challenged but not overwhelmed:

As Ms. M teaches each figure first without the recording, she refers to a "bird's eye view" map of the dance on the board, moving Xs and Os to represent dancers. Micah, who is easily overwhelmed when moving in a group of other children, especially when he does not know the figures, stands to the side and learns the figures from the board. While he does this, his partner temporarily dances with "Invisible Ed," a frequent (imaginary) stand-in partner for the class. Ms. M invites Micah to verbally review the dance for the class, using the map as a visual. As Micah leads the review, students move through the figures one more time. Micah then feels confident enough to join his partner.

Anisa uses a wheelchair. She moves well in it but needs both hands to propel the chair through the figures. The class makes sure to leave room in the formation for Anisa to maneuver her wheelchair easily. Students on each side of Anisa place their hands on her shoulders during the forward-and-back figure, when others are holding hands. Rather than right- and left-hand turns, Anisa and her partner perform the gypsy figure three times. Anisa propels forward and then backward down the set during the sashay, while her partner skips down and back beside her. By mutual agreement, Anisa's partner pushes her wheelchair during their dignified walk down the set so that Anisa can wave regally to her subjects.

Wyatt has autism and, while he has become more comfortable participating in dance activities, it can be a negative experience for him to have children moving and making noise all around him. Hand holding and eye contact are also challenges for him. Ms. M pairs Wyatt with a particularly mature and compassionate classmate, one of three students who take turns being Wyatt's buddies. Wyatt holds a scarf in each hand, which he uses for the hands-down-the-set figure and for right- and left-hand turns and the sashay. Because Wyatt is working on eye contact, he and his partner arrange to look at each other and count to three during the gypsy figure, and then they look away as they finish the figure. Ms. M notes Wyatt's success in this and reports it to his classroom teacher. Wyatt and his partner begin at the bottom of the set, where he only has other children on one side and where he can separate a little from the larger group if he needs to. Wyatt's partner helps him to decide if he would like to move up the set on each repetition or if he would like to stay at the bottom.

Jamie also uses a wheelchair and comes to music with a paraprofessional. He is nonverbal and has very limited motion. Ms. M has found that having the paraprofessional move Jamie through the movements is upsetting to him because he feels passive. She knows that Jamie is paying attention and is capable of following the music and the timing of the dance, and that he enjoys doing so. Ms. M has a large triangle set up for Jamie and has adapted a striker for him that he can hold to strike the triangle. Ms. M invites Jamie to strike the triangle as a signal for the beginning of each figure. Jamie, with a twinkle in his eye, takes it upon himself to add a "dinner bell" sound with the triangle at the beginning of each whole dance repetition.

Ms. M has shown her students some "fancy" moves and turns that can be added to figures when students are sure they can move through the dance comfortably. Students know they are welcome to try these, and many do, with some students even making up their own "fancy" moves. They enjoy the challenge of keeping the dance moving to the beat while adding extra moves.

Principle 1: Ms. Miragliotta knows that Micah is bright and likes to do things correctly (preferably on the first try!). She knows he learns well visually, but his spatial challenges can frustrate and even embarrass him. Allowing him not only to learn the dance visually but also to take a leadership role in reviewing figures for the class encourages Micah to concentrate to overcome challenges and to feel legitimately proud of his contributions and successes. When Micah joins in the dance, he is more comfortable making mistakes because his competence has been demonstrated and honored.

Principle 2: While it might seem that physically moving Jamie through the dance figures would be the best way to involve him fully, Ms. M actually honors his true needs and strengths by allowing him to participate actively rather than passively. Jamie's intelligence and sense of humor are allowed to shine as he performs independently. (Jamie's situation also illustrates Principle 1 well.)

Ms. M knows that Wyatt is working on making eye contact and interacting with other students. This activity allows him to make eye contact multiple times, but only briefly and for a predictable amount of time. Allowing him to progress up the set or not enables him to participate fully while remaining in a space that feels safe to him. Having three alternating buddies prevents "buddy burnout" while still making sure Wyatt is comfortable and familiar with his buddies and they with him.

Anisa is able to participate fully in the dance with minor modifications. While she normally prefers to move independently, and while this is optimal from an instructional and assessment point of view, inviting Anisa's partner to push her down the set at the end allows Anisa to participate in the dance's unique flavor.

Principle 3: Giving Micah time to help the class review the dance not only helps him but also allows others in the class who may need more repetitions of the instructions to have time and opportunity to be more successful.

Jamie, while participating musically in the activity, helps other students to stay on track and feel the phrases that denote each new figure.

PLAYING INSTRUMENTS

Musical instruments, specifically pitched and unpitched percussion instruments, can play an important role in the primary grade music classroom. Unpitched instruments can enhance rhythmic learning, as well as provide opportunities for children to experience varying tone colors and build motor skills. Pitched instruments, such as Orff instruments and other barred percussion, can add a visual-spatial and kinesthetic facet to the strong tonal skill building, both melodic and harmonic, that singing provides. Rhythm sticks, frequently the first instrument experienced in school, may first function as an extension of the hands. Just as children clap the steady beat, and later, various rhythm patterns, they may extend these activities to rhythm sticks. Children frequently demonstrate success at keeping a steady beat on rhythm sticks in roughly the same sequence with which they demonstrate beat keeping with hands alone. Figure 3.1 represents some of these beat-keeping motions in a sequence that many music educators have found to be effective. Additional beat-keeping motions may include performing alternating movements such as pat-clap-pat-clap (not pictured).

Students who struggle to accurately perform the steady beat or rhythm using sticks may be supported by first performing a comparable motion without the sticks—with the hands alone. By winding back to a simpler step in the beat-keeping sequence, teachers are able to ensure success for the greatest number of students. Instruments meant to be played by shaking, scraping, or other types of sound production can also be introduced by asking students to make comparable motions with their hands, with the instrument attempted only after the hand motion has been demonstrated successfully in a musical context.

Patting/tapping simultaneously (on lap or floor)

Patting/tapping simultaneously on head or other place

Clapping or tapping sticks together

Patting/tapping simultaneously, with arms crossed

Patting/tapping with dominant hand (and later, with non-dominant hand)

Patting/tapping with dominant hand (and later, non-dominant hand), crossing the midline

Figure 3.1

Patting/tapping with alternating hands

Stepping or marching

Figure 3.1 (Continued)

Pitched percussion instruments are frequently approached in one of two general ways: as melodic instruments (the player plays all or part of a song melody or sometimes a recurring melodic motive) or as harmonic or accompanying instruments (the player performs simple to highly sophisticated patterns or groups of patterns, such as borduns, as accompaniment to singing or to another instrument playing the melody). In either case, students might benefit from practicing the basic mallet pattern first with their hands (or fingers on the instrument) and then with mallets. A sequence for practicing mallets, as well as a sequence for mallet instruction, can be found in chapter 3 of the companion website. As many elementary general music programs include recorder instruction, a sample recorder lesson is also included in chapter 3 of the companion website as an example of winding back instruction.

Winding It Back

As with all musical activities discussed in this chapter, the most important step in ensuring student success is for the teacher to have designed a careful sequence, based on increasing levels of difficulty and incremental skill building, and to have considered the process he or she will choose to instruct students to perform planned tasks and activities. Inexperienced teachers (or those inexperienced at the activity at hand) will benefit greatly by writing the entire process in detailed steps. If the steps of a process (including the teacher's verbal instructions) are written and followed, the teacher will more easily and effectively be able to find the step at which a student or group of students began to be unsuccessful and then wind back to the previous step before asking for more difficult tasks. A number of instrument modifications are available for purchase. Children who cannot grip instruments or mallets may be aided by the use of Velcro fastenings and other adaptations. Instruments with easier-to-play surfaces are also available. Modifications to the process, the activity, or parts of the teacher's expectations can also help ensure ultimate success for every student, including those with learning differences. Yet again, teacher clarity about fundamental purposes and goals for the musical learning activity is critical.

Examine the following barred percussion lesson, thinking not only about how certain students are helped to be more successful through adaptations and modifications to the activity and materials, but also how the sequential and incremental process itself is conducive to a successful experience for all students.

MR. CARTER

Mr. Carter's second graders have been learning the song "I Know an Old Lady Who Swallowed a Fly." They have enjoyed showing the melodic contour on the "Perhaps she'll die" section:

Per - haps she'll die!

Mr. Carter plans to teach the students how to play that portion of the song on barred percussion instruments.

The students have previously been successful (with appropriate modifications) in playing simple borduns, including crossover borduns (see the following example), to accompany their singing and have learned correct mallet technique and pertinent vocabulary through these experiences.

This "I Know an Old Lady" activity will be the students' first experience in playing these instruments melodically (rather than as bordun accompaniment to songs).

Mr. Carter has prepared the Orff instruments by replacing the F tone bars with F-sharps. To follow is the basic process Mr. Carter uses to teach his students the pattern:

- Students sit in rows on the floor, all facing Mr. Carter. Throughout the process, Mr. Carter models the motions with opposite hands (mirroring).
- Isaac has leg braces that do not allow him to sit on the floor. Since the class routinely sits on the floor for music, Isaac is used to pulling his chair to the appropriate spot and using the rolling tray table for many activities. At Mr. Carter's instruction and with his modeling, students pat the floor (or tray) in front of them with their left hand (LH) and then their right hand (RH) to the right.
- Students cross their LH over their RH and pat the floor, then uncross their RH and pat the floor to the right.
  - Devin has trouble with left and right and with most activities that use spatial directions. Mr. Carter has several sets of colored wristbands (red for RH, lemon yellow for LH) and several poster board strips with colored, numbered hand prints to help with this process. Any student is welcome to use these. Devin and his friend Michael get these sets without being asked, because this routine has been established.
- Mr. Carter instructs the students (reminding them the goal is to stay together—not to race!) to repeat those motions again, very slowly, saying, "Left, right, cross, right."
- Mr. Carter invites students to practice the pattern on their own, each at his or her own tempo, at least five times. During this time, he walks around and checks students' progress, helping and correcting as needed.
  - Tara is not successful on her own but is able to complete the pattern when Mr. Carter sits right beside her and she copies his motions. He asks if she would like to choose a buddy to sit beside her. (He suggests several students he knows will help her well.)
- Mr. Carter asks students to return to patting the pattern all together, only this time, pretending the floor is red hot. Students bounce their hands quickly off the floor during the pattern.
- Mr. Carter invites students to sing the first verse of the song together, "playing" the floor on "Per-haps she'll die."
- Mr. Carter tells the class that their first and lowest note, which they will play with their LH, will be D. When they go to the instruments, they may use their LH pointer finger to silently touch the lowest (largest) D tone bar.

- The class follows the established routine for going to the instruments and all find their D.
  - ○ Mr. Carter takes a glockenspiel to Isaac's tray table.
  - ○ Mr. Carter has prepared several instruments with red and lemon-yellow stickers, numbered, for Devin and anyone else who would like one.
- Mr. Carter asks the students if they think the melody moves by step or by skip. One student answers, "skip," and Mr. Carter sings what that would sound like. The student changes his mind, and together, the class decides the melody moves all by step. Mr. Carter asks, "If D is our first and lowest note, and we're moving by step, what will our notes be?" The class decides together: "D, E, Feece, G" (having previously learned the one-syllable name for F-sharp is "Feece").
- Mr. Carter transfers the steps the class performed on the floor to the instruments, using left and right pointer fingers instead of patting. The class knows to "bounce" off the tone bars to "pull the sound out" rather than "pushing the sound in."
- Students transfer those motions to actual mallets, practicing the pattern together several times, beginning very slowly and progressing to performance tempo.
  - ○ Tara (mentioned earlier) and Pablo struggled with the crossover pattern with hands and then fingers on instruments but were eventually fairly successful. However, when mallets were introduced, they had difficulty again (as Mr. Carter had thought they might from previous crossover bordun experiences). Mr. Carter sees that Tara and Pablo are both becoming frustrated (Pablo's frustration manifesting as silliness and mallet antennae).

    Mr. Carter invites Tara, Pablo, and one other student to play a harmony part:

    on the bass bars and on a bass xylophone he has prepared with only those notes available. He tells them they may play that pattern or, if they wish, they may play only on the word "die." Pablo chooses the latter, deciding to play both the D and G together on that word. His classmates are impressed.
- The class performs the song together, singing the verses, and playing each time on "Per-haps she'll die" or, in Pablo's case, only on "die."

Are our three principles addressed in the previous vignette?

> **Principle 1**: In most cases, when modifications or adaptations are made to the activity, the expectations, or the materials, students are offered choices, and those choices are offered to all students, or not only to struggling students. In the case of Tara and Pablo, the harmony part they play truly does make the performance better and more interesting. Those students are held to a high standard and their abilities honored, rather than their struggles being allowed to hold them back.
>
> **Principle 2**: All students participate meaningfully, albeit differently, in the activity. All make music together, using their talents and abilities. In some cases, routines are in place to facilitate full participation. In other cases, Mr. Carter has thought ahead, anticipating where some students might struggle, and has provided options for those students to allow them to be successful.
>
> **Principle 3**: While Pablo and Tara play a different pattern, they still play together, with their classmates, contributing meaningfully to a musical whole.

AURAL AND MUSICAL LITERACY SKILLS

Teaching a child to love music without giving him or her the tools to read and notate it may be compared to teaching a child to love literature without teaching him or her how to read and write. As music educators, we hope our students will not only learn to love music and to sing and play well but also develop tools that allow them to access music independently, understand it, and document their own creativity in ways other musicians can then access. While musical literacy and a grasp of music theory are important goals for our students, these skills must be built on a solid foundation of strong aural skills; otherwise, the ability to read, write, and understand music becomes only a visual-intellectual exercise, unrelated to actual music in any meaningful way. For this reason, our discussion of rhythmic and melodic reading will be considered as inseparable from sequences involving aural skills.

RHYTHM

Many adult musicians recall first learning about rhythm reading through some version of a rhythm "pyramid" (see Musical Example 3.3) that places a whole note at the top, with half notes on the next line, followed by eighth notes, and then sixteenth notes.

Musical Example 3.3

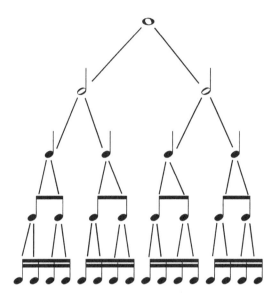

"This is a whole note. It has four beats," we were told. "These are half notes," the teacher continued. "They have two beats each. It takes two of them to fill the same time as a whole note." The explanation continued, either immediately or as we learned to count or play those rhythms—that is, as *some* of us learned to count and play those rhythms. Those of us who had already developed a sense of the beat were able to understand that "a whole note has four beats" (as far as this was true in that limited example assuming $\frac{4}{4}$ or $\frac{2}{4}$ time), but whether we were able to remember it was another issue.

Many other students, whose experiences had not given them a previous grasp of the beat, were not even able to gain that amount of meaning from the teacher's well-intentioned explanation. Beginning with the quarter note, as some other teachers did, was an improvement, but even that sequence put the proverbial cart before the horse, because in truth, the beat exists as a pulse—a feeling, and a feeling expressed in sound—and is most meaningfully felt, heard, and performed long before it is symbolized as any kind of mark on paper.

Steady Beat

Because children (as well as youth and adults) learn best when conceptual understanding is built upon a foundation of experience, rhythmic instruction must begin by providing the learner with sufficient experiences to make later theoretical understanding and symbolic representation meaningful. Gordon (2003) states: "Just as the audiation of tonality is the basis of tonal syntax, so the audiation of meter is the basis of rhythm syntax" (p. 161). Therefore, the fundamental experience upon which to lay a strong rhythmic foundation is the experience of keeping a steady beat (along with experiences of juxtaposing beat and no beat). See chapter 4 for ways in which creative movement may be used to aid this process. Beat competence is so important and so fundamental to all subsequent rhythm skills that careful sequencing, assessment, and winding back are especially crucial to this skill. While children can learn to keep the beat through many different beat motions and should experience a variety of beat motions throughout the learning process, it can be helpful in planning and winding back experiences if the teacher is familiar with an approximate order in which children are frequently able to perform the beat successfully. See Figure 3.1 to review the order of motions in which many music educators observe successful beat keeping in young children.

It is important to note that a natural beat-keeping tempo for young children tends to be considerably faster than that for adults, especially in the context of stepping the beat. Choksy (1999) writes: "The tempo at which earliest beat-stepping experiences are attempted must be the child's natural walking tempo, not the teacher's. Children's legs are shorter, and their natural stepping tempo is faster than that of adults" (p. 25). Think in terms of establishing tempos no slower (and preferably a little faster) than mm. 120 for initial beat-keeping activities. When keeping the beat as part of a faster/slower comparative activity, establish a tempo for "slower" that is much slower than the comfortable beat tempo, especially when stepping is involved, so that the child can actually shift weight from one foot to the other as he or she steps.

Introducing the Microbeat and Word "Rhythm"

Macrobeat and microbeat are fundamental components in the rhythm sequence. As children master beat keeping at various tempi and using various types of movement, experiences with the microbeat should also be introduced (Gordon, 2003). Internalization of the macro- and microbeat is the fundamental skill that allows for later success in hearing, feeling, reading, and writing rhythm. Experiences should include the following (in the context of singing, chanting, moving, and listening):

1. Teacher performs microbeat while students perform macrobeat.
2. Students perform microbeat while teacher performs macrobeat.
3. Students in two groups perform macrobeat against microbeat.
4. As a winding forward opportunity: Even primary grade students may be able to perform macrobeat and microbeat simultaneously (for instance, stepping the macrobeat while tapping the microbeat), especially when they have experienced moving to the macrobeat and moving to the microbeat, each while performing a contrasting skill (macrobeat, microbeat, or rhythm) vocally. Students should be offered this opportunity as a challenge choice (an opportunity to wind it forward) among other choices. For example, the teacher may say, "Now you have three choices: you may step the big beat; you may tap the little beat; or you may even try doing both at the same time!"

Word rhythm may be introduced by having students "catch the word pieces" by clapping their hands in front of their mouths while speaking a rhyme at a fairly slow tempo. When consistently successful, they may audiate the rhyme while clapping the word rhythm. The steps listed previously for macro- and microbeat may also be performed with combinations including word rhythm.

Training in a number of teaching approaches can suggest effective sequences to lead students to successful audiation, performance, reading, and writing of rhythm. The following vignette provides one basic outline and describes a classroom activity and some ways the teacher was able to wind forward and wind back to address his students' needs.

MR. VISVALINGHAM

Mr. Visvalingham is teaching a first-grade lesson segment on practicing quarter notes and paired eighth notes. His students have gone through the following basic sequence to arrive at this skill level. In the context of songs, rhymes, and recorded examples, they have done the following:

- Experienced and performed the macrobeat (in duple and triple microbeat meters) in the ways illustrated in the beat-keeping sequence chart in Figure 3.1
- Experienced and performed the microbeat
- Experienced and performed the word rhythm in songs and rhymes
- Tracked beat icons left to right

- Echoed rhythms using rhythm syllables:
  - Teacher spoke rhythms on neutral syllables and students echoed exactly
  - Teacher spoke rhythm syllables and students echoed exactly
  - Teacher spoke rhythms on neutral syllables and students "echoed" with rhythm syllables
- Improvised rhythms using rhythm syllables
- Distinguished (using icons to illustrate) between one sound on a beat and two sounds on a beat
- Discovered that (for now) a quarter note shows one sound on a beat and we read it as "tah," and paired eighth notes show two sounds on a beat and we read them as "tah-ti"
- Practiced reading a number of quarter and paired eighth-note patterns

Mr. V has used a number of engaging activities to assess his students' skill levels at all of the listed steps. He knows that:

Kelli came into class at the beginning of the year already able to perform all of these steps including rhythm reading and could read many more advanced rhythms as well.

Jennifer can keep a steady beat and associates the rhythm syllables with their symbols, but when asked to read rhythms individually, she cannot perform the rhythm with a steady pulse.

Leonard cannot yet keep a steady beat consistently through movement or when echoing rhythms alone. He does not yet associate quarter and eighth notes consistently with the rhythm syllables and has not yet successfully read rhythm patterns.

China can echo neutral-to-syllable very consistently and can improvise rhythms using rhythm syllables with great competence. She can articulate that ♫ says "tah-ti" and ♩ says "tah," but when asked to read a four-beat rhythm, she doesn't seem able to read the rhythm left to right.

Mr. V is leading students in a rhythm practice and partwork activity: students are invited to sing a simple familiar song together while he places a series of four-beat rhythm strips on the board.

After singing, students are invited to audiate and then read the rhythms, some individually, some together as a class.

Mr. V invites Leonard and Jennifer to join him at the gathering drum to be beat keepers for the next activity. Together with Mr. V, they play the beat on the drum while chanting the microbeat on "tah-ti tah-ti."

He invites Kelli and China to be rhythm pointers, using their fingers to tap the rhythms left to right as students read. China follows Kelli's lead, though it neither looks that way to the class nor feels that way to China.

He asks students on one side of the circle to sing the song while students on the other side of the circle read the rhythms using rhythm syllables and clapping musically, as Kelli and China track the rhythms. Then the two halves of the class switch and perform the opposite task.

The third time through, students are allowed to choose whether to be singers or rhythm readers. He asks Jennifer to partner with China and asks Kelli to sit with the group. (He is going to offer a winding forward opportunity he thinks Kelli will want to try.)

Mr. V offers a third option: he mentions that he has actually seen some people sing a song while reading an entirely different rhythm by clapping. He wonders if anyone might like to try clapping the rhythm on the board and singing the song at the same time. He expects Kelli to try this, and she does, largely successfully. Several others try as well, with varying degrees of success.

Many beg Mr. V to let them have one more try, which he does happily. More students try and more are successful.

What are some ways Mr. V winds forward and back, addressing each of our three principles?

Principle 1: While Mr. V does single out Leonard and Jennifer to address their needs, he does so in a way that allows them to play a highly desirable instrument. He honors them by giving them individual help, but in a context of collegial music making.

He does not ask Kelli to help China, only to be her partner. Both are also given desirable "jobs."

When challenges are offered, Mr. V offers the challenge to all students, allowing each to try and to make mistakes and experience challenge.

Principle 2: Mr. V has assessed his students' skill levels and is able to provide the activity that best suits each student's needs, from Leonard's work on steady beat to Jennifer's work on matching the "tah-ti" syllables with the beat and microbeat to China's work on tracking.

Mr. V. also provides a winding forward challenge for Kelli and for others who wish to try.

Principle 3: All of the winding listed previously is performed in the context of one musical activity, which not only reinforces each student's targeted skills but also provides a musically satisfying partwork activity as well.

UNIVERSAL PRINCIPLES
Sequence

When teachers plan and execute lessons based on well-designed, thoughtful sequences and teaching processes, it becomes much easier to discern possible reasons for students' lack of success at given tasks and, subsequently, easier to find effective ways to wind back for these students. For instance, when several second graders who have recently learned ♩♪ in the rhythm sequence mistakenly hypothesize that two sounds on one beat in a compound-meter rhyme should be written as ♫, the teacher must be able to wind back to the place in the sequence where that learning process became confused. Are those students not yet able to feel the difference between "marching" and "swinging"? Perhaps more echo patterns are needed. Perhaps those students have had insufficient movement experiences to inform their grasp of triple versus duple microbeats. Simply correcting the mistake will not result in true skill, true understanding, or accurate music making. When a clear sequence of skill built upon skill has been followed, the teacher can wind back intentionally, without having to guess where learning gaps may have occurred.

Goal Clarification

As students near the levels of beat, microbeat, and rhythm performance mastery that indicate readiness for notation, it will be helpful for the teacher, again, to keep in mind what his or her fundamental goals will be for this upcoming level of expertise. Will students be successful who name quarter notes and eighth notes? Will students be successful who use correct rhythm syllables? Will students be expected to maintain a steady beat and sense of the beat division as they read? All these skills are important, but it is the last one listed that we have been preparing students for as they have performed those myriad macrobeat, microbeat, and rhythm activities. Another question should perhaps be discussed at this stage, and that is in what order rhythmic units and rhythm notation symbols should be introduced. Beginning with a quarter-note beat makes sense, as that is the musical situation students will encounter most frequently for many years (followed closely by the dotted quarter-note macrobeat in compound rhythm, which will be discussed as well). While general agreement exists about beginning rhythm reading experiences with the quarter note, some music educators proceed next to half notes because the visual-intellectual explanation, "Two quarter notes tied together make a half note," can be easier and more straightforward. However, we have determined that developmental, experiential, and musical considerations, rather than visual-intellectual (subject logic) considerations, should drive our pedagogical sequencing decisions. The following factors suggest that introducing paired eighth notes along with, or directly after, quarter notes can make more sense than following the quarter note with sustained notes such as half notes:

- Introduction of concepts should follow the lead of the most appropriate repertoire for the age group. Songs and rhymes appropriate for young children are much less likely to contain primarily sustained notes than to feature the beat division.
- Use of rhythm syllables or speech syllables is a more effective rhythm reading approach for young children than "counting," which can be abstract and for which they may not yet possess the requisite knowledge or experience base. Rhythm and speech syllables make more musical sense with note values based on beat and beat division than on sustained notes, especially initially.
- As musicians of all ages sing and play, they do so more musically and with more rhythmic integrity when they have internalized not only the beat but also its divisions and subdivisions. They can then feel those divisions and subdivisions even in the context of reading and performing sustained notes. Beginning instruction with beat and beat division (microbeat), and rhythms based on them, can facilitate this important internalization so that when sustained notes are learned, somewhat later, they are informed not only by the beat but also by the beat division.

Student Independence

Without careful attention to student expertise, students may not have their needs met, simply because the teacher may be unaware that there is a problem. While formal assessment plays a part in teacher awareness of student mastery levels, far more important, from a practical standpoint, is one simple rule for the teacher: *Let the students do the work.* For example, if students have just learned to read ♪♪, and the teacher invites a student to read a rhythm containing this rhythm unit but taps the *rhythm* with his or her finger while tracking the rhythm on the board while the student reads, the teacher will not discover if that student is truly able to read that rhythm. Perhaps if the teacher had not tapped out the rhythm while tracking and had allowed the student to do the work of reading independently, the student might have read the rhythm incorrectly or simply stopped. This would have conveyed valuable information to the teacher about that student's skill level.

If the teacher sings a melodic pattern on a neutral syllable and asks a student to sing back in solfège, but the teacher "helps" by using body signs or hand signs while the student sings back, he or she will not discover whether or not that student can actually audiate the solfège pitches. Conversely, if the teacher allows the child to sing independently, that student's success *or failure* will provide accurate and valuable information to the teacher and to the child. Teachers (and students) must learn to embrace temporary and useful failure. Without allowing students to fail, teachers cannot be truly confident that each student has achieved the necessary expertise to proceed to the next step in the sequence. Opportunities must be provided for students to demonstrate skills independently of the teacher and independently of other students. Designing tools and establishing routines to make frequent assessment realistic help music educators discover the limits of our students' expertise and clarify the next steps for each student.

Students learn best from difference; therefore, triple meter instruction will deepen student understanding of duple meter. A chart to track student progress in preparation and presentation of triple meter can be found in chapter 3 of the companion website. For students who require more visual support for introduction to rhythm notation, the use of icons to wind it back may be helpful; see chapter 3 of the companion website for examples of visual icon use.

MELODY

Just as many opportunities for experiencing components of rhythm should be provided to children preceding and leading to the introduction of notation, ample experiences with pitch and melody should precede and prepare students for melodic reading from the staff. Activities mentioned previously, related to singing and to vocal exploration experiences detailed in chapter 5, offer some examples of readiness experiences that will prepare children to read melodically. Before discussing specific processes and strategies, it may be helpful to clarify exactly what is meant by melodic "reading." When competent readers read a book, it is not necessary that reading be performed aloud, nor is it necessary that some outside instrument help the reader to gain meaning from the printed page. Similarly, true melodic reading (and rhythmic reading as well) implies that the music reader sees the notation and instantaneously "hears" the melody (or rhythm, or harmony) "in his or her head" just as readers of words "hear" those words as they read them silently. This explanation is something of an oversimplification, but the ideas are useful as we clarify our goals for our students and their melodic reading. If the extent of students' melodic reading skills when they leave our classes includes only the ability to name the absolute (letter name) notes on the staff, to articulate some sense that when the notes go higher on the staff so does the sound, or even to label solfège pitches correctly based on a key signature, then that more fundamental and important goal of developing a strong link between the notation and the sound will not have been realized, and our students cannot truly be called musically literate. Vocal exploration activities can be used to aid in the introduction to melodic notation, providing needed scaffolding for some students; see chapter 3 of the companion website.

Forging this aural–visual link takes time and requires that music educators plan and sequence aural, kinesthetic, and visual experiences very intentionally. In addition to insuring that aural–visual links are created effectively, a well-considered sequence will allow the teacher to more effectively wind forward and wind back for students who need it.

MRS. GREENFIELD

Mrs. Greenfield's first graders have learned to sing, read, and write *sol-mi* patterns in solfège notation and on the staff, experiencing the following activities and others in sequence:

- Singing many songs that allow the *sol-mi* interval to be targeted
- Showing the *sol-mi* interval, when it arises in songs, with body solfège (*sol* on shoulders, *mi* on waist)
- Singing *sol* as the word "high" and *mi* as "low," showing with body solfège
- Echoing melodic *sol-mi* patterns:
  - Teacher's neutral syllable ("loo" or "bum") echoed exactly
  - Teacher's sung "high" and "low" echoed exactly
  - Teacher's sung neutral syllable to students' sung "high" and "low"
- Singing "high" and "low" with the teacher or another student "pushing buttons" (magnetic disks placed one above the other on the board, with a skip between)
- Singing correct pitches on a neutral syllable from the "buttons"
- Singing "high" and "low" from icons showing the melodic contour
- Discovering the "high" note as *sol* and the low note as *mi* and learning the Curwen hand signs for those solfège syllables
- Echoing:
  - Teacher's solfège to students' solfège
  - Teacher's neutral syllable to students' solfège (together and individually as aural assessment)

- Learning about the musical staff
- Learning "When *sol* is in a space, *mi* is in the space below it" and "when *sol* is on a line, *mi* is on the line below it"; reading *sol-mi* melodies from the staff; and using staff manipulatives to "write" *sol-mi* melodies

The first graders have been experiencing (singing, playing, hearing, echoing) songs containing *la* prominently and have been using body solfège (with the *la* pitch on the head) to show melodies containing *mi, sol,* and *la*. Mrs. Greenfield is beginning to assess students' readiness to make *la* conscious, naming it and learning the hand sign. She wants to make certain that students have aurally internalized that *la* is higher than *sol*.

While the majority of students in the class have mastered the skills and concepts described, several students need winding back or forward:

Jack demonstrates that he is audiating the intervals correctly. He can sing *sol-mi* patterns consistently correctly from Mrs. Greenfield's neutral syllables, and he can show *mi-sol-la* patterns (neutral and in song context) with body solfège. However, he still is not able to place *sol* and *mi* on the staff correctly.

Elias can sing correct *sol-mi* patterns and show them correctly with body solfège and hand signs, but when the teacher sings the *la* pitch or when it appears in a song and students are asked to show it on their bodies, he consistently shows it on his waist.

Kendra is new to the school. She sings on pitch and demonstrates high musical aptitude, but she hasn't learned any solfège, hand signs, or staff placement yet.

Rachel can usually show someone else's sung pitches correctly on body solfège (even when they sing a neutral syllable) and she can place *sol-mi* note heads correctly on the staff, but she is not singing on pitch at all. She sings consistently in a low, chesty near-monotone. Mrs. Greenfield is helping her to find her head voice.

Penny has limited movement and uses a wheelchair. She does not speak or sing words clearly but can often sing pitches correctly with the class.

Mrs. Greenfield has students sing the song "We Are Dancing in the Forest" and play the chase game.

We Are Dancing in the Forest

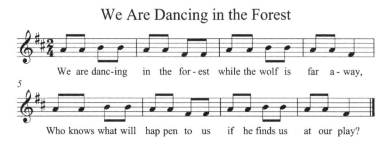

We are danc-ing   in   the   for-est   while   the   wolf   is   far   a-way,

Who knows what will   hap pen   to   us   if   he finds us   at   our   play?

Mrs. Greenfield has modified the singing (nonchasing) portion of the game so that, instead of moving in a circle and holding hands, students stand in place, facing outward, and show the pitches of the song on body solfège. While students can still see those to their right and left, the outward-facing position makes it less likely that students will be copying the motions of other students, and Mrs. Greenfield can do an informal, preliminary assessment of students' skill levels.

Mrs. Greenfield also takes advantage of this opportunity to target the needs of some of the students mentioned previously:

She invites several students, including Jack and Kendra, to take turns going to the floor staff and "hopping" *sol* and *mi* in the correct spaces or on the correct lines when they occur in the song ("in the forest," "far away," "happen to us," and "at our play").

She recruits a small "*la* team" to be in charge of only the *las*, singing only that pitch when it occurs ("dancing," "wolf is," "what will," and "find us") and showing it on heads. Of course, Elias is on this team with some other classmates.

Mrs. Greenfield encourages the "children" who are being chased to cry, "Help! help!" in their head voices (making sure not to scream or yell) and to throw their hands in the air dramatically. She makes sure Rachel gets to be one of the chased children and guides her to use her head voice in this play context. She is able to demonstrate a higher voice than she has used before, and Mrs. Greenfield and her classmates congratulate her on her success.

Penny is able to use a pointer to show the body solfège levels on a paper doll of herself that her teacher has taped to the tray on her wheelchair.

Students repeat the game several times. Penny's paraprofessional helps Penny to chase the children when it is her turn to be the wolf. Penny is able to tag the children with a pool noodle her teacher has adapted for her.

Mrs. Greenfield is able to address the three principles, winding forward and back in the context of a game.

> **Principle 1:** All of the "special jobs" Mrs. Greenfield devises to target her students' needs are desirable and enjoyable.
>
> Students are able to display competence while working on improving their weaker skill areas.
>
> **Principle 2:** Jack uses gross motor skills to reinforce the visual placement of *sol* and *mi* so that when the time comes to place note heads on the staff, he will be able to refer to this experience.
>
> Kendra can "copy" Jack and learn the *sol-mi* "rules" through experience, without Mrs. Greenfield needing to single her out to explain at length.

Both Jack and Kendra have their strong aural skills challenged, having to hear when *sol* and *mi* occur in the context of the song in order to "hop" the *sol-mi* parts of the melody correctly on the staff.

Elias is gaining experience in audiating *la* and repeatedly placing it correctly with body solfège. This kinesthetic cue and the concentration on that one pitch will make placing that pitch easier and more successful when back in the context of the other pitches.

Principle 3: All of these carefully chosen activities take place in the context of a game played together and a song sung together.

CLASSROOM CULTURE AND USEFUL FAILURE

Of course, it cannot be overstated that teachers must foster classroom cultures in which mistakes and risk taking are seen as positive and admirable, where persistence and work are valued over innate ability, and where the learning process is considered a higher good than correct answers. Allowing students to do the work and to make mistakes routinely will encourage the development of this type of classroom culture and allowing teachers to know exactly where each child is in the learning process. Too often, music teachers and directors perform and demonstrate skills along with their students—singing along instead of allowing students to sing independently, tracking rhythms on the board instead of allowing students to truly read on their own, and even sometimes holding students' hands to guide beat keeping or instrument playing. Not only does this teacher usurping of student skill demonstration inhibit learning and skill development, but also it keeps the teacher from accurately assessing what students actually know and can (or cannot) do.

Consider an activity as simple as teaching a song by echo rote. In this popular song-teaching technique, the teacher sings the entire song and then breaks it down by phrases, singing each phrase or motive and inviting students to echo. When each phrase is solidly learned, the teacher sings two phrases at a time, inviting students to echo this longer section. Progressively longer sections are sung until students sing the entire song from memory. The problem arises when, as is frequently the case, the teacher echoes each phrase along with the class. Often, when the teacher sings his or her own echoes routinely, the class simply allows the teacher to do the work, student singing becomes weak or nonexistent, and the teacher has no idea whether or not the students actually know the song. It takes some self-discipline on the part of the teacher to break this habit. The teacher must be willing to sing a phrase, give a gesture for students to sing, and then tolerate the initial silence or weak singing. When children realize they are actually responsible for singing the echo phrases and that the teacher trusts and respects their competence enough to allow them to fail on the way to success, they will rise to the challenge. There is almost nothing that inhibits confident and competent student singing like a teacher routinely singing along with the students.

The situation just described is offered as one example among many, where teacher performance can inhibit student performance and keep teachers from accurately assessing students' skill levels. Providing opportunities for students to demonstrate skills individually is also important as we work toward meeting the needs of all of our students and deciding where to wind forward and back. The solo singing games and the vocal exploration and question-and-answer activities mentioned earlier in this chapter can allow the teacher to assess and keep track of each student's singing development—but only if the student is allowed to demonstrate those skills without the teacher jumping in to "save" him or her when he or she fails. The teacher in a kindergarten or first-grade math class keeps track of which students can competently demonstrate one-to-one correspondence and number sense by counting objects. The teacher does not move in and begin counting the objects himself or herself if the child cannot perform the task, assuming the child will "get it eventually." Music educators need to take our skill assessments as seriously and be as accurate. The creation of user-friendly and effective record-keeping tools will help to keep track of each child's progress.

In contrast with an assessment record that simply states: "sings on pitch," as is seen commonly, an assessment chart such as the one in Figure 3.2 can help the teacher keep track of the "steps between the steps" of each student's progress.

Tools such as this may appear to add to the music teacher's already great workload. However, these steps-between-the-steps record-keeping charts can actually energize us, showing us a clear way forward with each child and eliminating some of the frustration we inevitably feel when we genuinely want to serve each student well but find that task overwhelming. Knowing exactly where each student is can clarify our task, telling us what questions to ask, what challenges to work toward solving, and what resources to seek to wind forward and back effectively. Many schools and school systems expect music educators to provide written feedback and even grades from music class. Having kept a clear record of where each student is in his or her

Student	Demonstrates "head voice"	If "no": Distinguishes between T's head voice/no head voice	If "no": Raspiness/vocal damage?	Sings "yoo-hoo" C'-A in tune	If "no": Sings in tune at other pitch level (indicate)	If "no": Distinguishes between T's matching/not matching	Sings in tune in song context F-C'	If "no": Sings in tune at other pitch level (indicate)	If "no": Distinguishes between T's matching/not matching
Giancarlo	✓			✓				C-G	✓
Levi	✓			✓			✓		
Eve		✓	✓ Parent called 10/13		✓ F-D	✓			✓

Figure 3.2 Steps Between Steps Assessment.

skill development can not only give parents and families an accurate picture of their child's progress but also lend the music program the credibility it deserves, as families and administrators realize we take our task and our students seriously.

Ms. Welsh's school system requires teachers to document student demonstration of certain basic skills in music. One of these skills, for first grade, is the ability to read quarter notes and paired eighth notes. Ms. Welsh knows that not all of her first graders are ready to perform this skill, but she is more concerned with what they *can* do. She designs an assessment tool that shows not only who has demonstrated the ability to read quarter notes and eighth notes, as her school system requires, but also where each student is in the sequence of skills leading up to reading those patterns (see Figure 3.3).

Student	Performs beat:			Tracks ♥ icons	Claps micro ♥ vs. T. beat	Claps Word rhythm vs. T beat	Echoes syllables from T. neutral	Decodes R. w/ icons	Reads ♩♫ rhythm correctly with steady beat
	Patsch	clap	step						
Angela	✓	✓	✓	✓	✓	✓	✓	✓	✓
Yogesh	✓	✓	✗	✓	✗	✓	✓	✓	✓
Jordan	✓	✗	✗	✗	✗	✗	✗	✗	✗
Emily	✓	✓	✓	✓	✓	✓	✗	✓	✓

Figure 3.3   Sequence of Skills.

Flexibility and Goal Adjustment

Flexible assessment tools not only provide clarity about student expertise and emphasize what students *can* do but also help indicate patterns that give teachers insight into why a child may be struggling. For instance, in the assessment chart in Figure 3.3, Yogesh is able to pat and clap the beat but cannot step it yet. He is able to demonstrate all other skills except for clapping the microbeat against the teacher's macrobeat. Perhaps Yogesh is not having trouble feeling rhythms. Stepping the beat and performing the microbeat both require mature motor skills. It may be immature motor skills that are keeping Yogesh from being able to perform the rhythmic skills he is actually able to feel. Knowing or surmising this can help Ms.

Welsh make decisions about how quickly Yogesh should progress and whether, for him, *winding to the side*—providing activities at a comparable skill level but delaying more difficult motor skill demonstration—may allow his motor skills to catch up to his true rhythmic ability.

It may seem daunting to envision the formatting, sequence, and design of a lesson appropriate for primary students that includes the many features discussed in this chapter. However, using the complete and detailed first-grade lesson plan included in chapter 3 of the companion website as a template may aid the creation of lesson plans incorporating the vocal, tonal, rhythmic, creative movement, folk dance, and instrumental concepts necessary for a comprehensive elementary general music lesson.

CONCLUSION

Teaching music in primary grades is a great privilege and a great responsibility. Providing rich, substantive musical experiences for our students that lead them to satisfying, artistic music making should be our primary goal. However, if we do not plan these experiences carefully and intentionally, and moreover, if we do not expect mastery from our young student musicians, we run the risk of allowing these students to fall short of their great musical potential and to miss out on the deep level of satisfaction that only comes with real expertise. Careful planning, frequent and honest assessment, and clear-sightedness about our goals for each student will allow us to wind forward and back so that every child we teach becomes an expert, an artist, and a true musician.

REFERENCES

Choksy, L. (1999). *The Kodály method I: Comprehensive music education* (3rd ed.). Upper Saddle River, NJ: Prentice Hall.

Csíkszentmihályi, M. (1990). *Flow: The psychology of optimal experience*. New York, NY: Harper & Row.

Gordon, E. E. (2003). *Learning sequences in music*. Chicago, IL: GIA.

Houlahan, M., & Tacka, P. (2008). *Kodály today*. New York, NY: Oxford.

Reynolds, A. M., & Valerio, W. H. (2015). Early childhood music curriculum. In C. M. Conway (Ed.), *Designing musicianship focused curriculum and assessment*. Chicago, IL: GIA.

CHAPTER 4

Using Movement to Foster Creativity and Deepen Musical Understanding

HEATHER RUSSELL, *Cleveland State University*
ROBERTA Y. HICKOX, *Halifax Area School District,*
Halifax, Pennsylvania

CHAPTER OVERVIEW

Creative movement can and should be incorporated into the entire pre-kindergarten though twelfth-grade music curriculum. In this chapter, we will describe how creative movement provides opportunities for all students to demonstrate their understanding in alternative ways, and how it fosters higher-order thinking skills, supports musical creativity, and strengthens students' understanding of the musical concepts they are representing in movement. We will describe ways to individualize creative movement experiences that meet all students at their current level of skill and understanding. The following topics and resources are included:

- Building movement awareness and a movement vocabulary
- Individualizing instruction by providing choice within structure
- Establishing a safe environment for creative movement
- Activity examples for elementary *and* secondary music settings

Movement has long been an important component of music education (Ferguson, 2005), particularly in the elementary general music setting, but also in the context of performing ensembles and instrumental instruction. Some types of movement to music are easily recognized, such as in folk dancing, singing games, marching band, and choreographed dance; other types of movement in music instruction are harder to recognize as movement. For example, when students are fingering notes on instruments, playing percussion instruments with hands or mallets, manipulating their voices to sing, or controlling their breathing to sing or play a wind instrument, the movement is not the product (musical sound), but movement is still essential to the music learning activity. Creative movement, or movement for expression or to represent musical understanding, is an important counterpoint to other types of movement, and it can and should be incorporated across the music curriculum, from early childhood through high school.

Creative movement provides opportunities for all students to demonstrate their understanding in alternative ways, fosters higher-order thinking skills, supports musical creativity, and strengthens students' understanding of the musical concepts they are representing in movement. In a school environment in which students must focus on deriving the one and only correct answer throughout the day in other content areas (and often in music classes), creative movement can be freeing and refreshing. It allows students opportunities to demonstrate their musical understanding and their unique ideas in an atmosphere in which there are no right or wrong answers, or at least many possible right answers and few wrong answers. For example, if the parameters of a creative movement activity only specify the use of high, medium, or low levels and smooth movement, students are free to move in general space or self-space, to move in a straight or zigzag pattern, to move with only one arm or one knee, or to move slowly or quickly. With this freedom, students can participate in whatever way they are able or at whatever skill level that will allow them to learn successfully; they can and do *wind it back* or *wind it forward* for themselves (or self-level). This is the essence of an individualized approach to teaching and learning that provides multiple access points for *all* students to engage in music. In this chapter, we will describe ways any music teacher can incorporate creative movement and support the development of creativity and musical understanding in every student.

CREATIVITY

If you want to be more creative, stop waiting for inspiration and start experimenting. **Creativity isn't creation at all**, it's reorganization.

Jon Wesley (2014)

What Wesley is saying is that creativity requires taking something one already knows or can do and changing it in some way. Creative people have a large vocabulary, or repertoire, of skills in and understandings of their fields of creativity. Jazz musicians, for example, have built a repertoire of typical jazz ideas, large and small, by playing others' compositions, copying others' improvisations, listening extensively to music in the jazz genres, and interacting with jazz musicians. Similarly, creative dancers have built a vocabulary of movements, simple and complex, by dancing others' choreography, copying others' movements, and watching and interacting with many fine dancers. The repertoire of ideas and movements is the foundation for creativity; it allows musicians and dancers to analyze and evaluate music they play and hear and choreography they dance and see, and to create new musical and movement ideas. (For more information on creativity in music, see chapter 7.)

Part of the understanding of creative people is an awareness of what they know and can do (metacognition), coupled with a vocabulary to describe it. Music teachers can facilitate creativity development in students by helping them build awareness of movement, a movement vocabulary, and a language vocabulary with which to describe what they know and can do. Teachers can build this base by providing examples of ways to move and opportunities to make choices about what to do in the context of musical activities, and by ensuring a safe environment in which to make those choices, thus addressing the individual needs of all students and creating an environment that honors learning differences.

A NOTE TO SECONDARY MUSIC TEACHERS

We would like to encourage secondary music teachers to incorporate creative movement in classes and ensembles. We most often hear two arguments against doing so: there is not enough time to rehearse already, let alone take time out for movement; and secondary-aged students will not want to do creative movement in band, orchestra, or choir, and therefore will not cooperate. The experiences of many ensemble directors refute those arguments. Two directors (Elizabeth Power and Malcolm W. Rowell Jr.) write of the benefit of movement in the foreword of Weikart, Boardman, and Bryant (2004, pp. xxi–xxii). Power, the education director of the Florida West Coast Symphony, writes that over the time her youth symphony members have been engaged in creative movement, they "have exhibited accelerated development in musicianship skills that not only have enriched their ability to play their instruments but also ...

have enabled them to understand the aesthetic values of music." Rowell, the former director of bands at the University of Massachusetts Amherst, writes that incorporating movement in rehearsals "allows the student to engage in the creative aspects of music-making in addition to the sequential development and refinement of executive skills."

When you use creative movement to help students understand the music they are learning to perform, they become better ensemble musicians. They may be reticent at first, but once they see the way it helps them grow as musicians, how they can apply it to repertoire, and how much fun it is, they quickly change their attitudes. We encourage you to try some of the activities in this chapter, in other chapters about creativity in this book, and in the resources listed at the end of the chapter and see what happens!

BUILDING A VOCABULARY/REPERTOIRE

A repertoire in creative movement refers to a vocabulary of basic movements (being able to move in a variety of ways), language to describe those movements (vocabulary), and self-awareness of movement. Students with little experience moving, little awareness of how they move, and a limited vocabulary to describe movement need teachers to model many simple movements that they can copy and label (by body part, by location, by movement terms). They may also need teachers to describe how they are moving for them and ask questions about how they are moving that increase their awareness. Teachers can use dance and physical education vocabularies, such as the themes developed by Rudolph Laban, as resources when choosing movements for students to copy. (See Figure 4.1 and the resources section of this chapter.) It is important to remember that even older students who have little experience or awareness of moving will need teachers to scaffold their movement development in these simple ways.

After students have copied the teacher's basic movements and developed an initial vocabulary of movement, they then need teachers to give them opportunities to use this vocabulary of movement in creative ways. Teachers can have students choose movements to perform and plan ways to vary them, often to meet a movement or musical goal established by the teacher or by the students.

Elementary music teachers may, for example, model walking in several ways: with feet in regular walking position (toes forward, heel-to-toe movement), toes in, toes out, on the heels, on tiptoe, with feet wide apart, crouched down, or in different pathways (curvy, zigzag, straight).

The teacher may label the different ways of walking (or ask the students to label them) and then ask students to plan a way to walk from one side of the room to the other, let them try their plan, and have them describe their plan and how it worked. In this example, students may choose to walk across the room in one of the ways modeled by the teacher or in another way. This is the beginning of creativity in movement—making choices. As students make choices or plan ways to move, try their ideas, and reflect on their choices or plans, they build their vocabulary of movement ideas.

Laban Themes			
Effort Factors	**Effort Elements (extremes on a continuum)**		
Flow	Free..Bound		
Weight	Light/Gentle...Heavy/Strong		
Space	Indirect...Direct		
Time	Sudden/Quick...Sustained/Slow		
Categories of Basic Movement			
Category	**Locomotor**		**Nonlocomotor**
Definition	Transferring weight		Anchored weight, no weight transfer
	In place or while traveling		In place only
	through space		
Examples	Walk/March		Twist
	Gallop/Slide		Turn
	Jump (land on two feet)		Swing
	Hop (one foot only)		Rock
	Skip		Bend/Straighten
	Crawl		Rise/Fall
	Leap		Curl/Stretch
			Push/Pull
Words to label or describe movement			
Slither	Soar	Dart	Dodge
Swim	Waddle	Fly	Twirl
Flick	Wiggle	Poke	Shiver
Twitch	Melt	Grow	Shrink
In/Out	Near/Far	Straight/Curved/Zigzag	Low/Middle/High
Start/Stop	Fast/Slow	Speeding up/Slowing down	Even/Uneven

Figure 4.1 Movement vocabulary.

Secondary ensemble directors can build a knowledge base of conducting gestures and ensemble skills for their students during a warm-up that includes creative movement. For example, students can create ways to signal stop and go using movement—not necessarily traditional conducting gestures. Students use these movements with partners in the ensemble to get them to start and stop singing a song, compare and contrast the gestures they chose and how well they worked, and apply the awareness gained from the movement activity to ensemble skills (i.e., Why it is important to stop and start together in an ensemble? How do you know when to do so?). Finally, directors can ask students to describe a place in their current ensemble repertoire in which starting and stopping together is important. This entire activity can take only a few minutes, but the creative movement can bring students' awareness to and build their knowledge of an important ensemble skill.

Winding It Back

Sometimes students move without awareness of how they are moving; they may move in simple or complex ways, but their movements are by chance rather than purposeful. In this instance, teachers can build students' vocabulary and self-awareness by describing for students how they are moving and by asking concrete questions about their movements.

STEVEN: AN EXAMPLE OF WINDING IT BACK

Ms. Smith, an elementary music teacher, asks her first-grade class to listen to a piece of music and move the way the music makes them feel. The music has a strong feeling of medium-tempo steady beat and an accessible, flowing melody. She notices that Steven is wildly flailing his arms, legs, and head during this activity; it is clear his movements do not match the music. Ms. Smith stops the music and says to Steven, "Tell me about how you moved." Steven replies, "I moved like this," and does the flailing movement again. She realizes Steven does not know how to describe his movements with words, so she winds it back and asks, more pointedly, "What did you do with your arms?" Steven says, "This," and flails his arms again. Ms. Smith tries again, asking, "Where were your arms when you moved them?" "Here," Steven says, flailing once more. Finally, Ms. Smith describes Steven's movements *for* him, saying, "I notice that your arms are out to your sides and are moving up and down very fast." Steven replies, "Yes, that's right."

In this example, instead of giving Steven a lower grade for creative movement or thinking that Steven was just fooling around, Ms. Smith winds it back by giving him labels for his movement that he can use himself and helping him attend to his movements (build self-awareness). She is able to note that, while his movements did not match the music, it was because of his level of knowledge and lack of self-awareness. She will be sure to give Steven more specific examples to copy and more parameters on choices for creative movement in the future, and she will describe his movements and how they do or do not match the music for him.

Winding It Forward

Some students have a lot of experience, self-awareness, and skill with movement. They are able to move in simple and complex ways with purpose. In this instance, teachers can build students' vocabulary and self-awareness by including or allowing their movements that may be more complex than instructed and by connecting what they are doing to musical awareness and understanding.

ASHAD: AN EXAMPLE OF WINDING IT FORWARD

Ms. Jones teaches her third-grade music class a simple hand jive to recorded music, but she notices that Ashad is embellishing the movements. She asks him to demonstrate his way of doing the hand jive and describe it. He says, "I made it smoother." Another student adds, "He made it faster." Ms. Jones says, "Yes, he is moving faster. In fact, he is moving twice as fast as it goes, which we could call 'double-time.'" Ashad answers, "Yeah, double-time." Ms. Jones recognizes an opportunity to wind it forward and connect it to music. She says, "When we do that with the notes of a melody, when we play it or write it twice as fast, we call it diminution. Can you do the opposite? Try stretching the hand jive movements out to twice as long. That's called augmentation."

In this example, instead of thinking Ashad was misbehaving, Ms. Jones recognizes he is changing the movement because he is ready for something more complex. She builds his understanding of movement *and* music by calling his awareness to and labeling how his movements are different and by encouraging him to take it even further. She is able to note that Ashad is able to handle more complex movements and plans to give him fewer guidelines for creative movement in the future as an opportunity to demonstrate his creativity.

Both of these examples illustrate reflection in action, in which a teacher recognizes that a student's current performance level is at a different level than expected and modifies expectations to meet that level. Teachers can also plan several levels, or access points, through which students can participate in creative movement and meet the musical objective of a lesson.

PROVIDING OPPORTUNITIES TO MAKE CHOICES

When students have a vocabulary of purposeful movements and language to label those movements, teachers can support creative movement by providing opportunities to make choices or multiple ways to engage in the lesson. The teacher sets parameters for movement choices, which can be narrow or wide, depending on the goals of the activity, and the vocabulary and current performance levels of the students. Examples mentioned earlier in this chapter were planning a way to walk across the room and trying some movements to signal start and stop. The parameters for student choice in those examples are the place and direction of movement (across the room) and the basic type of movement (walking), and the purpose of the movement (communicate start and stop). The first set of parameters (place, direction, type) is relatively narrow, and they support creativity with students who are relatively inexperienced; the second parameter (purpose) is relatively open ended and supports creativity with students who are more experienced. When choosing parameters for movement choices, teachers must be clear about what they want students to experience or achieve (the goals) (Figures 4.2 and 4.3).

Use word cards to direct student movement and label them. Have one set of index cards with locomotor movements written on them (one movement on each card) and another set with nonlocomotor movements. The sets of word cards can be different colors to aid in classification. Have students stand in stationary self-space, scattered throughout the space. Distribute one card to each student, who reads it without allowing other students to see it. Have students try the movement on their card, all students at the same time. Then, have them sit in self-space. Say, "When I call your name, please do your movement, but do not say what it is. We will describe and label the movement you are demonstrating." Call on students to move and invite other students to describe their movement. When they are done describing, have the student who moved read the word on his or her card and sit down. Repeat until each student has had a turn to move. (Adapted from Gilbert, 1992.)

Figure 4.2   Activity: Word cards (movement vocabulary).

Have students explore the idea of nonlocomotor, or anchored, movement by "gluing" or anchoring different body parts to the floor and seeing what else they can move while they are "glued." Say, "Put a dab of invisible glue on the bottom of one shoe. Glue that shoe to the floor. What body parts can you move while your shoe is glued to the floor?" (You might comment on what you see students moving, e.g., "I see someone moving his knee/elbow/shoulder. Can you also move your head? What about your belly?") Say, "Unglue your shoe, and put some glue on your forehead. Glue your forehead to the floor. What body parts can you move while your forehead is glued to the floor?" (Again, you might comment on what parts students are moving, and ask questions like, "Can you move two parts of your body at the same time? What about three parts?") Ask, "What other body parts could you glue/anchor to the floor? Summarize the activity by asking questions like, "Which body parts glued/anchored were easiest/hardest? Why? What does it mean to be glued/anchored? Where else can we be anchored besides the floor?" (a chair, the wall, etc.). (Adapted from Gilbert, 1992.)

Figure 4.3   Activity Example: Glue (nonlocomotor movement, body awareness).

Teachers can also use narrower choices (more parameters) when the goal of creative movement is experiencing a specific musical concept or when the next choice will build on the first choice. Even within narrow parameters, however, instruction is individualized, because students can choose a way to participate in which they can experience success and demonstrate their skill and understanding at individual performance levels (Figure 4.4).

Choosing ways to move to represent the feel of music, or exploring movements to represent a musical concept or idea (e.g., musical sequence), can be wound back or forward depending on the level of experience and

Divide the classroom space in two using a piece of masking tape. Have students stand in self-space on one side of the masking tape. Say, "Welcome to Slowland, where every movement is slow. This includes turning your head, taking a breath, and moving your arms, legs, and feet when you walk. Explore how you might move in Slowland." Give students time to try slow, sustained movements. If needed, suggest movements for students to try in Slowland, such as skipping, tiptoeing, walking, or jumping. Say, "On the other side of the tape is Fastland. When I play the slide whistle, please cross over the masking tape border into Fastland and explore how you might move there." Again, give students time to try quick, sudden movements and suggest movements to try as necessary. Questions for increasing self-awareness: "How is your movement different in each land? What do you have to think about to perform the same movements in each land?" Have students go back and forth between each side, using the slide whistle as the signal. Ask, "How will you move until you cross the border?" (This activity can also be adapted as "Heavyland/Lightland." to experience variations in weight.) (Adapted from Gilbert, 1992.)

Figure 4.4   Activity Example: Slowland/Fastland (time).

"Stand in self-space, scattered around the room. Move your hands as if you were swimming under water. Now move your hands as if you were painting a large painting. We can call this sustained movement 'smooth.' Show 'smooth' with another body part. Try moving smoothly as you travel in general space." Give students time to try traveling smoothly. "Now, try moving your hands suddenly or sharply. What are some activities in which we might move like that? Try showing 'sharp' with another body part. Try sharp movements while traveling in general space." "Listen to this music, which is sometimes smooth and sometimes sharp." Play the recording for students (enough so they can hear both parts): Track 12, *Stone Soup*, from Eric Chappelle's *Contrast and Continuum: Music for Creative Dance, Volume 1*. "Choose a smooth way to move when the music sounds smooth (when the violin is playing), and a sharp way to move when the music sounds sharp or sudden (when the drum is playing)." (Adapted from Gilbert, 1992.)

Figure 4.5   Activity Example: Smooth/Sharp (time/space/energy/articulation).

knowledge base of the students, and in response to the choices students make, regardless of their age or grade level (Figure 4.5).

After teachers give students a task with choices, they can decide whether to wind instruction back or forward by asking students questions, describing their movement, and having them describe the movements of others and how they represent the music or concept. Remember that parameters, or choices, when they are clear to both the teacher and students, create safety, which fosters creativity rather than stifles it. Initially, narrower parameters will facilitate safety and participation (and increase on-task behavior). Later on, wider parameters will do the same. Figure 4.6 contains a list of parameters teachers can use for student choice (see also Figure 4.1).

Representing Melody	Move your arms up and down in front of your body.	Walk a pathway across the floor (steady beat, contour only).	Choose a pathway to represent the melodic contour and a way to move that represents the melodic rhythm.
Representing Mood	Walk in a way that shows the feeling of the music.	Create a statue that represents the feeling.	Conduct in a way that communicates the feeling.
Representing Sequence	Explore different ways to do the same movement, plan an order to do them.	Choose a movement and do it using different levels.	Choose movements that represent the specific intervals and rhythm of the sequence pattern and do them in levels that match how they occur in the song.

Figure 4.6   Examples of planned choices for differentiating creative movement.

Representing Character	Sit, walk, skip, crawl, etc., the way the character's music suggests (e.g., Grandfather in *Peter and the Wolf*).	Move steady beat[1] using a hand or arm movement the character might perform.	Move around the room representing how the character feels in each part of the piece.
Representing Timbre	Move your shoulders to represent the cymbal crashes in this piece.	Explore ways to move to show the flute part.	Move as if you were an animal in a way that goes with one of the instrument parts you hear.
Representing Dynamics	Hold arms out wide to show loud and in close to show soft.	Explore big ways to move when the music is loud and small ways to move when the music is quiet.	Explore ways to move that show how the music is loud or soft.
Representing Phrase	Move your hands from one side to the other to show each phrase; change your statue pose on each phrase.	Walk steady beat and change direction for each phrase.	Plan a pathway that represents the sequence of four phrases in this song.
Representing Form	Choose a locomotor movement for the A section; choose a nonlocomotor movement for the B section.	Choose a way to move steady beat. Get in groups of three and choose an order in which to perform your movements, one for each of the three sections of the piece.	In small groups, create a dance for this song.
Representing Articulation	Sing your part at Letter A, use your fingers or hands while you sing to represent the articulation.	Explore ways to represent legato and staccato articulation by moving your body.	Explore gestures that communicate a style of articulation, conduct another person playing their part following your conducting for articulation.
Creating Movement Sequences to Go With Recorded or Sung Music	Choose two places to tap steady beat; alternate between them (e.g., head, stomach, head, stomach).	Choose four places to tap steady beat; alternate between them (e.g., head, stomach, legs, clap).	With a partner, create a hand jive using four movements.
Free Choice	Listen to this piece (1-2 minutes of it); choose a musical element you hear to represent through movement; explore ways to move to represent that element; choose your favorite way to represent the element to share with the class; demonstrate it, all copy it, describe the movement and how it represented the musical element.		

[1] We are using the phrasing "move steady beat" and "walk (or tap) steady beat" as a way to denote the internal, kinesthetic understanding of pulse and rhythm, as opposed to "move to a steady beat," for example, which denotes an external source for that understanding.

Figure 4.6 (Continued)

ESTABLISHING A SAFE ENVIRONMENT

Teachers support students' developing creativity in movement by establishing a safe environment in which to make choices about movement, to explore movement, and to allow for the individual needs of all students to be addressed. The individuality, and sometimes spontaneity, of moving creatively creates risk in the classroom—risk of being laughed at or risk of making "wrong" choices. Therefore, care in creating and maintaining an environment in which students feel safe to take risks in moving is of the utmost importance. A safe environment is one in which activities are free from right or wrong judgments to varying degrees. Figure 4.7 lists some ways teachers can establish a safe environment.

Technique	Examples
Define parameters for movement that allow for choice and individuality.	Students can and should stretch the boundaries of those parameters. There are many solutions!
Avoid qualitative judgments (positive and negative).	Avoid these: Good job; Be more creative; I like that; Excellent; Okay—but...; Is that all?; Nice try.
Describe movement for students (i.e., provide specific feedback)	I notice you are moving your ____ at ____speed; When you move your ___like that it looks like you are representing ____ in the music. I see you are walking with your legs stiff and toes pointed out.
Ask open-ended questions to clarify why students are moving in a certain way (whether or not their movement seems to fit the parameters given).*	What body part are you moving? How does your movement match the music? What kind of pathway did you choose? What are some words to describe how you are moving? How is your movement the same as/different from your classmate's movement?
Sometimes model movements, but sometimes do not model.*	When modeling, have students copy you exactly (no choice); When you want to give choice, do not model.
Move expressively or to represent a concept or element present in a piece.	Have students listen to the music before moving to it; then respond freely; then have them describe what the music sounds like and how their movement choices fit the music.*
Let students copy each other.	If they cannot think of a way to move, give students permission to get ideas from peers.
Recognize that students doing something different from what you asked, or varying the movement, can be okay.	If movement fits the purpose or task, it is okay; if not, it is a signal to wind it back or forward.

Figure 4.7 Important considerations for establishing a safe environment.

Have students try movements on their own first, all students exploring at once.	Before moving to music, moving in group tempo, sharing movement with the teacher or class, or moving with a partner, students need a chance to work out movements and ideas at their own speed, in their own space, and without the music—without class attention on them.*
Have students move with an object for expressive movement (especially students in 3rd-6th grades).	Moving a shaker, scarf, ribbon, hula-hoop, ball, piece of paper, or other object puts the attention on the object rather than the person.
Make it okay for students to participate at different skill levels.	Either plan more than one way to participate, or allow students to choose ways to move in which they can be successful. Some may choose to move in limited space or with small movements, which is okay if it falls within the parameters (sometimes due to social anxiety, or it could also be due to advanced skills).
Incorporate students' ideas.	Have students lead class movement, use their ideas for choreography, or have the class try each other's movements (and compare/contrast them). Teacher copies students' movements, too.

*Suggestions grounded in the work of Phyllis Weikart (2006).

Figure 4.7 (Continued)

Once teachers have helped students develop a beginning vocabulary of movements and labels, one of the most important things to do when asking students to express creativity in movement is to refrain from modeling movement or giving examples of movements. When teachers give examples of ways students could move, they are often just offering choices or starting ideas; however, students tend to simply copy the teacher's examples instead of trying something different. Even if teachers do not model movement ideas, they may have in mind ways students should move, but it is important to be open to all movements students may suggest or try (Figure 4.8).

Teachers need to remember they are not evaluating the movement itself; rather, they are evaluating how students' movements, and what they say about their movements, represent their understanding of musical concepts. Above all, the way teachers react to the creative movement choices of students establishes whether or not it is safe for students to be creative. Therefore, teachers should refrain from making qualitative judgments about the movement itself (e.g., "very creative," "good job," "I like that," or "Is that all?"). Instead, teachers should describe what they see and how it connects to the music or the concept, or ask questions to better understand the thought processes of their students. Sometimes students perceive their movement as the opposite of what it really is; in this instance, teachers can ask students to show the opposite of their current movement choice

Have students move to show texture in J.S. Bach's Cantata #167, BWV
167, *Sei Lob Und Preis Mit Ehren*.* Students stand in self-space, scattered
throughout the space. Explain that the piece has two sections. Sometimes
the orchestra plays together, or "tutti," and sometimes the cellist plays
by himself, or a solo. Say, "When the cello plays in solo, do a locomotor
movement in general space to match the music. When the orchestra plays
tutti, without the solo, freeze." Play the opening tutti and solo sections while
students move (repeat at least once, so students have a chance to determine
when to freeze and when to move). Switch parts, having students freeze
when the cello plays in solo, and do a locomotor movement during the
tutti sections. Play the opening tutti and solo sections while students move
(repeat at least once, so students have a chance to determine when to freeze
and when to move). Add to the movements for texture to also represent
expression/articulation. Ask, "Does the music tell us to dance smoothly
or sharply when the cello plays the solo part?" (smoothly). "Find a way to
do your locomotor movement smoothly to match the music of the cello.
Freeze during the tutti sections." Play the opening tutti and solo sections
while students move (repeat at least once, so students have a chance to
work out when to freeze and when to move). Ask questions to bring student
awareness to other musical elements, then have students add those ideas to
their movements. An example is the element, tempo. You might ask, "Does
the rhythm of the orchestral melody move at the same tempo as the cello
solo?" Later, in another lesson, have students choose one way to move for
the tutti sections and another way to move for the solo sections
(free choice).

*Recording: *Simply Baroque*, by Yo-Yo Ma and the Amsterdam Baroque Orchestra,
led by Ton Koopman BMV 167

Figure 4.8   Activity Example: Solo/Tutti (texture).

(e.g., slow instead of quick, heavy instead of light), which will help them
reflect on their intended movement. Often, when students compare oppo-
sites through movement, they understand the difference and correct their
original movement. If necessary, teachers can change the parameters/
directions or redirect students' attention to the concept, or they can simply say, "Thank you." When students recognize that the teacher will not
correct their movement, tell them they are "wrong," or embarrass them in
front of their peers, they will feel safer and will be more likely to participate
appropriately.

Another way to decrease risk is to have all students move and explore
movement ideas simultaneously. Doing so allows students to be anony-
mous and move without having the attention of the class. Having everyone
move simultaneously also frees up the teacher to observe the movement
of individual students, interact with them, and assess their understanding of musical concepts. If teachers ask students to move creatively to a
piece of music and they do not move at all, or there is not much variety

in the ways they move, that is okay; teachers should continue to provide opportunities for creative movement. If students cannot think of an idea, teachers can allow them to copy each other, which scaffolds their creativity by helping them get started. Then they can think of their own ideas as they are working toward the goal of creativity. Moreover, copying can even be taught as a strategy for building creativity (or a starting place for unique ideas).

If students are having trouble coming up with movement ideas, refrain from praising one student's movements or asking a student to try something different (i.e., "better" or "more creative"). Rather, describe in objective terms how students are moving (e.g., "I notice your arms are up high and I wonder if that is because the music sounds high"), which will support self-awareness, or change the parameters of the choices. Sometimes, students will still be self-conscious about moving creatively in front of peers. Moving with an object can alleviate self-consciousness by taking the attention off the person—because it is the object that is moving. Sometimes, especially with adolescents, social concerns of moving with others (e.g., partnering, coming up with movement together) increases risk. In this instance, teachers can support success by having students practice movements on their own before moving with another person. By taking individual student learning needs such as these into account when planning, teachers can create a safe environment that ensures success for all students.

EXPLORING CREATIVE MOVEMENT BY INTUITIVELY RESPONDING TO MUSIC

Mr. Patrick asks his second-grade class to listen to an excerpt of music and move like the music sounds. As the students move, he watches them, looking for movements he can connect to specific musical elements. When the excerpt ends, he says to the class, "I noticed Angela's circular movement. I think it illustrated the melodic contour of the piece. And Rayna's sharp, sudden movements highlighted the syncopated rhythm of the accompaniment. Let's copy Angela's and Rayna's movements and try them with the music playing."

Teachers can let students know that their choices for creative movement are acceptable by incorporating them into the class activity, by copying students' movements and having other students copy them, and by asking questions or describing what they observe about their movements. Teachers can use student movement ideas to highlight musical elements.

When teachers validate students' creative movement ideas in these ways, they assure students that their ideas are "good," which supports students' willingness to try new ideas of their own and of others. In Figure 4.9, children are exploring free and bound flow.

Figure 4.9 Free and bound flow.

Winding It Back or Forward

If a student is unable to participate in an activity that requires fine motor movement, teachers can plan a way to participate that uses gross motor movement, because gross motor movement is an earlier competency than fine motor. Conversely, if someone can successfully participate in a gross motor movement activity and seems to be bored with it, teachers can plan a way to participate using fine motor movement, because it is a later competency than gross motor. Students with proprioceptive challenges may need to perform more exaggerated movements or more subtle movements than other students, as their sense of where and how their body is moving in space is less developed. For example, if most students are marching, students with proprioceptive challenges may need to rock or stamp. Those movements provide stronger sensory information than marching. Rocking and stamping take longer to perform than marching, so students may need to be able to do those movements to the macrobeat instead of the microbeat. Students with challenges that affect balance (vestibular issues) or strength (e.g., muscle atrophy or nerve damage) may need to perform movements while sitting, while holding on to a chair or another person, or at a slower tempo. Figure 4.10 provides developmental information about the continuum of movement development from simpler to more complex or difficult.

Simpler	More Complex
Gross Motor	Fine Motor
Single movements (e.g., walk, walk, walk, walk...)	Sequenced movements (e.g., step, kick, step, kick)
Movements in Place (Self-space, stationary)	Movements through space (Traveling, general space)
Static (Move to a place and hold it)	Dynamic (Keep a movement going)
Tactile endpoint (e.g., on the body, on an object like an instrument or desk)	No tactile endpoint (e.g, in the air)
Moving without objects	Moving with objects (Except as noted)
Single type of movement (i.e., locomotor or nonlocomotor; upper body or lower body moving alone)	Integrated movement (Locomotor and nonlocomotor; upper body and lower body moving at the same time)
Locomotor Alternating sides Microbeat (approx. quarter note = 120)	Locomotor One side at a time (repeated) Macrobeat (approx. quarter note = 60)
Nonlocomotor Two sides moving symmetrically Macrobeat	Nonlocomotor Alternating sides Microbeat

Figure 4.10   Movement development: Simpler to more complex (from Weikart 2006).

This information can be useful when students struggle with movement in ways not already addressed in this chapter or when they clearly need more advanced choices.

Providing Multiple Access Points

Teachers can plan several ways students might participate in creative movement activities, present them and let students try each one, and then let students choose a way to move. Teachers can also ask students how they would be comfortable participating or let them choose not to participate. Students with social or emotional challenges may need to sit out and observe movement activities at first so they know what to expect. After they have seen the activity, they may be better able and more willing to try it. Even when teachers do not plan choice into an activity, they can make it safe to make choices and be creative by allowing students to vary the movement rather than insisting all students move in the same way. The earlier story in which Ashad modified the hand-jive movement is an example of allowing students to vary movement. Incorporating choice in these ways lessens risk and helps establish a safe environment for creative movement. Whatever the reason for creative movement activities, teachers can individualize instruction for all students by planning several ways to participate or by adjusting activities during instruction based on observations of student movements and what they say about their movements. Figure 4.11 gives specific examples of planned choices that are based on the information presented in the rest of this chapter.

Place or Direction		Purpose	Body Part	Other
Across the room	Straight	Give directions	Whole body	By yourself
In place	Curvy	Explore an idea	Arms, elbows,	With a partner
Next to	Zigzag	Express the mood	wrists	With a group
Alongside	Over/Under	Apply an idea	Legs/Knees	Sitting
On the body	In a line	Work together	Heels/Toes	Standing
In the air	Inside a space	Problem solve	Head, nose, chin	Lying down
On an instrument	In personal space	Demonstrate or	Shoulders	With an object
Toward/Away	In general space	represent	Back/Chest	At individual
from	In random	a concept	Hands/Fingers	tempo
In a circle	formation		Waist	At group tempo

Figure 4.11   Examples of parameters for student choices in creative movement.

SECONDARY ACTIVITY EXAMPLES

We present these activities in a separate section because secondary teachers unaccustomed to incorporating creative movement into rehearsals may not see them as applicable to their students if mixed with elementary examples. The activities in this section facilitate understanding of music and ensemble concepts through creative movement and allow for individualized participation by incorporating choice. As in previous examples, teachers can also suggest alternatives to the instructions based on knowledge of specific students and their needs. Remember that, initially, narrower parameters will facilitate safety and participation. Later on, once secondary students are used to exploring advanced musical ideas through movement, wider parameters will do the same.

These activity examples are adapted from the resources listed at the end of this chapter.

Synchronizing Ensemble Beat

You can use creative movement to have students synchronize their timing and transfer that skill and understanding to ensemble playing. Have stand partners work together for this activity. Ask one partner to move his or her arms in slow, flowing movements (nonlocomotor) while the other partner mirrors these movements, matching the timing of the movements and the location, and then switch roles. Repeat the copying activity, but have leaders choose other body parts to move and different ways to move for their partners to copy. Encourage students to explore using different flow, weight, space, and time as they move. Bring students' awareness to the aspect of timing by asking questions such as "What did you have to do to move at the same speed as your partner?" They should become aware that they had to focus their attention and that it was easier or more difficult with different movements. Tie the activity to ensemble timing by asking questions like "How is matching timing while moving different from matching timing while playing?" (You have to attend to others by listening, and by watching the conductor.) Apply the activity to ensemble repertoire: "In what piece are we having difficulty staying together, or matching our timing? What can we do to improve our group timing?"

Feeling and Performing Sustained Notes (Expressive Playing, Rhythm)

Use creative movement to explore ways to sustain pitch with accurate durations. Ask students to describe a sustained note and then locate and perform some sustained notes in current repertoire or in a warm-up. Have students individually explore using their voices or instruments to produce a long sound. With students in groups of two, ask one partner to play or sing a sustained pitch and the other partner to perform a movement that equals the length of the sustained pitch. (Students may need to repeat the activity in the same roles a couple of times to be successful.) Have partners switch roles. Then, in the same groups of two, ask one partner to perform a sustained movement (e.g., move fingers along a music stand, move arm in a sweeping motion) while the other partner plays a note that matches the length of the movement. Then the partners switch roles. Bring student awareness to performing sustained notes musically by asking questions such as "What strategies did you use to sustain a pitch? What strategies did you use to sustain your movement? How did you know how long to move or play? How can you perform sustained pitches in interesting ways?"

Understanding Accelerando and Ritardando

Ask students to define the terms *accelerando* and *ritardando* and represent them through movement (individually). With students in partners or small groups, have them explore fast or slow ways to move in personal or general space. Have them share their movements with each other, copy them, and describe how the movements represent the concepts of *slow* and *fast*. Then, have students explore ways to represent slow to fast or fast to slow with movement. Again, have students share ideas and describe how their movements illustrated the ideas. Bring student awareness to the concepts and apply them to ensemble playing by asking questions such as "What problems did you face when moving accelerando and ritardando? Which was more difficult to move? Why? What strategies can we use to accelerate or slow down evenly?"

RESOURCES
Books and Recordings

Many of the activity examples in this chapter are drawn from and adapted from the following books and recordings:

Creative Dance for All Ages. Anne Green Gilbert (1992), a movement and creative dance specialist from Seattle, Washington, founded the Creative Dance Center in 1981, where she began to develop a sequential and comprehensive dance curriculum based on exploring the concepts of dance. Her book, *Creative Dance for All Ages*, is an incredible resource for music specialists who may or may not have a background in dance. The ideas from this book can be taught as a daily lesson component or with less frequency. Many of the activities listed in this chapter have been adapted from *Creative Dance for All Ages* as examples of easily accessible movement activities based on Laban themes that are appropriate in the music classroom.

Music for Creative Movement. Music educator John M. Feierabend (2005) has compiled a set of three CDs containing classical music

excerpts that function as a soundtrack for movement exploration activities. *Music for Creative Movement* is organized into themes
adapted from the work of Laban including Light/Gentle, Heavy/Strong,
Sustained, Sudden, Slow/Bound, Quick/Free, Relaxed, Tense, Joyful,
and Combinations.

*Teaching Movement and Dance: A Sequential Approach to Rhythmic
Movement.* Phyllis S. Weikart (2006) is a movement and dance educator who developed an approach to teaching that uses music and movement to teach any curricular concept. She has also choreographed many
international folk dances in simplified ways, including a consistent
language-to-dance vocabulary. Her book, *Teaching Movement and Dance*,
outlines her teaching approach and movement development and includes
all of her dances. Some of the activities in this chapter are derived
from her approach and materials. Other resources from Phyllis Weikart
include:

> *Rhythmically Moving* (2003): a set of nine compact discs contain-
> ing the music for the dances in *Teaching Movement and Dance*.
> The music is useful for other movement activities, as well as
> dancing.
>
> *85 Engaging Movement Activities* (Weikart and Carlton, 2002)
>
> *75 Ensemble Warm-Ups* (Weikart et al., 2004), an excellent resource
> for band and choir directors working with students in grades four
> through twelve.

For an instructional sequence and examples of folk dance in the music
classroom, see the separate appendix "Teaching Students to Dance" on the
companion website.

REFERENCES

Feierabend, J. M. (2005). *Music for creative movement* [Compact disc set]. Chicago,
    IL: GIA.
Ferguson, L. (2005). The role of movement in elementary music education: A literature
    review. *Update: Applications of Research in Music Education, 23*(2), 23–33.
Gilbert, A. G. (1992). *Creative dance for all ages.* Reston, VA: American Alliance for
    Health, Physical Education, and Dance.
Weikart, P. S. (2006). *Teaching movement & dance: A sequential approach to rhythmic
    movement* (6th ed.). Ypsilanti, MI: High/Scope.
Weikart, P. S. (2003). *Rhythmically moving 1-9* [Compact disc set]. Ypsilanti, MI: High/
    Scope.

Weikart, P. S., & Carlton, E. B. (2002). *85 Engaging movement activities* [Book and Compact disc]. Ypsilanti, MI: High/Scope.

Weikart, P. S., Boardman, B., & Bryant, E. (2004). *75 Ensemble warm-ups: Activities for bands, choirs, and orchestras* [Book and Compact disc]. Ypsilanti, MI: High/Scope.

Wesley, J. (2014, February 2). The secret to creativity [Web log post]. Retrieved from http://www.pickthebrain.com

CHAPTER 5

Melodic Sequences

Accessing Tonal Content at Multiple Learning Levels

ROBERTA Y. HICKOX, *Halifax Area School District,*
Halifax, Pennsylvania
TAYLOR WALKUP, *New York City Public Schools*

CHAPTER OVERVIEW

Melody is the essence of music. I compare a good melodist to a fine racer, and counterpointists to hack post-horses; therefore be advised, let *well alone* and remember the old Italian proverb: *Chi sa più, meno sa*—Who knows most, knows least.

Wolfgang Amadeus Mozart (1826)

Melody is an integral part of music in all musical cultures (Randel, 1999). Making tonal content accessible to all students is crucial to their understanding and enjoyment of music. This chapter will do the following:

- Define melody
- Describe how tonal and rhythm factors combine to equal melody
- Present ideas for incorporating vocal exploration
- Discuss an approach to teaching tonal content
- Share examples of classroom activities and suggestions for *winding* the activities *back* and *forward* to meet the needs of individual students
- Offer assessment charts for use in tracking the progress of all students

The *Harvard Dictionary of Music* generally defines melody as "a coherent succession of pitches" in which "the succession of pitches is accepted as belonging together." It distinguishes melody as consisting of pitch combined with rhythm: "By its very nature melody cannot be separated from rhythm. Each musical sound has two fundamental qualities, pitch and duration" (Apel, 1972, p. 517). Tonal elements will be explored separately from rhythm elements in this book, as

> students who are just learning to audiate find it difficult to understand a tonal pattern combined with a rhythm pattern [that] remains the same tonal pattern when combined with another rhythm pattern. . . . Moreover, it would be almost impossible to teach combined tonal patterns and rhythm patterns – that is, melodic patterns – because only rarely can tonal and rhythm parts of a combined pattern share the same level of difficulty. Each student's individual musical needs are best met when instruction matches individual levels of tonal aptitude and rhythm aptitude in conjunction with tonal pattern and rhythm pattern difficulty levels. (Gordon, 2012, pp. 223–224)

THE KODÁLY METHOD

The sequenced nature of the Kodály approach fits particularly well with winding. Choksy (1999, p. 9), an early proponent of the Kodály approach, states that the Kodály method of music education has two objectives: "to aid in the well-balanced social and artistic development of the child, and to produce the musically literate adult—literate in the fullest sense of being able to look at a musical score and 'think' sound, to read and write music as easily as words." The *Merriam-Webster online dictionary* defines "method" as "a systematic plan followed in presenting material for instruction" ("Method," n.d.). Although instruction by a Kodály-trained teacher is certainly sequenced and systematic, the Kodály method (or Kodály Concept, as it is sometimes called) is best viewed as a philosophy through which instruction toward good musicianship is inspired. Kodály himself stated:

> On the basis of what has been said, the characteristics of a good musician can be summarized as follows: a well-trained ear, a well-trained intelligence, a well-trained heart, and a well-trained hand. All four must develop together, in a constant equilibrium. As soon as one lags behind or rushes ahead, there is something wrong. (Kodály, 1974, p. 197)

The use of the child's unaccompanied voice as the optimal instrument for music instruction, beginning music education "nine months before the birth of the mother" (Kodály, 1974), the use of the highest-quality music in the music classroom, and the ideal of universal musical literacy form the basis of the Kodály philosophy. As Kodály (1974) himself states, "Let us take our children seriously! Everything else follows from this. . . . Only the best is good enough for a child."

"A Kodály sequenced curriculum is an experience-based approach to learning rather than a cognitive developmental approach" (http://www.oake.org). Using singing as the primary instrument and movable *do* solfège and rhythm syllables as tools, proponents of Kodály music education sequence the introduction of pitches in the teaching of melody and individual rhythms in the teaching of rhythm that corresponds with a song repertoire highlighting a particular group of pitches or tone set. Kodály "considered that folk music represented a living art. It was not contrived for pedagogical purposes. It already existed and fit well into a systematic scheme for teaching the concepts and skills of music to young children" (Choksy, 1999, p. 2). Consequently, Kodály-inspired teaching utilizes predominantly authentic folk songs and singing games from a variety of cultures as its repertoire, to establish a solid foundation on which to expand into musical masterworks. Through the format of Prepare, Present, and Practice, each new pitch or rhythm element is studied as it relates to other known pitches or rhythms, so that the melody or rhythm becomes steadily more complex within a carefully constructed framework. The content of the Prepare, Present, and Practice categories is as follows:

> **Prepare:** All preparatory activities, such as tonal/rhythm patterning; learning of song/rhyme/singing game repertoire; comparison of known to new pitches/rhythms; naming of new pitches/rhythms with solfège or rhythm syllables; aural decoding, also called "generalization-verbal" (Gordon, 2012), of neutral syllables into solfège or rhythm syllables; and improvisation, that precede viewing standard notation of that new pitch or rhythm element
>
> **Present:** The initial viewing of the new pitch or rhythm element in standard notation in the context of a familiar song/rhyme
>
> **Practice:** All subsequent activities that deepen student understanding and audiation of the new pitch or rhythm element through reading and writing in standard notation

MUSIC LEARNING THEORY

Music Learning Theory, based on the extensive research and field testing of Edwin E. Gordon, is "an explanation of how we learn music. Although it has direct influence on method, it is not a method nor a theory of teaching" (Gordon, 2012, p. 25). Music Learning Theory utilizes sequential instruction to promote audiation for all students. Instruction is individualized according to each student's music aptitude (Gordon, 2012). Some of the central principles of Music Learning Theory are contrast (i.e., sameness and difference between tonalities and meters), the study of tonal and rhythm patterns within the context of tonality and meter, and the presentation of concepts and materials within "whole-part-whole" stages. These topics will be defined briefly later; a more in-depth understanding of Music Learning Theory can be acquired through Gordon's own writings.

Audiation, a term coined by Gordon, "is the process of assimilating and comprehending (not simply rehearing) music momentarily heard performed or heard sometime in the past . . . [or] reading in notation or composing or improvising. . . . Music is the subject of communication. Performance is the vehicle for communication. Audiation is what is communicated" (Gordon, 2012, p. 5). In short, "Audiation is to music what thought is to language" (p. ix). The growth of student audiation can best be measured when compared to an individual baseline of potential audiation (music aptitude) for each student. Gordon describes music aptitude as "a measure of one's potential to learn music. . . . Music aptitude is a hunger. Music achievement is satisfaction of that hunger" (2012). Through the information gleaned by administration of a valid and reliable music aptitude test, such as the Primary Measures of Music

MUSIC APTITUDE TESTING

Music aptitude is the potential for audiating music. The research of Gordon indicates that music aptitude is innate but not inherent, and is developmental until age nine. Two tools we use each year are the Primary Measures of Music Audiation (PMMA) and the Intermediate Measures of Music Audiation (IMMA). Both of these tests require no reading or music skills, can be used with students with limited English language skills, and can be administered to an entire class at one time. The purpose of administering a music aptitude test is to measure what each student audiates, in order to differentiate instruction. No music aptitude test has been normed for students with special needs at the time of this printing (Gordon, 2012).

Audiation (Gordon, 1986), the teacher can provide learning opportunities (termed "learning sequence activities" by Gordon and taught as pattern instruction) that conform to individual learning differences in audiation and maximize individual audiation potential. Music aptitude is innate but not inherent, and stabilizes after age nine. The urgency to nurture student music aptitude while it is still in the developmental stage is apparent in the focus on informal guidance and early childhood music programs by many proponents of Music Learning Theory.

MUSIC APTITUDE AND STUDENTS WITH SPECIAL NEEDS

Sarah's first-grade music teacher suspected that Sarah had high music aptitude, but she was unable to find an aptitude test that was standardized for students with special needs. Sarah was greatly affected by changes in the classroom (i.e., furniture that was rearranged) and was reluctant to hold hands with other students because "they were germy." Sarah's music teacher learned to alert Sarah to changes in the classroom setup or lesson, and Sarah began wearing gloves to class, after which she held hands and participated with great focus. Because Sarah demonstrated superior skills in music class, her music teacher challenged her as she would a student who was identified with high music aptitude: when the class's goal was for individual students to take turns pointing to the beat on the board and reading the notation in rhythm syllables, Sarah was asked to read the notation backward, which she did successfully.

Students learn what something is from what it isn't. "By comparing harmonic minor tonality with major tonality, students audiate characteristic tones in each tonality and, thus, differences between them.... Students best give meaning to different tonalities when they audiate significant similarities and differences" (Gordon, 2012, p. 163). Tonal patterns, a series of two to four pitches sung in a staccato fashion followed by a brief pause (audiation breath) before students perform, are used to support the main goal of audiation in a Music Learning Theory classroom.

> By their nature, individual pitches and durations advance linearly to and fro in flow of melody and therefore contribute minimally to pragmatic meaning in music. In contrast, tonal patterns move in irregular linear space toward and away from one or more tonal centers.... Thus, patterns, not isolated sounds, are compelling fonts of content and context in music. (Gordon, 2002, p. 217)

Tonal patterns and songs are first presented on a neutral syllable so that students do not become distracted by the text, and they are always preceded by establishment of the tonality and meter.

Instruction within Music Learning Theory occurs in three stages.

> In the first stage, students gain a vague impression of tonality and meter of a song or chant they hear and perform in classroom music activities. In the second stage, students study tonal patterns and rhythm patterns in that tonality and meter by using a skill in music learning sequence activities. Although these tonal and rhythm patterns need not be identical to those in the song or chant, by the third stage students audiate and perform the song again in classroom music activities with contextual meaning and more accuracy. (Gordon, 2012, p. 273)

This "whole-part-whole" structure is a fundamental part of Music Learning Theory lessons.

IDEOLOGY

"When teaching is based on learning rather than the reverse, any one of a potpourri of methods and techniques proves satisfactory" (Gordon, 2012). While the Kodály philosophy and Music Learning Theory differ in several ways, the core values are similar: begin music instruction as early as possible, use the voice as the primary instrument, have singing precede instrumental study, teach movable *do* with *la*-based minor solfège syllables and a rhythm syllable system as tools, and develop a culture of music. Regardless of the method used, music educators desire to inspire students to enjoy, through understanding, a lifetime of music: "He [Kodály] wished to see an education system that could produce a people to whom music was not a way to make a living but a way of life" (Choksy, 1999, p. 9).

WINDING IT BACK

Winding back is necessary when a student's needs will not be met by experiencing the same activity in the same way as described in the activity's general learning objective. Winding back can be accomplished through differentiation and individualized instruction.

Differentiated instruction is intrinsic within a sequence, as a sequence is linear: individual students can focus on different skills along the sequence as needed. Differentiation is a form of winding back instruction by teaching content from different points of a learning sequence to different students. Students who are not yet ready to work on a particular step in a sequence need more opportunity to practice or wind back the previous step in the sequence; each step becomes both the preparation for the subsequent step and an assessment of necessary skills for the subsequent step. Activities can be designed to address several levels of competence simultaneously so that each individual can work at a level that is personally challenging while contributing to the musical understanding of his or her peers. This chapter will present several activities that differentiate instruction that can be used as prototypes for creating activities suitable for your own classroom.

Instruction can be individualized when teaching patterns. Students interact with tonal and rhythm patterns of a specific level of difficulty based on each student's music aptitude. Solo singing is a crucial aspect of individualized instruction, as student performance reveals what the student has accurately audiated and allows diagnosis of the focus of continued practice for improvement. The teacher can then adapt or wind back future instruction based on student performance.

Students who learn differently are supported kinesthetically through the use of body solfa, hand signs, and movement; visually through the use of iconic and traditional notation; and aurally through the use of songs and chants in a variety of modes and meters. Photos of hand signs can be found in chapter 5 of the companion website; photos of body solfa can be found in chapter 3 of the companion website. The recurrence of tonal and rhythm skills within a sequence offers additional assistance: all students review *mi* and *do* in preparation to learn *re*; some remain focused on accurate intonation and decoding of *mi* and *do,* while most expand their knowledge of *mi* and *do* to discover the pitch *re* between. These steps, when presented sequentially within an activity, allow simultaneous learning for all students at their individual learning levels. Repetition of song material is rewarding when high-quality music is presented to students: the depth provided by high-quality song material offers opportunity to explore the tonal and rhythm patterns within the song, derive the melodic and rhythmic small form, and perform chord roots and ostinati to accompany the song. This chapter will include winding back ideas to aid all students, including those with learning differences.

EXPLORATION

Prior to the formal study of melody, in-tune singing must be developed to enhance the development of musical understanding. During childhood, the study of melody and vocal technique should develop simultaneously. Teachers must provide learning experiences to help children discover and learn how to use their head voices; however, this process can be both challenging and lengthy as singing is a learned behavior (Phillips, 2014). Teacher modeling is the most important teaching mode for the acquisition of melody; therefore, the teacher is responsible for producing an in-tune, pure singing voice (Choksy, 1999). The teacher should provide students with many opportunities for vocal exploration. The goal of beginning vocal exploration is to allow students the opportunity to explore the full range of their voices.

As children begin to differentiate between different types and registers of their voices, the teacher can use specific rhymes and short songs for them to use their head voices purposefully. During Exploration Activity #1, students are encouraged to explore the full range of their voices; during Exploration Activity #2, the teacher uses specific rhymes that require students to access their head voices for a limited amount of time; during Exploration Activity #3, the teacher adds the expectation of sustaining head voices within a specific amount of time; and during Exploration Activity #4, the teacher adds the expectation of using a singing voice while moving to very short songs. Each step provides the students with additional readiness for sustaining a head voice and singing songs for melodic decoding. (See the appendix for additional ideas for developing children's singing voices and providing readiness for melodic study.)

Vocal Exploration Activity #1: Voice exploration. *Using their voices, students will explore their speaking, whispering, shouting, and singing voices.*

- During this activity, the students are using their voices in different ways to "sing" the contour of a waving scarf. The goal is for students to explore the different registers of their voices. Using a scarf, the teacher presents a visual shape to the class and challenges the students to sing the shape of the scarf as it is moving. This activity requires students to use different registers of their voices to represent the movements of the scarf as they are happening. This can be especially challenging for students because they are often accustomed to having more wait time before responding.
  - **Variation #1** (Winding it back): For students who need more wait time to manipulate their voices, the teacher may show the movement of the scarf before asking the children to sing. By doing this, the student can identify and process the visual motion of the scarf before performing the "sound" of the scarf.
  - **Variation #2** (Winding it back): For students who are not able to access different registers of their voices yet, the teacher can reverse

the process and start with sound. A student can provide a sound and peers use the scarves to "draw" the sound in the air. The teacher can record the sound on the board and the class can practice drawing the shape with their scarves.

o **Variation #3** (Winding it back): For students who may be hesitant to use their voices in unusual ways, the teacher may provide stories or imagery to enhance the contour of the scarf. By using imagery or familiar experiences, the teacher provides something for the student to hold on to. For example, the teacher can tell a story about a roller coaster ride before using the scarf to show melodic contour. The students can use the specific imagery of the story to enhance their vocal exploration.

Vocal Exploration Activity #2: Accessing head voice for limited time. *Using their voices, the students will perform a chant using their head voices for one measure.*

• During this activity, the students are using their voices to speak a rhyme in both speaking and head voices. The goal of the activity is for the students to sustain their head voices for one measure. The students form a "train" around the classroom and begin speaking, "Engine, Engine #9" (Musical Example 5.1). The students speak the rhyme and use their head voices to perform the last four "toots." This activity requires the students to use their head voice purposefully for a limited time. The activity requires the students to use two different types of voices at specific times and requires students to think ahead to know when to use their head voice. Unlike Activity #1, this activity establishes the additional challenge of using head voice at specific times. This may create challenges for students unable to easily access their head voices or differentiate between different voices.

Musical Example 5.1

Engine #9

Traditional

En - gine en - gine num - ber 9,   go - ing down Chi - ca - go line.   If the train jumps off the track,

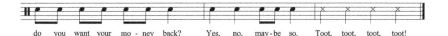

do   you   want your   mo - ney back?   Yes,   no,   may - be so.   Toot, toot,   toot,   toot!

- **Variation #1** (Winding it back): For a student unable to switch between speaking voice and head voice, the teacher may assign the student a specific part of the rhyme to speak. The teacher can ask the student to be the "train whistle" during the rhyme. This allows the student to use only his or her head voice for the last four "toots"; however, the student will still audiate the spoken chant to speak his or her part at the correct time. If the student needs more time to audiate the head voice tone, the teacher may ask the student to speak the rest of the rhyme and listen closely as the teacher or peers model the last measure.
- **Variation #2** (Winding it back): For students needing a visual or kinesthetic reinforcement of using their head voices, the teacher may create a movement to represent what their voices should sound like. Some students may be able to access their head voices, but only with visual cues to reinforce their aural recognition. The teacher can have the students use one arm to reach up to the ceiling and pull an imaginary string to sound the train whistle. As the students reach up high to sound the whistle, they can use the cue to remind them to switch into their head voice.

Vocal Exploration Activity #3: Sustaining head voice. *The students will use their head voices to speak a familiar rhyme.*

- During this activity, the students are using their head voices to speak a familiar rhyme. The goal of this activity is for the students to sustain their head voices for two to three phrases of a chant. The students perform a familiar rhyme while the teacher uses a pop-up puppet to signal head voice or speaking voice. During each repetition of the song, the teacher changes the phrase length and frequency of head voice or speaking voice. Consider starting with shorter durations of head voice and building to using only head voice to speak two or three phrases.
  - **Variation #1** (Winding it back): For students with shorter head voice stamina, consider reversing the process and allowing them to use the pop-up puppet to guide their peers. Between each repetition of the rhyme, the teacher says, "I really need a new teacher to be in charge of the pop-up puppet." The teacher can then select a student who may need more time to listen to a vocal model.
  - **Variation #2** (Winding it back): For students who may need scaffolding from peers, the teacher can have students work in a group. The teacher provides each group a different rhyme and a pop-up puppet. The students in the small group create different ways to perform their rhyme while sustaining their head voices. When the students are ready

to share, the teacher puts each phrase of the rhyme on the board. The small group shares their rhyme and the class chooses which phrases they think the students were sustaining in their head voices.

- o **Variation #3** (Winding it back): For students needing aural cues to perform and sustain head voice, the teacher may use a single message communicator to record a head voice model. The child can press the button and listen to the teacher speaking a short section of the rhyme in head voice and echo the sound individually.

Vocal Exploration Activity #4: Singing short songs. *Using their singing voices, the students will perform a two-note song using motions.*

- During this activity, the students use their singing voices to sing a folk song within a limited tone set. The goal of this activity is for the students to sustain their singing voices in an appropriate vocal range and tone quality. The teacher vocally models "See Saw" (Musical Example 5.2) using an appropriate singing voice.

Musical Example 5.2

See Saw

Traditional

While the students sing the song, they pretend to be a "see saw" by holding hands with a partner and taking turns standing up or squatting down to show high and low. This activity requires the students to sustain a healthy singing voice while moving up and down. This may be challenging for students because of the game motions and expectations to sing with a healthy, beautiful tone quality. Unlike the previous activities, the children are required to use one specific voice and match the students' singing around them.

- o **Variation #1** (Winding it back): For students unable to perform both the game motions and a singing voice, the teacher may simplify the high and low motions. The students may sing "See Saw" while alternating between high and low on their head and shoulders. Not only will the students continue to visualize the contour of their singing voice, but also they may be more focused on the physical aspect of breathing and vocal production.

○ **Variation #2** (Winding it back): For students unable to sustain their singing voice, the teacher may ask them to speak the words of the song in their head voice or create an ostinato to perform using their head voices. The teacher says, "Imagine you were playing on a see saw and saw another friend on the other side of the park. Let's say 'yoo-hoo' for them to come over and play." The teacher can then have a small group of students say "yoo-hoo" while the rest of the class sings "See Saw." By creating different parts to the song, the teacher can provide each student with learning experiences to meet his or her individual vocal needs.

○ **Variation #3** (Winding it back): For students unable to use an in-tune singing voice while singing with other children, the teacher may ask them to use a voice recorder to record their singing voice while singing "See Saw." The teacher may play the recording back to these students and allow them to self-monitor and evaluate their singing voice.

TRACKING VOCAL DEVELOPMENT

Singing is a learned skill. Students entering into the elementary music classroom will come with many different musical and vocal experiences that influence their stage of vocal development. It is the teacher's responsibility to implement a program of systematic vocal instruction for all students and assess individual student progress. Goetze (as cited in Bertaux, 1989, p. 93) states: "Accurate singing involves the continual evaluation of the singing pitch." She explains, "The singer listens to his own vocalizations and applies a recognition process to the sound he himself is making. The process is a continual monitoring in order to adjust for errors." For the young singer to develop in-tune singing, the teacher must serve as a facilitator in helping the student to develop vocal awareness and provide continual feedback through assessment.

According to Graham Welch, elementary students typically fall within four phases of vocal pitch-matching development (Phillips, 2014). In phase 1, singing is "chantlike" and uses limited tonal range and tonal patterns; in phase 2, there is growing awareness that changes in vocal pitch are controllable and vocal pitch range expands; in phase 3, melodic shape and intervals are accurate with some changes in tonality; and in phase 4, there are no significant melodic or pitch errors in relation to simple songs from the singer's musical heritage. To track this development, teachers can use charts to collect student data. This data can be used to assess student readiness for further melodic study. Figure 5.1 outlines ideas for head register and vocal assessment.

EXPLORE full range of voice	Fire engine	Roller coaster	Roadmaps	Zipper
USE head register at will	Johnny, Whoops	Pussycat	Way Down Yonder	I Saw You in the Ocean
SUSTAIN head register	Slinky	WAVE	Pop-up	Count to 10
SING a short song using head register	See Saw	Goodnight	Peas Porridge Hot	Lucy Locket

Figure 5.1   Tracking Student Progress Through Head Register

Students may require many practice opportunities and various experiences to consistently perform in a head register. Examples of vocal exploration activities have been included in chapters 3 and 5, as well as the appendix. Additional vocal exploration activities ("I Saw You in the Ocean" and "roadmap") can be found in chapter 5 on the companion website.

Preparation

After initial introduction to melodic pitches in the sequence outlined in chapter 3, a series of additional individual pitches may be presented to students, thus widening the tone set or collection of pitches to create a larger variety of tonal patterns. Gordon (2012, p. 219) states: "An interesting result of the research was difficulty levels of patterns has virtually no relation to frequency with which patterns are found in standard music literature." However, we believe that combining tonal pattern work within learning sequence activities and tonal pattern work within song repertoire offers the most opportunity for providing multiple access points for all students, as tonal learning sequence activities focus exclusively on audiation, while extrapolation of tonal patterns in song repertoire synthesizes resting tone and harmonic function in a broader perspective and advances a sense of musical culture. Additionally, language arts goals for students with learning differences may be supported through song repertoire (i.e., rhyming, phrasing, and story sequence). Preparation for each additional pitch consists of familiarizing the students with repertoire that includes known and new pitches and students echoing brief tonal patterns (two to four pitches, including the new pitch in a variety of contexts, performed without rhythm), sung on a neutral syllable and using solfège. Students are led to recognize that a song includes a pitch that is new to them, the relationship between that pitch and known pitches (i.e., higher than *sol*, lower than *mi*), and the interval between the new pitch and the closest known pitch (i.e., a step higher than *sol*). This aural discovery of the new pitch, leading students from recognition of a new pitch to comparisons and aural information about the new pitch, indicates when students are prepared to demonstrate knowledge of the new pitch (i.e., showing body solfa or hand signs, singing songs including the solfège of the new pitch, relating the sound of the new pitch in the context of a song or pattern through decoding). Solfège is used to connect sound to symbol: students see staff notation and audiate sound in the form of solfège syllables. Students must read notation before beginning to write with notation, just as students learn to read sentences before writing sentences.

The selection of appropriate song repertoire is determined in part by the personal musical taste of the teacher; however, some additional guiding practices for pedagogical song selection include the following:

- Select songs that contain the new pitch in an easily isolated or extractable motive.
- Select songs that contain the new pitch in a rhythmically simple motive. For example, the new pitch should not occur on the second of a pair of eighth notes, as this is too fleeting for students to hear without significantly slowing down the tempo and damaging the musical performance of the song.
- Select songs that approach the new pitch by the closest known pitch, as this makes it easier for students to aurally compare the new to the known (i.e., *la* is approached from *sol*, rather than from *do*).
- Select songs that you would enjoy singing and listening to very often. For example, folk songs of a variety of cultures have stood the test of time and have been passed on through the oral tradition (from singer to singer), demonstrating that people have enjoyed the songs and chosen to pass them on to future generations.
- Select songs that are beautiful! These may be interesting melodically or rhythmically, have a particularly good marriage of text and melody, set the text naturally with the rhythm, be in a mode and meter that suits the text and style of the song, or be beautiful for ineffable reasons.

The introduction of melodic elements can be effectively presented within a sequence by introducing an initial few pitches to establish a limited number of tonal patterns, then building on that foundation with the presentation of additional individual pitches to expand the repertoire of tonal patterns. Discerning a new (different) pitch from a group of known pitches (an aural literacy skill), associating the sound of the pitch with the corresponding solfège syllable (a correlation skill), and audiating from notation (a visual literacy skill) are recurrent musical skills that are useful in making music in many styles. These aural discovery, decoding (also known as verbalization-general), and reading skills will be examined in this chapter as three of the most important skills in a sequential strategy for presentation of new pitches. While these skills will be explored with the introduction of each new pitch in a complete approach to melody, this chapter will highlight these skills with the introduction of the new pitch *re* to known pitches *sol, mi, la,* and *do.* A possible sequence for introduction of subsequent new pitches will be included in the companion website.

Aural Discovery

Once a body of song repertoire including the new pitch has been heard, sung, enjoyed, and played with by students in numerous ways (e.g., sung in canon, with a partner song, or with ostinati; accompanied by instruments; improvised; or choreographed), select the song that most ideally isolates the new pitch and includes it in relation to the closest known pitch. With the introduction of the new pitch *re,* the ideal song can be one that includes only *re* and its closest neighbors, *mi* and *do,* as in the song "Hot Cross Buns" (Musical Example 5.3). This song's melody presents *re* in close comparison with both *mi* and *do,* isolates *mi-re-do* as a tonal pattern and repeats this pattern several times, and is a traditional and well-known folk song with implied tonic-dominant harmony in major tonality, making it optimal for improvisation and the study of functional harmony.

Musical Example 5.3

Hot Cross Buns

Traditional

Hot cross buns,   Hot cross buns,   One a pen-ny, two a pen-ny, Hot cross buns.

Students should be able to sing and decode tonal patterns and songs that include *mi* and *do* to begin aural discovery of *re,* as these pitches are included with *re* in many melodic motives and serve as the foundational and known pitches for the introduction of *re.* Students should also be able to sing "Hot Cross Buns" without the teacher, in order for the teacher to assess student independence and readiness to aurally analyze *re* in relation to known pitches. Some useful steps leading to aural discovery of a new pitch are as follows:

- Perform body solfa with known songs.
- Review "step" and "skip" in relation to intervals between known pitches.
- Add body solfa to a song containing the new pitch as a kinesthetic means of discovering the new pitch.

Using "Hot Cross Buns" as an example, students do the following:

1. Perform the song without the aid of the teacher.
2. Perform the resting tone and identify it as *do*.
3. Compare *do* to the starting pitch, identifying the starting pitch as *mi*.
4. Review the body solfa for *do* and *mi*, and sing the song using body solfa whenever the pitches *do* and *mi* occur in the motif "hot cross buns."
5. Attempt to identify the pitch that sounds between *mi* and *do*, on the word "cross," by first considering the pitch in relation to *mi* and *do*: is the pitch higher/lower than *mi*? Higher/lower than *do*? Students may suggest *sol, la, do,* or *mi*, as these are the pitches already known; the teacher should sing all answers given by the students (correct or incorrect) to allow the students to hear the suggested motif accurately and ascertain that none of these pitches are accurate.
6. Confirm that the pitch that sounds on the word "cross" is a new pitch and is a step higher than *do* and a step lower than *mi*.

To accommodate the learning of all children, a sequence like the aural discovery of "Hot Cross Buns" delineated previously will need to be flexible. Some ideas for winding back this sequence are outlined here:

- **Variation #1** (Winding it back): Teach body solfa and hand signs as a means for students to visually confirm and kinesthetically reinforce their audiation. Encourage students to use body solfa or hand signs as needed.
- **Variation #2** (Winding it back): Allow individual students to perform the familiar song in small groups or solo (step 1 of the previous sequence) while allowing other students to take the lead in aural discovery of the new pitch *re* with steps 3 through 6. All students are not required to do all work; instead, students do the work that is most meaningful to them at a particular point in time. "It should go without saying that for a child who cannot sing a minor third accurately to call what he or she *is* singing *so-mi* is patently absurd" (Choksy, 1999).

- **Variation #3** (Winding it back): It is possible, even likely, that some students will not yet be audiating *re* in tune while the majority of the class is ready to discover *re* in familiar songs. Continue tonal pattern echoes using a neutral syllable and solfège syllables to allow these students ample opportunity to hear the tonal patterns performed with accurate intonation.

Another repertoire option for the aural discovery of *re* might be a song such as "Great Big House in New Orleans" (Musical Example 5.4.). This song isolates *re* in relation to its closest neighbors, *mi* and *do*, in the final cadence, but offers a more expansive tone set with the inclusion of *sol* and *la*, which can be more appealing to older students. Another traditional folk song, "Great Big House" can be sung to the simple movements of a play-party and also implies a tonic-dominant harmony in major. Consider carefully the tonal content of song materials chosen to discover *re*, as song selection itself can be a form of winding back or forward.

Musical Example 5.4

Some strategies for winding it back using "Great Big House" that honor the individual learning needs of all students are highlighted here:

- **Variation #1** (Winding it back): Sometimes performing two jobs at once (singing and kinesthetic reinforcement) can be overly difficult for a student. Allow individual students to accompany the singing of the class with body solfa or hand signs and other students to sing without the use of body solfa or hand signs as discrete microsteps building to the eventual combination of skills. One group may benefit from the physical support of body solfa or hand signs performed by a second group to correspond with what the first group is singing.

- **Variation #2** (Winding it back): Students who are not yet ready to learn the new pitch *re* can review the known pitches included in measures 1 and 3, *mi, sol,* and *la*. The repetition found in these measures increases the students' participation while allowing them a means to wind back the sequence to suit their learning needs.
- **Variation #3** (Winding it back): While the majority of students are singing the text and showing body solfa, individual students could sing "chick-en pie" as an ostinato, showing body solfa.
- **Variation #4** (Winding it back): Divide the class into four equal groups and assign each group to perform the text of one measure using body solfa. Strategically assign the group containing students in need of winding back to sing the final measure that includes the motive *re* in its simplest form.
- **Variation #5** (Winding it back/forward): After the students have aurally discovered *re* and are able to sing the song in solfège, assign small groups or individual students to sing only one solfège syllable, wherever those pitches occur within the song (i.e., one group sings only the pitch *mi,* another group sings only the pitch *sol,* etc., to achieve a handbell effect). Strategically assign the pitch *mi* to those who need to wind it back, as *mi* occurs on strong beats in a somewhat regular pattern. Assign the pitches *la* and *re* to those who need to wind it forward, as those pitches occur in more rhythmically tricky places within the song.

These activities demonstrate some of the many ways to design lesson segments that allow simultaneous learning at a variety of learning levels.

Decoding

Proficiency in correlating groups of neutral pitches within the context of a song or tonal pattern with solfège syllables can greatly aid students' ability to audiate, improvise, read, and write music. Tonal patterns "translated" from neutral syllables (e.g., "bum") to solfège in this way can be used to create music by arranging those patterns in a new order or inferring new patterns. A repertoire of tonal patterns is the foundation of what is often referred to as "sight-singing" or "sight-reading": previous audiation of a tonic pattern in major can be referred to when visualizing that same tonic pattern in staff notation. A repertoire of tonal patterns that has been read in staff notation becomes the foundation for writing music (dictation and composition). Thus, the ability to audiate or decode tonal patterns in solfège is a valuable foundational skill for musicians.

A sequence for aural decoding of tonal patterns from neutral syllables to solfège syllables builds on the aural discovery sequence outlined in the previous section. Once students have discovered the presence of the new pitch *re* and can sing known songs and tonal patterns using solfège syllables, students are challenged to relate the solfège syllables to pitches performed using neutral syllables. A sample sequence for decoding is outlined here:

1. Students echo tonal patterns performed using neutral syllables.
2. Students echo tonal patterns performed using solfège syllables.
3. Students hear tonal patterns performed using neutral syllables and respond by performing the same tonal patterns using solfège syllables.

Decoding Activity

Students individually decode a tonal pattern from a neutral syllable into solfège syllables. The teacher differentiates by performing tonal patterns that are suited to each student's current level of challenge, and the final pitch of one student's tonal pattern becomes the first pitch of the next student's tonal pattern, establishing a chain of patterns that relate to each other and share the same resting tone.

Student A	*la-sol-mi*					
Student B		*mi-re-do*				
Student C			*do-re*			
Student D				*re-mi-sol-la*		
Student E					*la-sol-do*	
Student F						*do-mi*
Student A							*mi-re-do*

Figure 5.2   decoding chain

Some strategies for winding back this activity are described as follows:

- **Variation #1** (Winding it back): Include tonal patterns that do not include the new pitch *re* as needed for winding it back (e.g., *sol-mi-sol-la*).
- **Variation #2** (Winding it back/forward): Ask students to decode out of turn as needed to allow additional practice and challenge. For example, student A decodes a pattern without *re* (e.g., *la-sol-mi*), listens as other students decode patterns including *re* (e.g., *mi-re-do, do-re-mi, re-mi-do*), and then is asked to decode a *re* pattern previously decoded by another student (e.g., *mi-re-do*). See Figure 5.2.

- **Variation #3** (Winding it forward): Individual students are asked to decode tonal patterns that contain *re* in a less common context, such as *re-sol* or *la-re*.

These activities demonstrate how lesson segments can be designed to encourage simultaneous learning at a variety of learning levels.

DIFFERENTIATING TONAL PATTERNS

Jodi's class was decoding melodic patterns, including the pitches *sol, mi, la,* and *do*. The teacher differentiated the decoding phrases for each student and chained the patterns so that the last pitch of one student's pattern became the first pitch of the next student's pattern. Taking turns around the circle, the first five students decoded the following patterns:

Sam	*do-mi-sol*
Emily	*sol-la-sol-mi*
Brian	*mi-la-do-sol*
Jodi	*sol-mi-sol*
Luke	*sol-mi-la-sol*

Jodi's and Sam's patterns did not include the newest pitch *la* yet, and Jodi's pattern was in a very familiar context. Brian's pattern included all the known pitches because he needed the additional challenge.

USING A DRONE TO WIND IT BACK

Most of Mrs. Anderson's third graders have been at her school since kindergarten and have learned to hear, read, and write songs and tonal patterns containing *do, mi, sol,* and *la*. They are comfortable singing back with correct solfège and hand signs when Mrs. Anderson sings *do-mi-sol-la* patterns on a "loo," and they can read tonal patterns containing those pitches accurately from the staff.

For several weeks, the class has been singing songs and working with tonal patterns containing *re*, and most students have aurally discovered that this "new note" (not yet identified as *re*) is higher than *do* and lower than *mi*. Mrs. Anderson has assessed this skill by singing patterns containing *re* on a neutral syllable and having students decode the patterns into solfège, using body solfa. Mrs. Anderson has students perform this activity with eyes closed, showing her who is really ready to name the new note and who needs more time and experience to be able to audiate the patterns.

Giancarlo loves music class but has only recently begun to sing on pitch fairly consistently. He can echo short *do-mi-sol-la* tonal patterns accurately and sings simple, limited-range songs in tune most of the time. Using body solfa, he has just begun to demonstrate the ability to hear that *mi* is lower than *sol, la* is higher than *sol,* and *do* is the lowest of all. However, he is not consistently accurate, and his reading of those pitches and patterns from the staff is still developing.

To challenge and engage the majority of the class, who are ready to discover *re*, Mrs. Anderson presents *re*, while she winds it back for Giancarlo by continuing to give him opportunities to strengthen his singing and aural grasp of the more familiar solfège. She allows Giancarlo (and a friend of his choice) to play and sing a *do* drone, and later, a *mi* drone, while the rest of the class sings and signs *mi-re-do* patterns on "Hot Cross Buns" and other *mi-re-do* songs. As the class's tone set expands from *mi-re-do*, Mrs. Anderson introduces the song "Rain, Come Wet Me," which includes a repetitive *sol-mi* along with *mi-re-do*. Giancarlo and some volunteers are responsible for reading all of the *sol*s and *mi*s when the class reads from the staff.

Giancarlo is excited to be successful at skills and is ready to take ownership of those skills. The isolation of the *sol-mi* interval (and later, others) in the context of a larger tone set continues to strengthen his audiation skills. Mrs. Anderson continues to assess Giancarlo's developing skills separately, holding him accountable for the skills that are appropriate to his musical development.

MUSIC READING

Reading from staff notation is often considered a hallmark of a visually literate musician. With aural decoding as a foundation, a possible sequence for reading from staff notation is outlined here:

1. Have students echo tonal patterns using neutral syllables and solfège syllables.
2. Have students decode tonal patterns from neutral syllables into solfège syllables.
3. Have students echo familiar tonal patterns using solfège syllables and show those tonal patterns in staff notation, perhaps on flashcards.
4. After several tonal patterns have been introduced in staff notation in this fashion, change the order in which the patterns are presented so that the notation triggers audiation rather than requiring memorization.
5. Expand from reading individual tonal patterns into reading a series of two or more familiar tonal patterns.

6. Present other familiar tonal patterns previously decoded into solfège syllables without students first echoing the pattern (i.e., students have echoed and decoded the pattern *re-mi-do* but have not yet seen it notated on the staff). In this way, the teacher can assess students' ability to apply what they've audiated to the new notation, indicating that the notation triggers previous audiation. Effective sight-reading involves reference to the repertoire of tonal patterns previously learned in solfège as a means to read tonal patterns, which share a resting tone and often outline harmonic function, rather than attempting to read through interval or pitch retention, which lacks the context of centering around a resting tone and its implied harmonic functions.

The addition of visual staff notation to the kinesthetic and aural aspects of melody previously established can trigger difficulties for some students and an appropriate challenge for others, creating a wide range of learning levels to balance within a lesson segment. Winding back strategies can increase the efficacy of a lesson segment goal by allowing all students to learn simultaneously at an appropriate level of challenge. Some strategies for winding back melodic reading are highlighted here:

- **Variation #1** (Winding it back): Provide tonal patterns using fewer pitches for selected students to decode and read (e.g., *sol-mi-do* instead of *la-sol-mi-re-do*).
- **Variation #2** (Winding it forward): Provide tonal patterns using more difficult combinations of pitches for selected students to decode and read (e.g., *re-sol* or *mi-do-sol*).
- **Variation #3** (Winding it back): Maintain a familiar order for reading of tonal patterns for some students.
- **Variation #4** (Winding it forward): Shuffle the tonal pattern flashcards to create a different order for some students.

Melodic Reading Activity

Ask students to select the corresponding tonal pattern performed from a selection of flashcards containing tonal patterns notated on the staff. Encourage students to audiate the tonal patterns notated on the staff before selecting the flashcard that corresponds to the tonal pattern performed.

- **Variation # 1** (Winding it back): Allow students the opportunity to decode aloud the tonal pattern performed before asking them to select the corresponding flashcard.
- **Variation #2** (Winding it back): Ask selected students to decode aloud the tonal pattern performed and ask another student to select the corresponding flashcard.

- **Variation #3** (Winding it back): Number the selected flashcards. Ask all students to indicate the number of the corresponding flashcard by holding up the appropriate number of fingers where only the teacher can view them. Begin by performing the least challenging tonal pattern, repeat the same pattern occasionally, return to a pattern already performed, and slowly increase the level of challenge.

After experience with *re* in the context of *mi-re-do*, students will experience *re* in other contexts, such as *do-re-mi* and *re-sol*. A chart like the one in Figure 5.3 can be used to track individual progress to aid in winding back instruction.

	mrd	smrd	drm	drms	rs	sr
Emily						
Caleb						
Mason						
Madison						

Figure 5.3   Tracking progress for *re*

Students who have not previously experienced sequential music instruction may enter your music program lacking the prerequisite skills to master the current learning objective. The following vignette illustrates a technique to wind back instruction for that student while maintaining the intended lesson focus.

WINDING IT BACK FOR A NEW STUDENT

Sophia is a new student in Mrs. Johnson's third-grade music class, having moved to the school district from another state. Although Sophia is willing and interested in participating, it is evident that she does not have a background in reading music, as Mrs. Johnson's students do. To wind it back for Sophia, Mrs. Johnson asks the class to read from a tone ladder and instructs Sophia that she is to sing only the *sols* when Mrs. Johnson points to the "s." Mrs. Johnson proceeds to point to various patterns focusing on *mi-re-do*, while occasionally including *sol*:

s

m

r

d

> When Sophia is successful with this task, Mrs. Johnson asks her to sing the *sol*s and the *do*s when they occur. Mrs. Johnson continues pointing to patterns on the tone ladder and Sophia participates successfully. Mrs. Johnson makes a note on the lesson plan to assess Sophia's singing of *sol* and *do* from the tone ladder with a buddy during the next lesson before adding additional solfège pitches.

There are several possibilities for the order of presentation of melodic elements; the selection of melodic hierarchies is dependent on skill level, age, cultural background, and classroom setting. The repertoire and tone set for beginning students who are young will be different than that for older elementary students or those within an ensemble setting: *sol-mi* songs may be more appropriate for the first group, and extracting *mi-re-do* from a song containing a larger tone set may be more appropriate for the other groups. Chapter 5 of the companion website contains additional assessment charts to track student progress for a complete introduction of *sol-mi*, adding *sol-mi* to the staff, and preparing *do*, as well as a template for tracking the introduction of new pitches. A description of several possible melodic hierarchies, including the advantages and disadvantages for selection, and a sample melodic sequence, titled "Generic Melodic Sequence," which provides the context for the aural discovery, decoding, and reading segments highlighted in this chapter, can also be found in chapter 5 of the companion website. Students with special needs may progress at a slower pace, requiring additional microsteps or goal modifications. Some ideas for winding that include modifications and adaptations for preparing for *sol-mi,* reading *sol-mi* on the staff, and preparing for *la* are also included in chapter 5 of the companion website. A template for customizing assessment charts to track individual progress can be found on the companion website as well.

Melodic Practice Activities

Providing multiple access points for all students can be more easily accomplished if a variety of tools are available. Repetition of the same task in different ways offers both frequency of practice and diverse approaches, both of which aid students of all learning levels and styles. Some learners need to experience the skill many times to master it, while others need to experience the skill in a particular way for learning to take place. This segment of the chapter offers descriptions of a variety of melodic practice activities from which the reader can choose or adapt to suit the needs of his students.

AUDIATION ACTIVITIES

A new melodic concept is introduced in one context, then practiced in other contexts for reinforcement of the concept. Practice activities can deepen student understanding of a concept and reinforce the original context. Activities that reinforce audiation of the new melodic element before notation is introduced are of particular importance, as audiation forms the basis for reading and writing.

The following practice activities reinforce audiation.

> **Audiation Activity #1:** Small groups of students or individuals are assigned one solfège syllable to sing throughout a known song or abstract exercise (handbell effect):

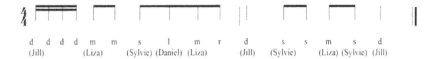

> **Audiation Activity #2:** Small groups of students or individuals are assigned a specific measure or phrase to sing in a known song or sight-read an abstract exercise:

Students should perform these activities without cues from the teacher. This allows the students to rely on their audiation rather than an external source. If the syllables, measures, or phrases are assigned to small groups out of order, the work of the students will be more independent, and this is a means of winding forward the skill.

By singing only one beat in solfège before passing to the next person, the students will audiate the song in a different way. To follow are two ways to do this:

> **Audiation Activity #3:** Each student sings one beat of solfège before passing the song to the next person in the circle. The next person sings the next consecutive beat of the song in solfège and passes to the next person in the circle (i.e., chaining).

Audiation Activity #4: Students chain the solfège around the circle, passing by phrase.

Similarly, students can be asked to audiate the entire familiar song but only perform a specific solfège syllable. By asking students to perform only part of the song but audiate all of the song, the solfège syllables of the song are repeated frequently but with more challenge. This type of activity can be used when students sight-read as well:

Rising Tide: Students are asked to sing only one pitch in solfège each time it occurs in the notation but must audiate all of the notation. Additional pitches are added successively, until the "tide has risen" and the entire song is being sung on syllables.

Sinking Ship: Students sing the entire song in solfège from notation. One solfège syllable is subtracted (audiated only) with the remaining pitches sung aloud. Additional pitches are subtracted successively, until the "ship has sunk" and the entire song is being audiated.

Audiation is also used in the following examples, in which a familiar song, "Great Big House" is notated with pitches missing (Musical Example 5.5):

Audiation Activity #5: Students must sing the song in solfège to discover which pitches are missing and then dictate to the teacher or have individuals write the missing pitches.

Musical Example 5.5 "Great Big House" with missing pitches.

Great Big House

Traditional

Audiation Activity #6: The teacher performs a familiar song from notation but sings some changes. The students must identify, locate, and write the changes in the notation.

Audiation Activities #5 and #6 can be made more challenging when the notated song is unknown to the students and therefore abstract. The teacher sings the example on a neutral syllable with several changes from what is notated. Students must audiate the notation to detect the "errors" the teacher is performing.

Each of the audiation activities can be wound back to include challenges that match the individual learning needs of all students. If many students in a class need to experience a more difficult activity, the activity can be sequenced such that lower-level skills are reviewed to establish the foundation upon which the more challenging work is built; all students experience challenge at their individual learning levels but do not necessarily perform all of the work.

WINDING IT BACK WITH AN AUDIATION ACTIVITY

Erin's third-grade class was reviewing low *la* by singing "Hush, Little Baby" using text and switching to solfège on the teacher's signal (reading from the staff). Although the class had done the same activity with other melodic and rhythmic elements in previous years, Erin was anxious that she would not be able to switch languages successfully at the tempo used by the rest of the class. The teacher, anticipating Erin's anxiety because of her previous experiences with this activity, moved the class forward through a sequence in a deliberate manner. The class moved quickly through the following sequence:

1. The class sang "Hush, Little Baby" using text.
2. The class sang "Hush, Little Baby" using text, switching to audiation on the teacher's signal.
3. The class sang "Hush, Little Baby" using solfège.
4. The class sang "Hush, Little Baby" using solfège, switching to audiation on the teacher's signal.
5. The teacher sang "Hush, Little Baby" using solfège; when she stopped, the class continued in solfège.
6. The teacher reminded the class to sing the text and the solfège in their heads at the same time.
7. Half the class sang "Hush, Little Baby" using text; on the teacher's signal, the other half of the class continued in solfège. Then they switched jobs.
8. The teacher demonstrated switching between text and solfège.
9. The class sang using text, switching to solfège on the teacher's signal. The teacher signaled halfway through the song (only one switch in the song), then after each phrase (three switches in the song), then randomly (more switches in the song), making sure that she signaled a beat before the class would switch languages.

By moving very sequentially, the teacher hoped to build Erin's skills and confidence. When Erin faltered on step 7, the teacher made a note in her lesson plan about Erin's progress on the activity.

PARTWORK AND MELODIC GAMES

Practice of a melodic or rhythmic concept can be made more challenging and more harmonically interesting through the use of partwork. When students are asked to perform more than one musical task at a time, their audiation and their musical understanding increases. The addition of partwork is also a means of winding forward an activity. Some practice activities that include partwork are listed here:

> **Partwork Activity #1:** Students sing using text and conduct.
> **Partwork Activity #2:** Students sing using text while a small group performs an ostinato.
> **Partwork Activity #3:** Students sing using text while a group sings in canon.
> **Partwork Activity #4:** Students sing using text and perform an ostinato on a barred percussion instrument.
> **Partwork Activity #5:** Students sing using text while a group sings a partner song.
> **Partwork Activity #6:** Students sing using text while a group sings the chord roots.

Any of these activities can be used with the students singing in solfège or absolute letter names instead of the text. These activities can also be used when students are sight-singing in solfège or absolute letter names. To wind back, students perform with others in a small group; to wind forward, students perform individually.

Sight-Reading and Partwork

As an additional challenge, students can be asked to sight-read from the staff while performing the beat and beat division, conducting, or walking the beat and tapping the rhythm. Ask students to audiate more than one musical language simultaneously when they are reading notation. When students know several songs that they are able to sing using text, solfège, rhythm syllables, and perhaps absolute letter names, they can:

- sing using text, then switch to rhythm syllables within the song;
- sing using text, then switch to solfège within the song;
- sing using text, then switch to solfège and again to rhythm syllables within the song;

- sing using text, then switch to solfège and again to absolute letter names within the song;
- sing using text, then switch to solfège and again to rhythm syllables and again to absolute letter names within the song; or
- sing, switching from the soprano to alto part, the soprano to bass part, the alto to tenor part, and so forth (e.g., using text, solfège, rhythm syllables, and absolute letter names).

Students who might struggle with this activity could be assigned to sing only the text when the teacher holds up the "text" sign, while others might be alternating between "text" and "solfège." These students could then sing only the solfège when the teacher holds up the "solfège" sign, while the class alternates between singing the "text" and the "solfège," thus winding back the sequence through the use of scaffolding. The teacher can signal by clapping, tapping a woodblock, or raising his or her hand, or with a different visual or aural signal. The teacher could also assign an interval (e.g., every phrase or every measure) at which the job would change.

Canon Activities

The use of canon as a technique to aid students in simultaneous audiation in multiple musical languages is an extension of the previous activities. Some uses of canon as partwork are as follows:

> **Canon Activity #1:** Some students sing the melody in solfège; others sing solfège in canon with the first group.
>
> **Canon Activity #2:** Students sing in solfège while showing hand signs of the same song in canon.
>
> **Canon Activity #3:** Students sing in solfège while clapping the rhythm of the same song in canon.
>
> **Canon Activity #4:** The notation of any familiar song, flashcards, or composed exercises can be read and performed backward in solfège, as this takes the patterns out of the context of the familiar and makes the melodic or rhythmic patterns abstract.

Again, students may sing in small groups to wind back or in solo to wind forward the level of challenge of the activity.

Sudoku

The melodic puzzle in Figures 5.4 and 5.5 can be used as a Sudoku, in which each row and column must contain only one of each melodic element. Students solve the Sudoku by identifying and writing the missing melodic element in a particular row or column. That melodic element must also fit in the corresponding perpendicular row or column. A Sudoku can be made less challenging by leaving only one box empty in a row or column; a more challenging Sudoku would have more than one box empty in a row or column, making it essential that the student decide in which order to complete the boxes for the solution to be made evident. Students sing pitches by row or column.

d	m		s
	r	m	d
m		s	r
r	s	d	

Figure 5.4 Sudoku#1

d		s	l	r
	r	d	m	
m		l		d
r	d		s	l
	l	r		m

Figure 5.5 Sudoku#2

Tone Ladder and Tone Set

Tone Ladder

l

s

m

r

d

The teacher points to one letter at a time; students sing the solfège associated with each letter.

Musical Example 5.6 Do pentatonic tone set.

The teacher points to one pitch at a time in the tone set (Example 5.6). Students sing the solfège associated with each pitch. Differentiation can occur when the teacher chooses specific patterns for each student: patterns can be made more accessible for some students by excluding the newest melodic concept or asking a student to read patterns that are extracted directly from song material. The activity can be made more challenging by asking a student to read patterns that are more unusual and not often found in song materials (e.g., *re-la* or *sol-re*).

Note by Note

The teacher establishes the tone set (selection of pitches) to be practiced. She plays one pitch on the piano/recorder; the class echoes that pitch in solfège. The teacher continues to play one pitch at a time within the given tone set; the class echoes each pitch in solfège, alternating with the teacher's playing. As with the tone ladder and tone set activities, differentiation can occur when the teacher chooses specific patterns to challenge each student at his or her particular level. This activity can also be used to practice absolute letter names, when the students' response to the teacher's playing is to sing the absolute letter name.

Concentration

Students are seated in a circle. The teacher defines the tone set being practiced. The following rhyme is spoken while performing the ostinato: Patsch, clap, snap right, snap left (Musical Example 5.7).

Musical Example 5.7

Concentration

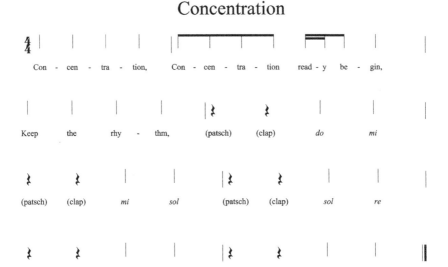

Each student sings a different solfège syllable on beats 3 and 4 of the ostinato pattern; the first solfège syllable sung must match the last solfège syllable sung by the preceding player. For example:

> Student #1: (patsch), (clap), *d, m* (sung)
> Student #2: (patsch), (clap), *m, s* (sung)
> Student #3: (patsch), (clap), *s, r* (sung)
> Student #4: (patsch), (clap), *r, m* (sung)
> Student #5: (patsch), (clap), *m, l* (sung)

This activity could be wound back by beginning the activity with a specific student, who would sing the assigned starting pattern. A student could also be asked to echo the pattern sung immediately before his or her turn, and the next successive player would continue the game.

Solfège Simon

The teacher (or a student) sings a melodic pattern containing two to four pitches within the designated tone set. Each consecutive student improvises a melodic pattern containing two to four pitches but must begin on the last pitch of the previous person's pattern. For example:

drm
msl
lsmd
dr
rdm
msls
srmd
dmd, etc.

An adaptation might be for a student to echo the pattern sung previously, with the next successive player continuing the game. Another option would be for the student to sing the last pitch of the previous pattern repeatedly (e.g., *mmm*), and the next successive player would continue the game.

Through the use of an assortment of practice activities, students receive the repetition and frequency necessary for all to learn the new melodic concepts at their own pace. Practicing the melodic concepts in many ways allows each student to practice in the learning modality that is most comfortable for him or her, and for all students to enjoy the various approaches. An additional activity, "Improvisation Chain," can be found on chapter 5 of ▶ the companion website.

The presentation of tonal content in a sequential manner and in the context of high-quality music makes the work relevant and meaningful, and decoding, improvising, reading, and writing music will be lifelong skills. In addition, a background in this melodic sequence will provide students with the prerequisite audiation and knowledge to continue study of scale types and intervals, as found in chapter 9. Chapter 7 contains many ideas for students to use vocal exploration and solfège to improvise and compose their own ideas. Notation of songs cited in this book can be found under ▶ "Songs" on the companion website; sources for the song material can be found in "Folk Song Sources" on the companion website. It is of paramount importance that each student learn to audiate melody in a way that is most meaningful. The teacher's use of melodic sequence in creating and implementing lessons to wind it back and forward increases the opportunity for all students to experience the beauty of melody.

REFERENCES

Apel, W. (1972). *Harvard dictionary of music*. Cambridge, MA: Belknap Press.
Bertaux, B. (1989). Teaching children of all ages to use the singing voice. In: *Readings in music learning theory*. Chicago, IL: GIA.

Choksy, L. (1999). *The Kodály method I: Comprehensive music education*. Upper Saddle River, NJ: Prentice-Hall.

Gordon, E. E. (1986). *Primary measures of music audiation*. Chicago, IL: GIA.

Gordon, E. E. (2012). *Learning sequences in music: A contemporary music learning theory*. Chicago, IL: GIA.

Kodály, Z. (1974). *The selected writings of Zoltán Kodály* (L. Halápy & F. Macnicol, Trans.). London, England: Boosey & Hawkes, 1974.

Method. (n.d.). In *Merriam-Webster's online dictionary*. Retrieved from http://www.merriam-webster.com/dictionary/method

Mozart, W. A. (attributed, 1826). *Reminiscences of Michael Kelly, of the King's Theatre, and Theatre Royal Drury Lane, including a period of nearly half a century; with original anecdotes of many distinguished personages, political, literary, and musical* (2nd ed., Vol. I). London, England: Henry Colburn. Digitized 2006. Retrieved from http://www.oake.org

Phillips, K. (2014). *Teaching kids to sing*. Boston, MA: Schirmer.

Randel, D. M. (1999). *The Harvard concise dictionary of music and musicians* (2nd ed.). Cambridge, MA: Belknap Press.

CHAPTER 6

Accessing Rhythmic Sequences at Multiple Learning Levels for All Students

ROBERTA Y. HICKOX, *Halifax Area School District, Halifax, Pennsylvania*

CHAPTER OVERVIEW

Music creates order out of chaos: for rhythm imposes unanimity upon the divergent, melody imposes continuity upon the disjointed, and harmony imposes compatibility upon the incongruous.

Yehudi Menuhin

Rhythm is a critically important aspect of music: it is experienced in movement, dance, poetry, and drumming, and it is combined with pitch to create melody. Through sequenced rhythm content, careful scaffolding, and winding strategies, all students can gain audiation skills in rhythm that are foundational for experiencing all genres of music and creating new music. This chapter will do the following:

- Define rhythm
- Discuss the importance of continuous flow movement in audiating rhythm
- Examine macrobeat and microbeat and their functions within the context of meter
- Present beat function rhythm syllables
- Introduce an approach to teaching rhythm content

- Share examples of classroom activities and suggestions for *winding* the activities *back* and *forward* to meet the needs of individual students
- Offer assessment charts for use in tracking the progress of all students

The ideas of Music Learning Theory offer a research-based approach to rhythm instruction; the Kodály approach outlines a sequential process as well. Sequence is a powerful tool in winding as it encourages the teacher to consider prerequisite understandings in preparation for subsequent learning. Sequence also enables the design of activities that simultaneously address the needs of different learning levels: the prerequisite understandings are reviewed and assessed before new learning concepts are introduced. This allows at least three levels of instruction: (1) review and wound-back material, (2) the lesson objective, and (3) a more difficult degree of challenge for winding forward. Through winding, rhythm instruction can be individualized. The *Harvard Dictionary of Music* defines rhythm fundamentally as "the whole feeling of movement in music, with a strong implication of both regularity and differentiation" (Apel, 1972, p. 729). Indeed, "Rhythm has foundation in movement. Regardless of music style, rhythm is compromised without free flowing, continuous movement in audiation" (Gordon, 2012, p. 190). The use of large, sustained, and flexible movements is central to internalizing rhythm and for audiating what happens between beats. "Remember, rhythm comes from the Greek *rhythmos*. It means flow, as water in a river. . . . Flow and coordination of movement in audiation seems to be the basis of rhythm aptitude" (p. 174). With the continuous flow movement in audiation, externalized foot tapping or beat keeping is superfluous.

As with tonal aptitude, rhythm aptitude is developmental until approximately age nine. Through the use of learning sequence activities, rhythm content can be individualized. Based on a student's rhythm aptitude score from a valid, reliable, and age-appropriate music aptitude test such as the Primary Measures of Music Audiation (PMMA), specific rhythm patterns are selected for the student to echo, decode, and identify. All students are listening to the variety of rhythm patterns that are presented to others, offering the repetition necessary for some to audiate their individual pattern. Because music aptitude is not correlated with intelligence, all students are instructed according to their potential, regardless of learning differences or intelligence. "At most, there is only a five to ten percent relation between music aptitude and any type of intelligence test score. A student with high music aptitude may be expected to have any level of intelligence and a student with high [or low] intelligence may be expected to have any level of music aptitude" (Gordon, 2012, p. 56). Therefore, knowledge of student aptitude scores can aid music teachers in teaching all students at their appropriate musical skill level, regardless of other factors such as academic success or identified special needs. Neurotypical students benefit from winding just as students with special needs do because all students benefit from instruction focused on their individual learning needs.

Macrobeats are the large beats felt when music is audiated.

> Microbeats are shorter than macrobeats and are derived from the equal division of macrobeats. When macrobeats are divided into two microbeats of equal length, the first of two coinciding with a macrobeat, the result is usual duple meter. When macrobeats are divided into three microbeats of equal length, the first of three coinciding with a macrobeat, the result is usual triple meter. (Gordon, 2012, p. 175)

Audiation precedes notation; therefore, rhythm patterns audiated in usual duple meter can be notated with a variety of meter signatures (e.g., $\frac{2}{4}$, $\frac{2}{2}$, or $\frac{4}{4}$), as can rhythm patterns audiated in usual triple meter (e.g., $\frac{3}{4}$ or $\frac{3}{8}$). Rhythm patterns (content) are audiated concurrently with macrobeats and microbeats, providing an aural comparison for meter (context). When students do not audiate the macrobeats and microbeats while listening to or performing rhythm patterns, meter is not implied, and they will struggle to make sense of the rhythm patterns (Gordon, 2012).

To establish the context of meter, the teacher should chant a four-beat rhythm pattern containing macrobeats and microbeats in the meter and tempo in which the subsequent rhythm patterns will be performed. Ultimately, student audiation develops to the point where flow, meter, macrobeats, microbeats, and rhythm patterns are thoroughly internalized.

> Audiation is a matter of concentrating on one set of musical sounds while at the same time attending to or performing one or more sets of other musical sounds.... When they are performing and audiating, musicians are unconscious of what they are doing and music absorbs them. Fine musicians know when they are audiating: it occurs when ears become more important than fingers and arms. (Gordon, 2012, p. 6)

Students demonstrate audiation when they sing or play with good intonation and a consistent tempo. Activities for promoting audiation include performing patterns, the resting tone, chord roots, the macrobeat, and the microbeat. Tools such as solfège and rhythm syllables label and externalize musical understanding; those tools gradually become unnecessary for audiation.

For clarity of audiation, rhythm patterns are best separated from tonal patterns. Oftentimes rhythm is imposed on tonal patterns to create melodic patterns.

> Gordon's research indicates that children have difficulty conserving the tonal and rhythmic characteristics of music. Upon hearing the same tonal pattern performed twice with different rhythms, for example, they will often insist that the second pattern was a different tonal pattern. For this reason, tonal and rhythm content are kept separate in learning sequence activities. Tonal patterns are performed without rhythm and rhythm patterns are performed without pitch. (http://giml.org/mlt/lsa-teaching/)

As a tool for performing rhythm content, rhythm syllables based on beat function, not time value, are recommended. Rhythm syllables relate to the way the rhythmic element is audiated, rather than the way it might be notated. Macrobeats in all meters use the same syllable, regardless of their placement within a measure. However, microbeats use different syllables, dependent on the meter (e.g., microbeats in duple are audiated DU-DE, while microbeats in triple are audiated DU-DA-DI). Rhythm syllables are taught as a tool to aid audiation: "Ideally, as students' level of skill increases, they gradually discard syllables for use with familiar patterns and use syllables only occasionally for learning unfamiliar patterns" (Gordon, 2012, p. 89). An extensive comparison of several rhythm syllable systems is presented in chapter 10 of the companion website.

When notating rhythm, it is optional to show only the rhythm stems in most instances. "Only the note stems are used initially for rhythm reading. The body of the note is not necessary to rhythm reading except for half notes and whole notes. In all other cases the rhythm is determined by the note stems" (Choksy, 1974, p. 13). For some students with learning differences or those with fine motor challenges, this rhythm shorthand can be more efficient; and can be notated with popsicle sticks used to represent rhythm stems as a kinesthetic reinforcement for all students.

When rhythm content is highlighted within the context of songs or chants in classroom activities, all students are offered multiple access points at a variety of learning levels. This chapter will delineate the rhythmic learning process and provide strategies for including *all* students in

WINDING IT BACK THROUGH SCAFFOLDING

Samuel's third-grade class was practicing sixteenth notes by reading the rhythm notation of the song "Paw Paw Patch" from the board. As an added challenge, Samuel's music teacher directed the students to tap the sixteenth notes in their hands, pat the eighth notes on their legs, and stamp the quarter notes when these rhythms occurred in the song. Samuel was not yet able to speak the rhythm syllables or tap the rhythm successfully for the sixteenth notes and was struggling to keep up with the class. His music teacher wound it back and suggested that Samuel speak and pat the eighth notes only, while the class performed the entire song. When Samuel was successful, his music teacher asked him to speak and stamp the quarter notes in addition to his work with the eighth notes. Because the work was scaffolded, Samuel was able to successfully demonstrate his understanding of quarter notes and eighth notes. Samuel was able to speak the rhythm syllables for all the rhythms at a slower tempo as the class was lining up to leave music class.

each activity by showing how to wind the rhythmic sequence back and forward to address individual students' learning needs. In addition, practical examples will be provided both within the chapter and in chapter 6 of the companion website to illustrate how winding for multiple levels can be accomplished simultaneously.

PREPARATION FOR LEARNING SEQUENCE ACTIVITIES

After experiencing creative movement (see chapter 4 for activities and statement of purpose), students show continuous flow movement while listening and responding to the teacher's singing and chanting. Students learn to move purposefully to macrobeats in both duple and triple. Macrobeats are then subdivided into microbeats (groups of two microbeats in duple meter and groups of three microbeats in triple meter), and macrobeats and microbeats are performed simultaneously for a physical and aural comparison. Macrobeats, microbeats, and rhythm patterns can then be experienced simultaneously in various combinations (e.g., macrobeats and microbeats, macrobeats and rhythm patterns, microbeats and rhythm patterns). A detailed sequence of these beginning rhythm concepts can be found in chapter 3 for younger students and in chapter 8 for older students. This chapter presumes student understanding of and experience with macrobeats, microbeats, rhythm patterns, and rhythm syllables in duple and triple meters.

Through learning sequence activities that target specific functions of rhythm patterns (e.g., macrobeats and microbeats only, divisions of microbeats, and elongations), students receive guidance, based on music aptitude test scores, in rhythm skills. This individualized instruction, which occurs during a five- to ten-minute block at the beginning of each lesson, sequences rhythm content through several stages of learning. Students **echo** rhythm patterns on neutral syllables and rhythm syllables between performances of the teacher's song/chant to place the rhythm patterns in the context of the meter of the song/chant in a whole-part-whole sequence. While neurotypical students imitate the teacher's rhythm patterns without pause, students with processing delays or verbal challenges might need two beats of rest to prepare to echo or to participate in rhythm patterning at a slower tempo.

The context of triple meter is established through performance of "My Friend and Your Friend" (Musical Example 6.1).

Musical Example 6.1 "My Friend and Your Friend"

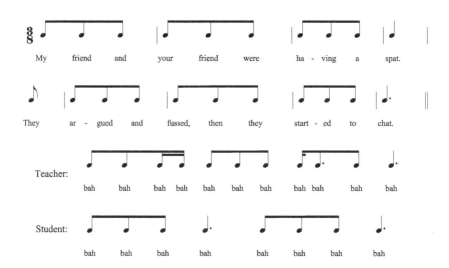

The teacher performs two macrobeat-microbeat patterns. Students **identify** the two rhythm patterns performed by the teacher as "same" or "different" as a way of experiencing the contrast necessary to audiate thoroughly. Students with processing delays may need a longer pause between the teacher's query about "same" or "different" and their answer. They may also need to consider another student's answer and agree or disagree as a means of identifying "same" and "different."

Students **create** rhythm patterns on neutral syllables and rhythm syllables as examples of "different," as in the teacher/student rhythm conversation in Musical Example 6.2.

The teacher and students can use hand signs to indicate whether the subsequent pattern should be echoed ("same") or created ("different"), as in

Musical Example 6.2

Figure 6.1. (See chapter 7 for more ideas and activities on creativity.)

Students **name** the meter and function in duple and triple meters so

Figure 6.1 Same and different signs

that they have audiated and classified rhythm syllables as belonging to a particular meter (i.e., duple) and function (macrobeats and microbeats). Additional functions are added (i.e., divisions and elongations) to expand the students' repertoire of rhythm content. Students are asked to **decode** or generalize their understanding of rhythm patterns by echoing individual patterns chanted on a neutral syllable by the teacher using rhythm syllables (see Musical Example 6.3). Students with verbal challenges can name the meter and function by selecting from a choice of cards (i.e., "duple" and "triple"). As an interim step prior to decoding, students can echo the teacher's pattern with a neutral syllable. Students who are not yet ready to decode rhythm patterns can create rhythm patterns on a neutral syllable for other students to decode.

Musical Example 6.3

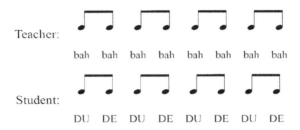

These learning sequences are introduced initially in duple meter and triple meter, before continuing into unusual paired and unusual unpaired meter. Students should, at a minimum, experience rhythm patterns in duple meter and triple meter so that the contrast between the feeling of the two meters reinforces audiation of each meter.

Individualized instruction is supplemented with classroom activities, during which all students experience songs and chants in a variety of meters and modes. These classroom activities can be scaffolded to include the substeps needed by some learners and can be designed to challenge a variety of learning levels simultaneously, thus winding back/forward the instruction.

The instructional sequence described in this chapter is modeled after the one detailed in Gordon's *Learning Sequences in Music* (Gordon, 2012). While most of the terminology and ideas are from Gordon and Music Learning Theory proponents, I prefer the term "decoding" to "generalization-verbal" for use with younger students and have made adaptations to some of the more traditional Music Learning Theory activities.

PRESENTATION OF RHYTHM NOTATION

With the extensive background of rhythm audiation engendered by echoing, identifying, creating, naming, and decoding (also called "generalization-verbal") specific rhythm content, students are now prepared to view rhythm notation. A sample sequence for initial presentation of rhythm notation is itemized here:

1. The teacher chants a familiar four-beat rhythm pattern containing macrobeats and microbeats in rhythm syllables.

DU DE DU DE DU DE DU DE

2. Students chant the rhythm syllables to the same rhythm pattern.

DU DE DU DE DU DE DU DE

3. The teacher shows a flashcard containing the notation (standard or stick notation) for the rhythm pattern and chants the rhythm syllables.

4. Students chant the rhythm syllables while looking at the rhythm notation.
5. Steps 1 through 4 are repeated with several familiar patterns in duple meter.
6. The teacher shows each flashcard in the same order without first chanting the rhythm syllables; students chant the rhythm syllables while looking at the rhythm notation.
7. The teacher rearranges the order of the flashcards and shows them without first chanting the rhythm syllables. Students chant the rhythm syllables while looking at the rhythm notation.
8. The teacher shows a new flashcard containing a familiar four-beat rhythm pattern in duple; this rhythm pattern has been previously echoed, decoded, and even used in creating, but has not been previously seen in notation. Students read the rhythm pattern, chanting rhythm syllables.

Any teaching sequence describes the logical order of steps leading to student understanding and mastery of the objective. Because students come to a music classroom with a variety of learning levels, a sequence must be flexible to accommodate the learning needs of all students.

The presentation sequence just detailed can be wound back/forward as follows:

- **Variation #1** (Winding it back): The student is unsuccessful at chanting the rhythm syllables while viewing the rhythm notation when the teacher does not chant first (step 6). The class chants the rhythm syllables while viewing the rhythm notation, and then the student individually echoes the class's rhythm syllables.
- **Variation #2** (Winding it back): The student is unsuccessful at reading the rhythm notation when the flashcards are in an unfamiliar order (step 7). He or she could be asked to chant the rhythm syllables to the flashcards individually when the flashcards are in the familiar order.
- **Variation #3** (Winding it back): The student is unsuccessful at reading the rhythm notation when the rhythm patterns have not previously been presented in notation through steps 1 through 4. The class reads the unpresented rhythm notation using rhythm syllables; the student echoes the rhythm syllables while looking at the rhythm notation.
- **Variation #4** (Winding it forward): The student needs an additional challenge. He or she is asked to individually read an unpresented rhythm pattern from notation using rhythm syllables.

READING OF RHYTHM NOTATION

Once students have begun to read from rhythm notation, the teacher continues to present other previously echoed and decoded rhythm patterns in rhythm notation, establishing a familiar order. The teacher's chanting of the rhythm patterns prior to the class's chanting decreases, and an unfamiliar order is created by shuffling the flashcards. Additional reading activities are introduced that include these familiar patterns in unfamiliar ways. A reading activity example that incorporates differentiation is highlighted here:

1. Flashcards containing rhythm notation to all known rhythm patterns are shuffled.
2. The teacher reveals one flashcard, moving the flashcard to the back of the pile after the students begin chanting the rhythm syllable(s) for beat 4.
3. Step 2 continues as students become comfortable with the rate of change of the flashcards.

4. The teacher reveals one flashcard, facing it and the remainder of the flashcards toward the floor after beat 3, allowing the students to finish chanting the rhythm syllables for beats 3 and 4 while no longer seeing the rhythm notation.
5. Step 4 continues as students become comfortable with the rate of change of the flashcards.

This pattern continues, with the teacher moving the flashcard to the back of the pile after beat 3, then beat 2, then beat 1, challenging the students to chant one rhythm pattern while viewing the notation of the subsequent rhythm pattern. This sequence decreases the amount of time the students view the rhythm notation, accelerating the imprinting of the notation as a pattern in the students' audiation, rather than the students reading each rhythm element separately. Students are forced to "read ahead" in the way experienced musicians sight-read, so that the eyes are ahead of the sound being produced, and sight-reading is by pattern or measure rather than by beat. It is unlikely and unnecessary that this sequence be attempted within one lesson; rather, this skill is best built over time. With the challenges of unfamiliar order and increasingly rapid rate of change, winding will be necessary to teach to each student's individual needs.

- **Variation #1** (Winding it back): Always review the step prior to the current lesson objective. For example, if the current objective is step 4 (moving the flashcard to the back of the pile after beat 3, allowing the students to finish chanting the rhythm syllables for beats 3 and 4 while no longer seeing the rhythm notation), begin the sequence for that lesson on step 2 and review steps 2 and 3 briefly before moving ahead to step 4. Some students will need that quick re-examination of the process to meet the challenge of the current lesson objective. For other students, this will become their learning objective.
- **Variation #2** (Winding it back): Utilize individual responses to differentiate within the sequence, allowing the students with the most challenges to do their work at the beginning of the sequence and asking students in need of more challenge to read as the sequence becomes increasingly more difficult (the rate of change is faster). This adaptation can be performed within the same lesson segment: student A may not yet be ready to read flashcards containing the newest rhythm content and will be challenged to read previously presented flashcards with familiar rhythm content in an unfamiliar order; student B may need to audiate a flashcard out of tempo before individually chanting its rhythm syllables aloud; student C may be challenged to read the flashcards when the flashcard is moved to the back of the pile after

beat 3 and a new flashcard is visible, and will be most successful reading the flashcards when the new card is hidden; and student D is comfortable working at the level of the current lesson objective. This is an example of lesson segment design that provides for simultaneous learning.

- **Variation #3** (Winding it forward): At the most difficult level (changing the flashcards after beat 1 while the new flashcard is visible), individual students can read a series of flashcards after most of the students in the class have achieved their own level of challenge. All students do not need to do all work: each student thrives when challenged to work at his or her particular level of learning.

WRITING WITH RHYTHM NOTATION

Students who have read familiar patterns in rhythm notation have the prerequisite background to begin to write in rhythm notation. Writing can take many forms, culminating in rhythmic dictation with paper and pencil. Simpler versions of writing involve selecting the appropriate rhythm notation from a field of several choices, manipulating popsicle sticks to form rhythms, and ordering beat cards containing one rhythm element to form the rhythm pattern desired. Additionally, peer helpers can dictate for individual students who may need to hear the rhythm pattern numerous times. Using a variety of approaches to writing, especially ones that involve the kinesthetic modality, provides the repetition and reinforcement needed for all students to learn their best. Some students will have their "light bulb" moment after the sixth repetition, others will need to experience a variety of approaches for the concept of writing to be made clear, while for others only a particular approach strikes home. A sequence for presenting writing is detailed here:

1. Students are able to read familiar rhythm patterns in familiar and unfamiliar order, alone and in groups.
2. Students scatter to "perfect spots" around the room. Distribute a set of beat cards to each student; each set contains several quarter-note cards and several paired eighth-note cards.
3. The teacher chants a familiar rhythm pattern on a neutral syllable; students respond by chanting back the rhythm syllables of the same pattern.
4. Students write the rhythm pattern by selecting the appropriate beat cards and arranging them in the order of the chanted rhythm pattern.
5. Students float their fingers underneath the written pattern to track while reading the rhythm pattern in rhythm syllables.

With each new skill, students will require differing levels of scaffolding, repetition, and modifications to be challenged appropriately. Therefore, a writing activity like that described previously, which provides individualization and layers of challenge, can be an efficient way to allow multiple access points for all students. Some ideas for winding this writing activity are highlighted next:

- **Variation #1** (Winding it back/forward): Differentiate by chanting individual patterns to individuals as needed (less challenging patterns to wind it back and more challenging patterns to wind it forward). The teacher must keep track of the main class pattern, the easier pattern, and the more difficult pattern.
- **Variation #2** (Winding it back): Individual students decode the rhythm pattern into rhythm syllables aloud before writing.
- **Variation # 3** (Winding it forward): Students audiate the rhythm syllables before writing, rather than speaking them aloud.
- **Variation #4** (Winding it forward): Individual students can receive two sets of beat cards, allowing them to write an eight-beat rhythm pattern for an added challenge.

WRITING RHYTHM PATTERNS

The students in Zariah's class were writing four-beat rhythm patterns in duple meter. Each student had a set of beat cards containing rhythm elements over one beat (quarter note, paired eighth notes, quarter rest, four 16th notes) and two beats (half note), and students were scattered throughout the room in "perfect spots." Zariah's teacher chanted a rhythm pattern on a neutral syllable and the students were asked to select and order their rhythm cards to represent the teacher's pattern in rhythm notation. When the teacher noticed Zariah's hesitation, he wound it back by asking Zariah to echo the pattern on a neutral syllable, then decode the pattern into rhythm syllables. Zariah was then able to write the pattern correctly. Another student, Luke, struggled when asked to echo then decode the same pattern. The teacher asked the class to read the rhythm pattern using rhythm syllables from their assembled beat cards; Luke was able to write his pattern after hearing the correct rhythm syllables.

Instructional sequences and assessment charts for introducing two-meter and half notes in duple meter and triple meter, and sixteenth notes in duple meter, as well as additional vignettes, can be found in chapter 6 ▶ on the companion website.

ASSESSMENT

At times, a student may require a modified curricular goal to meet his or her learning needs. Other students will be able to achieve the main curricular goal with adaptations of size (e.g., reading three flashcards rather than five), color (e.g., all quarter notes appear in red, all eighth notes appear in green), pace (e.g., student performs at a tempo of his or her choosing), or modality (e.g., student writes the rhythm pattern by choosing the matching flashcard from a selection of five flashcards). A chart such as the one in Figure 6.2 can help document modifications and adaptations that might be appropriate for each rhythmic goal.

Curricular Goal	Modified Curricular Goal	Adapted Curricular Goal
Students will speak quarter rest patterns using neutral syllables.	Student will approximate quarter rest patterns following individual prompt by teacher.	Student will speak quarter rest patterns using neutral syllables at a tempo of his choosing.
Student will speak quarter rest patterns using rhythm syllables.		Student will speak quarter rest patterns using rhythm syllables at a tempo of his choosing.
Student will show quarter rests in well-known rhymes/ songs while speaking rhythm syllables.	Student will tap the rhythm of well-known rhymes while speaking words.	Student will show quarter rests in well-known rhymes/ songs while speaking rhythm syllables at a tempo of his choosing.
Students will decode abstract quarter rest patterns from neutral syllables into rhythm syllables.	Student will chant rhymes that contain quarter rest with other students.	Student will decode quarter rest patterns from neutral syllables into rhythm syllables at a tempo of his choosing.

Figure 6.2   Modifications and adaptations for quarter rest in duple meter.

To adequately assess each student, the goal of each assessment must be clear: What learning is expected to have taken place? How should this learning be measured? What is the best way for each student to demonstrate his or her learning? Students reading three flashcards instead of five flashcards should be assessed accordingly. Some students may be asked to write rhythm patterns by selecting the appropriate flashcard from a selection of several, while others may use popsicle sticks.

Tracking rhythmic progress	Duple meter	Triple meter
ECHO rhythm patterns (neutral syllable-neutral syllable)		
ECHO rhythm patterns (rhythm syllable-rhythm syllable)		
SHOW macrobeats and microbeats while chanting the rhyme		
CHAIN after each beat or phrase while chanting the rhyme		
CONDUCT in 2 while chanting the rhyme		
DECODE rhythm patterns and familiar rhymes (neutral syllable-rhythm syllable)		
IMPROVISE using rhythm syllables, including the new rhythm		
READ familiar rhythm patterns from notation		
WRITE familiar rhythm patterns from notation		

Figure 6.3   Tracking rhythmic progress.

A chart such as the one in Figure 6.3 can be adapted to aid in tracking each student's individual progress through a sequence of learning.

PRACTICE ACTIVITIES FOR RHYTHM CONCEPTS

Because students in any given classroom can be at many different skill levels at any given time in any given area of study, it is helpful to have many different ways to approach the same task (lots of tools in your tool bag). By repeating the task in different ways, an individual student can find a way to experience the task that makes sense to him or her. By repeating the task many times, an individual student can experience the task with enough frequency that he or she is able to perform the task. And by repeating the task many times in many different ways, an individual student can learn in the way that is most organic to him or her because the necessary repetition of the task has been varied in approach.

Best practice for music educators, as for educators in other content areas, is to present the information through visual, auditory, and kinesthetic means. While many activities can be scaffolded to have students experience the concept through all learning modalities simultaneously, practice activities can focus on one learning modality in one lesson because a different modality will be a focus in subsequent lessons. Practice activities that focus on only one learning modality are often more challenging to the students, as some are being asked to learn outside of their primary learning modality. An example is a decoding activity in which students are only using their aural skills to translate an unknown rhythm pattern into rhythm syllables. Another example is an activity in which students are using their kinesthetic abilities to reinforce the rhythm syllables of a familiar song by patching the quarter notes, tapping the eighth notes, and clapping the sixteenth notes. When offered many practice opportunities in each learning modality, students have an optimal chance to audiate and comprehend the material through their primary modality while also being challenged when practicing through their secondary modalities.

AUDIATION ACTIVITIES FOR STUDENTS AT DIFFERENT LEARNING LEVELS

When a rhythmic concept is being prepared, students may have experienced the new concept in one song successfully; however, they need to recognize that the new concept is present in other songs and in other contexts. The new information and audiation prerequisites will need to be reinforced before new information and audiation are presented. It is possible for students to experience the new concept in a different song in the exact same manner as the new concept was introduced. Unfortunately, this type of repetition may cause students to learn music by intellectualizing it, rather than through audiation: they will "figure it out" rather than feel it or hear it, and that approach is less musical and does not promote audiation. Practice activities to reinforce a particular step in the rhythmic sequence are described here:

> **Audiation Activity #1:** Small groups of students or individuals are assigned one rhythm syllable to sing/chant throughout a known song or sight-sing an abstract exercise (handbell effect) (Musical Example 6.4).

Musical Example 6.4 Assigning rhythm symbols.

(Jeff)   (Scott)   (Claire)   (Lexi)   (Scott)   (Nola)   (Jeff)

> **Audiation Activity #2:** Small groups of students or individuals are assigned a specific measure or phrase to sing/chant in a known song or sight-read an abstract exercise (Musical Example 6.5).

Musical Example 6.5 Assigning measures or phrases.

(Scott)   (Lexi)   (Jeff)   (Nola)

In these activities, students will work without cues from the teacher. This allows the students to be guided by their audiation rather than relying on the teacher to tell them when to start and stop singing. If the syllables, measures, or phrases are assigned to small groups out of order, the work of the students will be more independent.

Performing rhythm syllables by singing only one beat of music before passing to the next person will help students audiate the song in a different way. To follow are two ways to do this:

> **Audiation Activity #3**: Each student sings one beat of rhythm sylla-bles before passing the song to the next person in the circle. This person sings the next consecutive beat of the song in rhythm syl-lables and passes to the following person in the circle (chaining).
> **Audiation Activity #4**: Students chain the rhythm syllables around the circle, passing by phrase.

Similarly, students can be asked to audiate the entire familiar song but only perform a specific rhythm syllable. By performing only part of the song but audiating all of the song, students are repeating the rhythm syl-lables of the song frequently but with more challenge. This type of activity can be used for sight-reading as well.

> **Audiation Activity #5**: Students are asked to fill in the missing rhythms for a familiar song, "Dinah" (Musical Example 6.6). Students must sing the song in rhythm syllables to discover which rhythms are missing and then dictate to the teacher or write the missing rhythms.

Musical Example 6.6 Fill in the missing rhythms.

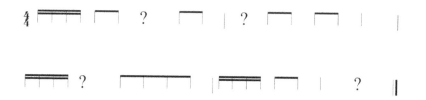

> **Audiation Activity #6**: The teacher performs a familiar song from notation but sings some changes. The students must identify, locate, and write the changes in the notation. This activity can be made more challenging for specific students when the notated example is unknown and therefore abstract. The teacher sings the

example on a neutral syllable with several changes from what is notated. Students must audiate the notation to detect the "errors" the teacher is performing.

Not all work must be performed by all students: this would be unfair if the work is outside of their current ability level. Instead, lesson segments can be designed that take advantage of the sequential nature of instruction by incorporating lower-level skills as review before moving on to unfamiliar contexts or skills. In this manner, the individual learning needs of students with challenges are honored, and students in need of additional challenge have their learning needs met as well.

PARTWORK AND RHYTHM PRACTICE ACTIVITIES

Practice of a rhythmic concept can be made more challenging and more harmonically interesting through the use of partwork. When students are asked to perform more than one musical task at a time, their audiation and musical understanding increase. As such, partwork activities are an excellent means of winding forward. Some practice activities that include partwork are listed here:

> **Partwork Activity #1:** Students sing using text and tap the macrobeat with one hand and the microbeats with the other hand simultaneously.
>
> **Partwork Activity #2:** Students sing using text while walking the beat in place and tapping the rhythm.
>
> **Partwork Activity #3:** Students sing using text and add body percussion as an ostinato.
>
> **Partwork Activity #4:** Students sing using text and conduct.
>
> **Partwork Activity #5:** Students sing using text and perform an ostinato on a rhythm instrument or barred percussion instrument.
>
> **Partwork Activity #6:** Students sing using text while walking the rhythm and tapping the beat.
>
> **Partwork Activity #7:** Students sing using text while clapping the rhythm of a different song.

Any of these activities can be used with the students singing rhythm syllables instead of the text. These activities can also be used when students are sight-singing in rhythm syllables. To wind back, students may sing in small groups; to wind forward, students may sing individually.

Canon Activities

The use of canon as a technique to aid students in simultaneous audiation in multiple music languages is an extension of the previous activities. Some uses of canon as partwork are as follows:

> **Canon Activity #1:** Some students sing the melody in rhythm syllables; others sing in rhythm syllables in canon with the first group.
> **Canon Activity #2:** Students sing using text while clapping the rhythm of the same song in canon.

Flashcards

The context of a rhythmic element (the placement of the element within a pattern) can predict the difficulty of the rhythm pattern. For example, in my experience, a rhythm pattern that begins with paired eighth notes is more easily audiated and performed than a rhythm pattern that ends with paired eighth notes. When rhythm patterns are audiated out of the context of a familiar song or chant, the abstract nature of the rhythm pattern increases the level of difficulty. Therefore, students need to read abstract rhythm patterns in a variety of contexts to truly experience the level of sight-reading that experienced musicians encounter. Some suggested activities to practice abstract rhythm patterns are as follows:

> **Flashcard Activity #1:** Students read each rhythm flashcard forward, then backward.
> **Flashcard Activity #2:** Students read rhythm flashcards upside down.
> **Flashcard Activity #3:** Students clap four-beat rhythm patterns from flashcards while singing the text of a familiar song.
> **Flashcard Activity #4:** Students read rhythms from a rhythm ladder with the teacher pointing to the beat (Musical Example 6.7).

Musical Example 6.7 Rhythm ladder.

Flashcard Activity #5: Students read from a chain of beat flashcards with the teacher changing the order of the beat flashcards as the previous pattern is being spoken. A video clip of students reading from beat flashcards can be found in chapter 6 of the companion website.

The notation of any familiar song, flashcard, or composed exercise can be read and performed backward in rhythm syllables, as this takes the patterns out of the familiar context and makes the rhythmic patterns abstract, thus winding forward the content.

Other games practicing rhythm concepts are described as follows:

Who Has This Rhythm? Each student holds a card with two rhythm patterns. The teacher chants, "Who has this rhythm?" and reads her rhythm pattern in rhythm syllables. The student holding the card with that rhythm pattern as his A (answer) pattern chants, "I have that rhythm" and reads the same rhythm pattern to confirm. That student then chants, "Who has this rhythm?" and reads his Q (question) pattern. The game continues with individual students confirming their A patterns and asking their Q patterns until the final student's question is answered by the teacher (Musical Example 6.8).

Musical Example 6.8

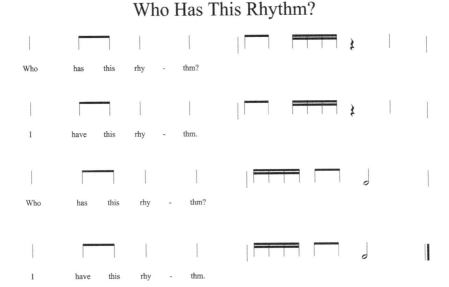

Rhythm Puzzle: The teacher notates a rhythm puzzle on the board, including the new rhythm concept in each four-beat pattern (Musical Example 6.9). Students read in rhythm syllables as the teacher points to each possible four-beat pattern horizontally, vertically, and diagonally. Individual students can speak one of the rhythm patterns on a neutral syllable and another individual student can locate and circle the pattern in the puzzle (like a word search puzzle).

Musical Example 6.9 Rhythm puzzle.

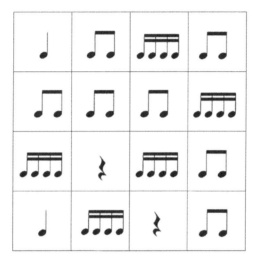

Sudoku: A similar rhythm puzzle could also be used as a Sudoku, in which each row and column must contain only one of each rhythm element (Musical Examples 6.10 and 6.11). Students solve the Sudoku by identifying and writing the missing rhythm element in a particular row or column. That rhythm element must also fit in the corresponding perpendicular row or column. A Sudoku can be made less challenging by leaving only one box empty in a row or column; a more challenging Sudoku would have more than one box empty in a row or column, making it essential that the student decide in which order to complete the boxes for the solution to be made evident. Students complete their individual Sudoku puzzles, then read them simultaneously as the teacher calls out the direction (1-down, B-across, D-diagonal, etc.).

Musical Example 6.10 Rhythm Sudoku #1.

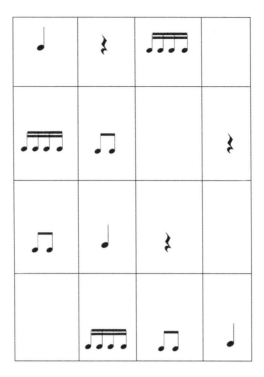

Musical Example 6.11 Rhythm Sudoku #2.

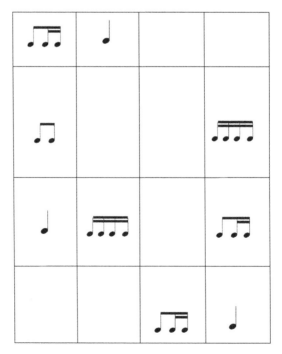

Rhythm Card Game: Another rhythm practice game is described in the vignette that follows, and a video clip can be found in chapter 6 ⊙ of the companion website.

DIFFERENTIATING WITH THE RHYTHM CARD GAME

Ronnie's class was playing the rhythm card game. Each card contained three rhythms: the top rhythm, written in red, was an easy pattern containing difficult patterns from the previous rhythm element and easy patterns from the newest rhythm element. The middle rhythm, written in blue, was a medium-level pattern containing the newest rhythm element. The bottom rhythm, written in black, was a difficult pattern containing the newest rhythm element. The class stood in a circle with one student in the center, and each student held a card. The student in the center spoke one of his card's patterns (pattern X) in rhythm syllables; all students whose cards contained pattern X switched places in the circle, with the last player taking the position in the center. The students who needed more of a challenge held two or three cards so that they read all six to nine rhythm patterns quickly before determining whether they needed to switch places. Ronnie and some other students were encouraged to look at the top pattern in red only to match the rhythm syllables being spoken to the rhythm notation on one pattern.

King of the Mountain: Students are seated in a circle, each with a rhythm flashcard facing them on the floor. The king is designated at the top of the mountain; the person to the right of the king is at the bottom of the mountain. The king speaks his or her rhythm pattern followed immediately by the rhythm pattern of another person. This person speaks his or her own rhythm pattern and then that of another person. Students attempt to trick others, particularly the king, by causing them to slow the tempo, make an error, or stop. When this happens, that person is "out" and moves to the bottom of the mountain, to the right of the king. The other players move up the mountain by one place, leaving the cards in their original positions. Only the students who are lower than the person who gets out are allowed to move up the mountain.

Rhythm-Go-Round: Students stand in a circle, each with a rhythm flashcard facing them on the floor. Students read their own flashcard in rhythm syllables, then move one card to their right while audiating four beats of rest. All read their new flashcards, then continue to their right, audiating four beats of rest between each new card. The teacher may wish to assess students by placing an easy rhythm pattern, a medium-difficulty rhythm pattern, and a difficult rhythm pattern in consecutive order in the circle. By standing in the middle of the circle in front of those three cards, the teacher can assess each student on the appropriate rhythm pattern as the rest of the class continues the activity. Improvisation can be added to the activity by replacing some of the rhythm flashcards with blank flashcards: when a student reaches the blank flashcard, he or she will improvise a four-beat rhythm including the new rhythm concept before continuing on to the next rhythm flashcard. Video clips of this activity with and without improvisation can be found in chapter 6 of the companion website.

Memory: The teacher sets up a grid of rhythm flashcards face down on the floor. A student flips over any two flashcards, attempting to match them. He or she must chant the rhythm patterns notated on each flashcard to determine if they match. Nonmatching flashcards are both flipped face down. When two flashcards match, both flashcards remain face up. This game is best played in multiple small groups around the room so that students do not have to wait long before their turn and remain engaged in the activity. The rhythm flashcards used in each of the small groups can be differentiated so that the more difficult rhythm patterns are being practiced by those students ready for that challenge, the new rhythm element used in a more familiar context is practiced by the majority of the class, and rhythm patterns focusing on the previous rhythm element are used for those who need continued practice (Figure 6.4).

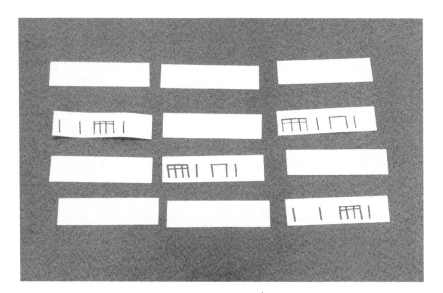

Figure 6.4 Memory game.

Rhythm Rondo: "ABACADAEA" is written on the board. The teacher (or a student) improvises a four-beat rhythm pattern including the new rhythm concept. This is the A pattern. The students conclude that the B pattern will sound different than the A pattern; the C pattern will sound different than the A pattern and different than the B pattern, and so forth. Students will improvise a four-beat rhythm pattern including the new rhythm concept when B, C, D, and E occur. The Rhythm Rondo can be performed in several ways:

- All students speak the A patterns and improvise the B, C, D, and E patterns.
- All students speak the A patterns; individual students improvise the B, C, D, and E patterns.
- All students speak the A patterns; individual students improvise the B, C, D, and E patterns, according to a specific parameter (e.g., their patterns must include a quarter rest or start with a half note).

Through the use of an assortment of practice activities, students receive the repetition and frequency necessary for them to learn the new rhythmic concepts at their individual pace. Practicing the rhythmic concepts in many ways allows each student to practice in the learning modality that is most comfortable, and for all students to enjoy the various approaches.

Through the sequential presentation of rhythm concepts, students will benefit from a logical progression of tasks, each building on the task before it. While many students may not need to progress through every discrete step, students in every class will benefit from such a sequential approach. If the teacher can accurately identify the specific step of a sequence a particular student is struggling to achieve, he or she can easily wind it back for that student, increasing the likelihood that the student will ultimately be successful and appropriately challenged. A generic rhythmic sequence can be found in chapter 6 on the companion website, as well as possible ⊙ rhythm hierarchies. In addition, song materials cited in this book can be found under "Notation of Songs" on the companion website.

CONCLUSION

By sequencing rhythmic content to meet each student's learning needs, multiple learning levels can be addressed simultaneously, leading to an efficient use of lesson time and honoring student learning differences while they make joyful music. When a variety of practice activities are included, the needs of individual students may be met meaningfully, creatively, and frequently. Learning modalities can support those who learn primarily through one modality while challenging those for whom that modality is secondary. Winding back and forward within a rhythmic sequence establishes a framework for review, assessment, and added challenge that individualizes learning for all students.

REFERENCES

Apel, W. (1972). *Harvard dictionary of music*. Cambridge, MA: Belknap Press of Harvard University Press.

Choksy, L. (1974). *The Kodály method I: Comprehensive music education*. Upper Saddle River, NJ: Prentice-Hall.

Gordon, E. E. (2012). *Learning sequences in music: A contemporary music learning theory*. Chicago, IL: GIA.

Gordon, E. E. (1986). *Primary measures of music audiation*. Chicago, IL: GIA.

CHAPTER 7

Vocal Creativity

Exploration, Improvisation, and Composition

JILL REESE, *The State University*
of New York at Fredonia

CHAPTER OVERVIEW

Vocal creativity is a fundamental skill in which students synthesize past experiences (skills and knowledge) while generating musical ideas to express themselves meaningfully. By varying levels of structure and support, teachers can scaffold students to ensure successful experiences creating with the voice and the development of musical independence. This chapter will do the following:

- Define exploration, improvisation, and composition and describe how they are different but related
- Consider factors that contribute to successful vocal creativity
- Share examples of classroom activities and suggestions for *winding* the activities *back* and *forward* to meet the needs of individual students
- Suggest ideas for documenting, sharing, and celebrating students' creative processes and products

---

The concept of creativity is synonymous with the arts and is considered part of the framework for twenty-first-century teaching and learning (Partnership for 21st Century Skills, n.d.). Creativity allows students with different experiences and abilities to represent their understanding in new ways that are personally meaningful. It provides an opportunity for students to synthesize their knowledge and skill in the form of something original and expressive. Because there are often multiple acceptable responses during creative activities, teachers can structure learning activities in ways that allow all students to participate successfully, and students can respond in ways that are appropriate for them. Though creativity is often broadly conceived in educational contexts, generative musical creativity in the music classroom typically includes inventing and documenting musical ideas and often takes the form of exploration, improvisation, and composition.

Exploration is the spontaneous trying out of "different sounds and combinations of sounds in a loosely structured context" (Kratus, 1991, p. 38). Exploration may not be based in audiation (Gordon, 1989) and is primarily process oriented (Kratus, 1991). Students who are exploring their voice, body, and instruments may not be able to predict what will occur from certain actions (Kratus, 1991). Examples of music exploration are when students are inventing new sounds or timbres with their voices and inventing nontraditional ways to play standard instruments. A fundamental cognitive goal during exploration may be the concept of "same and different." During exploration activities, children discover and invent sounds and movements they may never have experienced before and identify how these sounds are the same as and different from each other. Children who are exploring are primarily focused on divergent thinking: they are creating as many new ideas as possible.

Improvisation is the spontaneous combining of musical ideas within a prescribed context that provides varying degrees of structure without the intent to revise in the future (Brophy, 2001). Unlike exploration, improvisation is both process and product oriented (Kratus, 1991) and based in audiation (Gordon, 1989; Kratus, 1990). Students who are improvising using their voice, body, or instruments are "able to predict the [products] of certain actions" (Kratus, 1990, p. 35). This prediction makes improvisation different from exploration. Examples of music improvisation are when students play a new tune on the recorder based on the harmonic structure of "Hot Cross Buns" and when they use their repertoire of familiar folk dance choreography to create new movements during the B section of "Shoo Fly." During improvisation activities, children use their previous knowledge of and experience with tunes, patterns, and movements to create something new within a structure. Children who are improvising are focused on divergent thinking and convergent thinking: they are recalling and inventing many different musical ideas and deciding which of those ideas to use.

Like improvisation, composition involves thinking in music, but it also includes documenting and revising a musical product (Wiggins, 2005). Similar to exploration and improvisation, composition is a process, but it is often associated with a tangible product such as a recording or a document. The process for composition may be enhanced by audiation and may include exploration and improvisation, but the intention extends beyond spontaneous creation to include elements of revision and preservation. Students who are composing are combining and revising musical ideas until they have a finished product they preserve in some way (e.g., notation or recording). Examples of music composition are when students create a new tune using only the notes they can play on the recorder. They preserve the rhythm using stick notation and the letter names of pitches for the recorder melody, and add a rhythmic accompaniment using iconic notation below the stick notation and letter names of the recorder melody. They revisit their creation over multiple class periods to fine-tune it before performing their original song in a concert.

Though these three forms of creative expression are related (Burnard, 2000), the intentions behind them are different (Reese, 2005). Explorers are discovering, improvisers are creating and performing simultaneously, and composers are creating and revising a product for future performance. From a pedagogical perspective, each of the three types of creative expression serves as readiness for the next: exploration is a readiness for improvisation, and improvisation is a readiness for composition (Gordon, 2003; Kratus, 1990). All musical creativity is informed by previous experiences and a vocabulary from which to draw. These experiences include listening, singing, playing instruments, and moving; the vocabulary includes terms such as "pitch," "rhythm," "harmony," "movement," and "style," among others. The amount of experience and size and quality of vocabulary influence the success students experience with each type of creative expression. The younger students are when they begin their journey with musical creativity, the more comfortable they will be with the process of exploration, improvisation, and composition. As students get older, they often experience fewer opportunities for divergent thinking and are increasingly focused on finding the one right answer.

Other factors that contribute to students' success with creativity are the frequency with which their teachers include opportunities for exploring, improvising, and composing in the curriculum, and the frequency with which teachers model the creative processes and share their own improvisations and compositions with the students (see Figure 7.1 regarding considerations about modeling). Students will be more comfortable and successful creating musically if they have many opportunities to practice generative music creativity. They will be more comfortable and successful creating if they are learning in a culture where their teacher, other students, and members of their community share products and processes of generative musical creativity. Unfortunately, creating (including exploration, improvisation, and composition) is the national standard that typically receives the least amount of instructional time (Orman, 2002) and is often perceived as the most challenging to teach (Byo, 1999; Louk, 2002). In this chapter, I attempt to demystify musical creativity and provide activities (structured from simple to more complex) and strategies adults can use with students of all abilities to help them build readiness for successful creative expression. Students' voices are a natural starting point for creativity, as their voice is most closely related to their musical thinking.

> Children are much better able to audiate their vocalizations at an early age than
> they are their instrumental performances, because they have many more experiences in using their voices than they have in playing an instrument, and the
> voice is easier for them to control than is an instrument. (Kratus, 1996, p. 31)

Though many children are able to successfully use their voices to express themselves creatively, some struggle to control their vocal mechanism due to physical, medical, or auditory processing differences, and some hesitate to use their singing voice due to lack of experience. I will suggest ways to use the voice to explore, improvise, and compose, and I will suggest strategies to engage students with various communication differences.

For the activities and variations of activities described in this chapter, teachers should consider if their students would be helped by experiencing a model of the process (including metacognitive narrative describing the thought process) and product before they are asked to create. The model can be provided by the teacher or a student who has been successful. Understand that a model might help some students, but for others, the model might limit their thinking and might communicate that there is one correct process for creating and one correct answer.

Figure 7.1.   Idea to consider #1: Modeling.

EXPLORATION

Vocal exploration activities provide students opportunities to discover different ways to make sound with their voices, manipulate their vocal mechanism, and experience the idea of difference and sameness using their voices. The goal of beginning vocal exploration activities is just to be different; as students gain experience with vocal exploration activities, teachers can begin to impose structure and expectations on the activities. During Exploration Activity #1, students are encouraged to explore divergent thinking and the various sounds possible; during Exploration Activity #2, the teacher begins to add the structure of creating within a specific amount of time; during Exploration Activity #3, the teacher begins to add the expectation of exploring with a specific type of voice (singing voice). Each progressive addition of structure provides additional readiness for improvisation. (See chapters 2, 3, and 4 for other ideas about establishing building blocks and providing readiness for creativity.)

Exploration Activity #1: Timbre exploration. *Using their voices, students will be able to create/invent new sounds or timbres.*

- During this activity, the students use their voices in different ways without specific musical parameters (meter, tonality, form, etc.). The goal is for students to explore the different facets of their voices and to think divergently. The teacher presents a visual image to the whole class and challenges students to use their voices in different ways to represent the image. This activity requires students to consider that there might be multiple possibilities and correct answers. This can be especially challenging for students because they are often used to searching for the one correct answer.
  - **Variation #1** (Winding it back): For students who might need the scaffolding provided by peers, the teacher can have the students work in groups (see Figure 7.2 regarding the importance of creativity in small groups). The teacher provides each *small group* of students a different image. The students invent a way to use their voices to represent that image. When the students are ready to share, the teacher shows the class three different images (one is the image the teacher gave the small group). The students in the small group share their vocal representation of the picture, and the class chooses which image they think the students were representing with their voices and provides evidence to support their choice.
  - **Variation #2** (Winding it back): For students who are not yet able to coordinate their voices to represent the picture provided for them, the teacher can turn the activity on its head and begin with sound. A student can provide a sound, and peers draw a picture that represents that sound. The teacher can record the sound to replicate it as needed for others to draw.
  - **Variation #3** (Winding it back): For students who are not yet comfortable sharing their voices, consider using technology to facilitate the activity. The teacher can provide each group with an iPod, iPad, or other audio-recording device. Students can explore using their voices to create different sounds and record the one they think best fits the image. The teacher can then share the recording and the image.

o **Variation #4** (Winding it back): Older students who have not had previous experiences using their voices or with vocal exploration may be especially hesitant to use their voices in unusual ways. With these students, the teacher may consider using text from a poem for the activity. By using text, the teacher provides students something familiar to hold on to. The teacher can give each student a different stanza from a poem. Students can use programs such as GarageBand to record themselves speaking their stanza and then use the various features of GarageBand to modify the pitch, speed, and other musical qualities. The teacher can then have students listen to their peers' recorded and modified stanza and attempt to replicate the recording using only their voice.

Though it is important for teachers to include opportunities for individual (solo) responses (singing, playing, improvising) to assess students' achievement as individuals and to individualize instruction to meet each student's needs, it is also important for teachers to include opportunities for students to work in small and large groups. Not only do these experiences provide opportunities to develop certain social skills, they also provide the opportunity for students to learn from each other and to scaffold each other's development. The teacher does not always need to be the only "more-knowledgeable-other" in the classroom. Wiggins (2005) suggests

> one of the main reasons for engaging students in small-group work is that it enables them to scaffold one another. As students work together toward a common goal, they can fill in gaps in one another's understanding, enabling the overall competence of the group to move forward. (pp. 40-41)

By progressing from large group creating to small group creating, and then to individual creating, teachers provide students with supported introductory experiences before they are expected to try something on their own. Of course, when planning collaborative work for small and large groups, teachers must understand the various strengths and challenges each student brings to social situations, and they must be prepared to adjust the activity so all students can experience success.

Figure 7.2.   Idea to consider #2: Group work.

Exploration Activity #2: Timbre and rhythmic exploration. *Using their voices, students will be able to create an interlude between repetitions of a familiar song.*

• During this activity, the students use their voices in different ways within a specific parameter of time. The goal is for students to explore the different facets of their voices within a musical context of time. The teacher performs the chant "My Voice" (Music Example 7.1), and between repetitions of the chant, students create an eight-beat interlude using their voices creatively (see Figure 7.3 about creating a musical sandwich by inserting opportunities for creativity between repetitions of a song or chant). The teacher can either have the whole class create simultaneously during the interlude (indicating this by gesturing with two hands toward the class) or have individuals create (indicating this by gesturing with one hand toward an individual). Unlike Exploration Activity #1, this activity establishes the additional challenge of exploring within a specific time parameter. Depending on the experiences and abilities of each student, some will explore in a way that expresses the meter and awareness of the interlude's eight-beat length, whereas others will explore freely and focus more on their voices and less on the meter.

> By "sandwiching" opportunities for creativity between repetitions of a song or a chant (essentially making the improvisation sections an interlude), the teacher maintains the musical context for creating. If the students struggle to create within the context or stray from the key or meter, the teacher can help re-establish the context for the students by returning to the song or chant. The song or chant also connects the creating to "real" music and contributes to the relevance of the activity.

Figure 7.3.   Idea to consider #3: Sandwiching.

Musical Example 7.1. "My Voice."

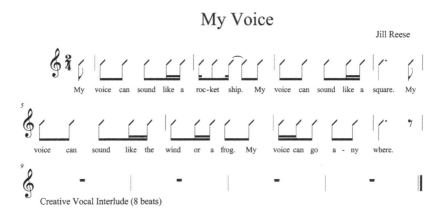

° **Variation #1** (Winding it back): For students who are struggling to create new sounds with their voices and need a bigger vocabulary of sounds, consider encouraging them to imitate sounds of various "sound makers" (traditional and nontraditional). The teachers can introduce a number of sound makers (e.g., ratchet, wind chimes, bulb honk horn, kazoo, slide whistle, spiral notebook and pencil to "zip" the spiral) and ask students to use their voices to replicate the sound makers. When students successfully imitate the timbre of the sound makers, the teacher can add the challenge of imitating a rhythm played on that sound maker. The teacher can play a rhythm for the first four beats of the interlude, and the students imitate that rhythm while matching the timbre with their voices during the last four beats of the interlude. The teacher returns to "My Voice" and picks up another sound maker, then adds it during the next interlude.

o **Variation #2** (Winding it back): For students who are hesitant to use their voices in front of their peers, teachers can use an iPad app such as MadPad (Krudge, 2011) to record students performing a sound they create with their voices. By touching the record button on each of the twelve squares provided, the teacher and students can record twelve different sounds made by the students with their voices. Hesitant students can even record themselves in the hallway without performing in front of their peers. Then, students can use the recorded voices on the MadPad app like an instrument to create an eight-beat rhythmic interlude between repetitions of the chant "My Voice."

Exploration Activity #3: Tonal exploration. *Using their singing voices, students will be able to explore creating different combinations of pitches.*

• During this activity, the students use their singing voices to create a "beep" for their car horns. The goal is for students to explore their singing voices to create something different. The teacher performs "City Line Avenue" (Music Example 7.2) while the students move in various pathways, holding their paper plate steering wheels. Between each repetition of the song, the class creates a new horn sound for their cars using their singing voices and the word "beep" or other phoneme that works for them (see Music Example 7.2). The teacher can either have the whole class create simultaneously (indicating this by gesturing with two hands toward the class) or have individuals create (indicating this by gesturing with one hand toward an individual). Consider providing space and silence for students to think before asking them to perform their new beep (see Figure 7.4 regarding the importance of silence).

Musical Example 7.2. "City Line Avenue," Exploration Activity #3.

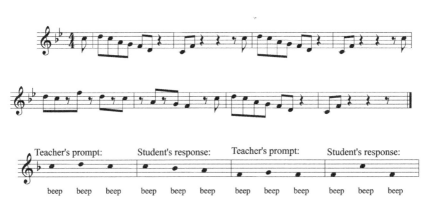

City Line Avenue

Jennifer Bailey

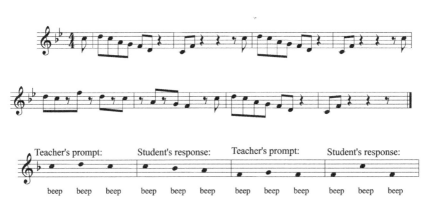

> Silence is often a valuable tool that provides students time to think and to imagine before being asked to respond or share their creative ideas. Teachers can provide silence in the space students might typically respond (e.g., during the length of the interlude for Exploration Activity #2) for students to imagine/think/audiate their response before sharing their responses with the class. This opportunity for silent practice is often extremely valuable for most students, but it is especially valuable for those who have less experience or need more processing time. By providing a couple silent times through the space students might typically respond, teachers are honoring the idea that there's more than one correct answer, and they are providing students a safe space to try out different ideas.

Figure 7.4. Idea to consider #4: Silence.

- **Variation #1** (Winding it back): For students who have a limited vocabulary, consider having them echo "beeps" created by the teacher. Between phrases, the teacher sings various tonal patterns on "beep" and gestures for the whole class or individuals to echo the tonal pattern. After students imitate a couple of the teacher's patterns, the teacher returns to the song and the students return to driving their cars. (See Music Example 7.3.)

Musical Example 7.3. Exploration Activity #3, Variation #1.

o **Variation #2** (Winding it back): For students who are struggling to create something new, consider exploring the concepts of same and different. Sometimes students are more familiar with being asked to imitate the teacher and, therefore, struggle to do something that is different. Variation #2 provides students with the opportunity to identify same and different and provides more examples to build their vocabulary. Between phrases, the teacher says, "Listen to these two beep songs. Do they sound the same or different? First [while holding up one finger, teacher sings a tonal pattern using "beep"]; second [while holding up two fingers, teacher sings a different tonal pattern using "beep"]. Raise your hand if you think the two beep songs sounded the same. [Check for understanding.] Raise your hand if you think they were different. [Check for understanding.] The two sounded different." The teacher repeats the same/different activity alternating between various patterns that are the same and those that are different. After a couple comparisons, the teacher returns to the song and the students return to driving their cars. (See Music Example 7.4.)

Musical Example 7.4. Exploration Activity #3, Variation #2.

#1. Teacher sings first pattern: Teacher sings second pattern: #2. Teacher sings first pattern: Teacher sings second pattern:

beep   beep   beep   beep   beep   beep   beep   beep   beep   beep   beep   beep

VOCAL IMPROVISATION

Vocal improvisation activities focus on spontaneously creating music *within specific parameters* (e.g., form, tonality, meter, harmonic function). Improvisation includes divergent thinking developed during exploration activities but challenges students to purposefully move beyond the minimal requirement of being different. To do so, teachers must provide parameters and restrictions within which students consider divergent possibilities and make choices. Making choices within limits is more challenging than just doing something different. This type of creativity is akin to what musicians do while creating in a vocal jazz group or in a Celtic fiddle ensemble: they must be aware of the context and structure while spontaneously creating within those boundaries.

During Improvisation Activity #1, students improvise different rhythm patterns within a specific metric context; during Improvisation Activity #2, they improvise different tonal patterns within a tonal context; during Improvisation Activity #3, they improvise tonal patterns within a specific harmonic function; and during Improvisation Activity #4, they improvise melodically (combine rhythm and tonal content) to improvise a new melody over a familiar harmonic structure. Each progressive addition of structure provides additional readiness for the next activity and readiness for composition.

Improvisation Activity #1: Rhythmic improvisation. *Using their chanting voices, students will be able to improvise rhythms in call- and-response format within specific rhythmic limitations (i.e., meter, durations/rhythms).*

• During this activity, the students are using their chanting voices to create a "response" to the "call" chanted by the teacher. The call remains the same, while the response is different each time. The goal is for students to improvise a rhythm pattern that is different from the teacher's using rhythmic syllables. While the teacher performs the "Charlie the Fish" chant (Music Example 7.5), students move (using a paper cutout of a fish mounted to a popsicle stick in each hand) as if their fish are swimming in curvy pathways through the ocean (see Figure 7.5 for ideas about using props to elicit creative responses). Between repetitions of the chant, the teacher chants a four-beat rhythm pattern (the same pattern each time) using rhythm syllables. The teacher gestures on beat 4 of the pattern for the class or for individuals to create a different pattern using syllables. After providing a couple opportunities for students to create, the teacher returns to the chant and the students "swim" with the paper fish. For the purposes of demonstrating that any rhythm syllable system could be used with the examples that follow, I chose to use the Takadimi syllables for each example in this chapter. Teachers should feel free to substitute the system they use with their students when using the examples. For consistency, teachers should choose and consistently use one same rhythm syllable system (e.g., Kodály, Gordon, Takadimi, numbers) within their curriculum (see "Selecting Rhythm and Tonal Syllables" in chapter 10 of the companion website for descriptions of various syllable systems).

Musical Example 7.5. "Charlie the Fish," Improvisation Activity #1.

Charlie the Fish

Gretchen Cole

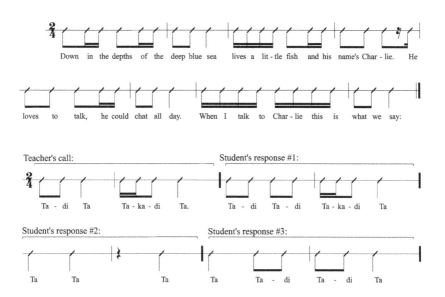

Though it is sometimes valuable for the students to see a successful example of an improvisation, teachers may not always have another adult (e.g., student teacher or aide) or child in the room who is capable of providing a successful model. If this is the case, teachers can use objects, such as puppets or stuffed animals, to demonstrate their expectations. By holding two objects and demonstrating the call with one and the response with the other, the students can observe a successful model of the expectations.

Teachers might also find that some students are less self-conscious when they are holding an object and sharing their musical creativity through the object than when the focus is on the student doing the musical creativity.

Figure 7.5.   Idea to consider #5: Props.

- o **Variation #1** (Winding it back): For students who have limited experience with rhythm syllables, the teacher can use a neutral syllable (e.g., "bah," "ch," or "blub" like a bubble sound) and ask students to use combinations of short and long sounds. (See Music Example 7.6.)

Musical Example 7.6. Improvisation Activity #1, Variation #1.

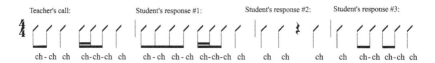

- **Variation #2** (Winding it back): For students who are struggling to create a different pattern, the teacher might choose to return to an exploration activity, like identifying same and different patterns. (See Music Example 7.7.)

Musical Example 7.7. Improvisation Activity #1, Variation #2.

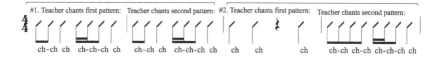

- **Variation #3** (Winding it back): For students who imitate their peers' previous pattern rather than creating an original pattern, or for groups who seem to get stuck on one pattern (e.g., every student seems to chant *Ta-di, Ta-di, Ta, Ta*), the teacher can change the call pattern to the pattern the students are stuck on, rendering that pattern unusable by the students.
- **Variation #4** (Winding it back): For students who need more modeling or who need a larger vocabulary of patterns, the teacher models the call and response using a red fish for the call and a blue fish for the response to provide examples of improvisation (see Figure 7.5 for more ideas about using props to support teaching). This type of modeling also helps the students build their repertoire of patterns. (See Music Example 7.8.)

Musical Example 7.8. Improvisation Activity #1, Variation #4.

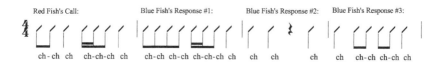

- **Variation #5** (Winding it back): For students who are familiar with rhythm syllables but could benefit from more structure, the teacher could choose to focus on a limited number of rhythm patterns. The teacher might choose to focus on three types of patterns and could tell the students, "Today, we are only going to use combinations of *Ta, Ta-di*, and *Ta-ka-di*." Students would create their improvisations using only the patterns the teacher specifies.
- **Variation #6** (Winding it forward): For a different challenge, the teacher can specify rhythmic values the students should avoid using. For example, the teacher could tell the students, "Your responses can include all sorts of rhythms, but they may not include *Ta-di-mi*."

Improvisation Activity #2: Melodic improvisation. *Using their singing voices, students will be able to improvise a consequent phrase in relation to an antecedent phrase (question-and-answer format).*

• During this activity, the students use their singing voices to improvise a consequent phrase (melodic answer) in response to an antecedent phrase (melodic question) sung by the teacher. The goal is for students to improvise a melody that is related to (similar in tonality and meter) the antecedent phrase sung by the teacher. Returning to "City Line Avenue" (Music Example 7.9), the teacher can provide additional parameters and change the original exploration activity to improvisation by establishing expectations for more structured responses. Between repetitions of the song, the teacher sings a new melody (antecedent phrase that is eight beats long) using the word "beep," then gestures to the class to improvise a related consequent phrase (eight beats long) using their singing voices and the word "beep." The teacher can also have individuals respond (indicating this by gesturing with one hand toward an individual). Depending on the experiences and abilities of each student, some will improvise in a way that clearly expresses the meter and tonality, while others will be less clear. Some students will end the consequent phrase on the tonic pitch or another pitch that logically indicates the end of a phrase, while others will not. Some students will relate the content of their consequent phrase to the content in the antecedent phrase, while others will not.

Musical Example 7.9. "City Line Avenue," Improvisation Activity #2.

City Line Avenue

Jennifer Bailey

o **Variation #1** (Winding it back): For students who have a limited tonal/ melodic vocabulary, have less experience with improvisation, or are not yet consistently using their singing voices, consider removing the tonal content and asking students to improvise rhythmically using their chanting voices. Between repetitions of the song, the teacher chants an antecedent phrase (rhythm content only) using the word "beep," then gestures to the class to respond with a related consequent phrase (rhythm content only) using "beep." The teacher can alternate between class responses and individual responses. (See Music Example 7.10.)

Musical Example 7.10. Improvisation Activity #2, Variation #1.

o **Variation #2** (Winding it back): For students who were successful with Variation #1, consider adding pitch, but limiting the pitch to the tonic note (resting tone). Between repetitions of the song, the teacher sings an antecedent phrase (rhythm content only) on the pitch of the resting tone using the word "beep," then gestures to the class to respond with a related consequent phrase (rhythm content only) on the pitch of the resting tone using "beep." The teacher can alternate between class responses and individual responses. (See Music Example 7.11.)

Musical Example 7.11. Improvisation Activity #2, Variation #2.

o **Variation #3** (Winding it back): For students who were successful with Variation #2, consider adding pitches beyond the tonic note (resting tone). Depending on the experience of the students and the methods used by the teacher, the teacher can have students toggle between a diatonic pitch such as *sol-la-ti* (*sol* being the tonic in Mixolydian), or arpeggiated tonic patterns such as *sol-ti-re*. Between repetitions of the song, the teacher sings an antecedent phrase on the predetermined set of limited pitches using the word "beep," then gestures to the class to respond with a related consequent phrase using the same limited predetermined pitches and the word "beep." The teacher can alternate between class responses and individual responses. (See Music Example 7.12.)

Musical Example 7.12. Improvisation Activity #2, Variation #3.

Teacher's antecedent phrase: Student's consequent phrase:

beep   beep beep beep beep beep beep   beep beep beep beep   beep   beep beep beep

- o **Variation #4** (Winding it forward): For students who are successful, consider challenging them to lead the antecedent phrase, or challenge students in pairs to take turns with the antecedent and responses jobs! (See Figure 7.6 about using the analogy of a conversation to support improvising.)

> By comparing the process of improvisation to the process of having a conversation, teachers can encourage students to connect their previous understandings of turn-taking and contingent responses (relating their response to the context) to their new understandings of improvisation. "If I asked you a question like, 'What did you eat for lunch today?' you would not respond by saying the same thing, 'What did you eat for lunch today?' You would respond by saying something different. But not just anything different like, 'My favorite color is blue,' because that wouldn't make sense. That doesn't answer the question. You might say, 'I had pizza and an apple.' That would make sense because it is different and it is related to my question."

Figure 7.6.   Idea to consider #6: Musical conversations.

Improvisation Activity #3: Tonal improvisation.

Using their singing voices, students will be able to improvise tonal patterns within specific tonal parameters (tonality, harmonic function, pitches).

- During this activity, the students are using their singing voices to improvise tonal patterns within a structure (minor tonality). The goal is for students to improvise a tonal pattern that is in a tonality and harmonic function specified by the teacher. While singing "Going Fishing," the students are rocking forward and back to the beat (pretending to cast and reel back their fishing line). Between repetitions of "Going Fishing" (see Music Example 7.13), the teacher sings tonal patterns in minor tonality using solfège syllables. After each pattern, the teacher pauses to allow students to think of a new pattern, then breathes and gestures for students to sing a pattern that is different from the teacher's but in the same harmonic function (e.g., if the teacher sings *la-do-mi*, the student could sing *mi-do-mi*). (See Figure 7.6 regarding the importance of guidelines for creativity.) The teacher can alternate between having the whole class respond (indicating this by gesturing with two hands toward the group) and having individuals respond (indicating this by gesturing with one hand toward an individual). After a couple patterns, the teacher and students return to "fishing" from the pond as they sing the song.

Musical Example 7.13. "Going Fishing," Improvisation Activity #3.

Going Fishing

Traditional

- o **Variation #1:** If students need a different challenge, consider using four to five popsicle sticks ("fish sticks"): some sticks have the letter T (for teacher) written on the end and others have the letter S (for student) written on the end. The teacher holds the sticks with the letters buried in her hand. At the end of the song, one student chooses a stick. If it has a T on it, the teacher creates a pattern using syllables and the student improvises a different pattern (same function as the teacher's); if it has an S on it, the student creates a pattern using syllables and the teacher has to improvise a different pattern (same function as the student's). Either way, the student is improvising!
- o **Variation #2** (Winding it back): If the students struggle to improvise using solfège syllables, consider removing the syllables and using a neutral syllable such as "bum." Then ask the students to improvise a pattern that uses the same sounds, but in a different order. (See Music Example 7.14.)

Musical Example 7.14. Improvisation Activity #3, Variation #2.

- o **Variation #3** (Winding it back): If the students improvise a different pattern but are confusing the solfège syllables (syllables do not match the pitches), consider singing the pitches the student supplied with the accurate syllables, then singing the pattern with the syllables the student supplied and the accurate pitches, and asking the student which one he or she intended. (See Music Example 7.15.)

Musical Example 7.15. Improvisation Activity #3, Variation #3.

- o **Variation #4** (Winding it forward): If students are successful with the original activity, consider asking them to improvise a pattern that uses a different harmonic function. For example, if the teacher sings a minor tonic pattern, the student could improvise a minor dominant pattern. For students to experience success, the teacher must have previously introduced the concept of various tonal patterns and the labels for their harmonic functions. For example, the teacher must have taught that minor tonic patterns are combinations of *la-do-mi* and minor dominant patterns are combinations of *mi-re-ti-si*. (See Music Example 7.16.)

Musical Example 7.16. Improvisation Activity #3, Variation #4.

- o **Variation #5** (Winding it forward): If students are successful with the original activity, consider asking them to improvise not just one pattern, but a series of patterns using different functions. For example, if the teacher sings a minor tonic pattern followed by a minor dominant pattern, the student could improvise a different minor dominant pattern followed by a minor tonic pattern. (See Music Example 7.17.)

Musical Example 7.17. Improvisation Activity #3, Variation #5.

la   do   mi   mi   si   ti   si   ti   re   mi   la   do   la

Improvisation Activity #4: Melodic improvisation. *Using their singing voices, students will be able to improvise a new song based on the harmonic structure of a familiar song.*

• During this activity, the students use their singing voices to improvise a new song based on the harmonic structure of the song "Hey Lolly, Lolly, Lo." The goal is for students to become familiar with and internalize the harmonic structure of a song, and then improvise a melody using the harmonic structure of that song. (See Figure 7.7 for more information about the importance of structure and guidelines.) The teacher and students sing "Hey Lolly, Lolly, Lo" (see Music Example 7.18) while demonstrating sequenced movement (pat-clap) to the steady beat.

  Step 1: The teacher demonstrates singing the chord roots as the students sing the song. Students sing the chord roots on the steady beat. Once the class can successfully sing the chord roots, the teacher can ask for small groups or individual volunteers to sing the chord roots as the class sings the song. Teachers also can invite students to sing duets: one student on the chord roots, the other on the song.

  Step 2: The teacher demonstrates improvising new rhythms using the chord root pitches. Then, students improvising new rhythms use the chord root pitches while the teacher sings the song. Once the class is improvising new rhythms using the chord root pitches, the teacher can ask for

> Though many teachers associate creativity with total freedom, imposing some structure and using guidelines actually helps beginning creators! Kaschub (1997) believes limitations and restrictions are important for beginning improvisers and composers. "Inexperienced musicians may simply be overwhelmed when asked to [create] without guidelines or rules. The musical options are infinite.... For the novice musicians, so many options can prove stifling—so stifling, in fact, that they suppress the divergent aspect of the creative process" (Kaschub, 1997, p. 27). By allowing students to make choices within limits, the teacher is providing a safe place for students to practice both divergent and convergent thinking. When students are successful within limitations, the teacher can expand the options and loosen the restrictions. Musicians need to learn to play within the rules before they can break the rules with intention!

Figure 7.7. Idea to consider #7: Structure and guidelines.

Musical Example 7.18. "Hey Lolly, Lolly, Lo," Improvisation Activity #4, Step 1.

Hey Lolly, Lolly, Lo

Traditional

small groups or individual students to improvise new rhythms using the chord root pitches while the class sings the song. Teachers can also invite students to sing duets: one student improvising new rhythms using the chord root pitches, the other singing the song. (See Music Example 7.19.)

Musical Example 7.19. Improvisation Activity #4, Step 2.

Traditional

Step 3: The teacher demonstrates improvising a new melody as the students sing the chord roots on the macrobeat. Then, students sing a new melody while the teacher sings the chord roots. Once the students are singing new melodies simultaneously as a class (which might sound a bit chaotic), the teacher can ask for small groups or individual volunteers to sing their new melodies as the class sings the chord roots. Teachers can also invite students to sing duets: one student on the new melody, the other on the chord roots. (See Music Example 7.20.)

Musical Example 7.20. Improvisation Activity #4, Step 3.

- ○ **Variation #1a** (Winding it back): If students are struggling to improvise a new melody over the chord root melody, consider reducing the number of choices they are making during each chord root. For example, during the tonic chord, students could toggle between *do-mi-sol*, and during the dominant chord, students could toggle between *sol-fa-re-ti*. (See Music Example 7.21.)

Musical Example 7.21. Improvisation Activity #4, Variation #1a.

Example using only tonic chord tones during tonic harmony, and dominant chord tones during dominant harmony.

- ○ **Variation #1b** (Winding it back): Simplify even further by having them toggle between *do* and *mi* during the tonic function of the chord root melody, and between *ti* and *re* during the dominant function of the chord. The teacher could add notes for students to choose from (similar to Variation #1a) when students demonstrate success. (See Music Example 7.22.)

Musical Example 7.22. Improvisation Activity #4, Variation #1b.

Example using only *do* and *mi* during tonic harmony, and *re* and *ti* during dominant harmony.

- ○ **Variation #2** (Winding it back): If students are struggling to improvise even when provided minimal notes to toggle between, consider going back to step 2 and providing students with more experience improvising new rhythms using the chord root pitches.
- ○ **Variation #3** (Winding it forward): If students are successful improvising a new melody over the chord progression of a familiar song, consider advancing to a song that is in a different tonality (this would require the students to have experience with many songs in that tonality) or choosing another song that has additional chord functions. For example, if the students are successful with the song "Hey Lolly, Lolly, Lo" (which contains tonic and dominant functions), consider using a song like "Camptown Races" (which contains tonic, dominant, and subdominant functions) and use the same process as the original activity to challenge the students further.

VOCAL COMPOSITION

With *exploration* and *improvisation* activities, the students and teacher do not intend on preserving, revising, or editing the product. The focus is on the spontaneous creation of something in the moment. The product and process are one. When students have experience with exploration and improvisation, the skills, musical vocabulary, and processes used during exploration and improvisation activities often inform the process and product of their composition. Exploration and improvisation are readiness and prerequisites for composition. "Prior to any composing experience, students need to engage in sufficient performing and listening experiences to help them frame the work they are being asked to do" (Wiggins, 2005, p. 39).

When composition is informed by exploration and improvisation, the compositions are based in musical thought, rather than based in mathematics or chance. The idea that composition is based in musical thinking or "thinking in sound" is one that can be easily overlooked when teachers begin composition assignments with notation, rather than beginning with sound and using notation as a tool to record what the music students create (Kaschub and Smith, 2009). When I first began engaging students in composition early in my teaching career, I gave students the beginning note, ending note, and a variety of pitches and rhythms to combine while composing. After working hard on their compositions, students would often ask, "Can you play my composition for me? I want to know what it sounds like." While the experience had some value for the students, it was rarely connected to their musical thinking and seemed more an exercise in mathematics and chance. While there is a place for mathematics and chance in composition, the following suggestions for classroom activities focus on providing experiences with composition that are connected to students' musical thinking.

For students who have few experiences with notation (iconic or standard), consider audio or video recording the composition process and the product. That way, the teacher and students have documented the musical ideas for future revision or to inform future performance of the composition. Students who have little to no experience with iconic or standard notation might also benefit from watching the teacher model the process of notating the students' vocal compositions using iconic or standard notation. For students with few experiences using standard notation but some experience with iconic notation, consider asking them to use iconic notation to represent their creations. Regardless of whether icons or standard notation are used, consider audio or video recording the product, as a way of refreshing the composer's memory; icons and even standard notation are not always the most exact representation of the composer's intent (hence leaving room for artistic interpretation). For students with some experience with iconic notation and some experience with standard notation, consider translating the icons into standard notation for and with the students (a process similar to that used by preschool and kindergarten teachers when they translate the students' meaning behind their early attempts at writing).

Composition Activity #1: Rhythmic composition. *Using their chanting voices, students will be able to compose a rhythmic ostinato to accompany a familiar chant.*

- During this activity, the students use their chanting voices to create rhythmic patterns (based on words) they will combine in various orders to compose ostinati to accompany the chant "Muffins" (see Music Example 7.23). The goal is for students to create, revise, and document rhythm patterns as ostinati. The teacher and students demonstrate a stirring motion while chanting "Muffins." The teacher asks students to think of an ingredient they could use to make muffins (e.g., chocolate chips) and writes the word and rhythmic notation on a three-by-five card. The students chant the word rhythmically as an ostinato while the teacher performs the song. They repeat the same process for additional ingredient words until they have compiled a variety of ingredients. The teacher models arranging the ingredient cards in various combinations to create an ostinato. The teacher performs the song as the students perform the ostinato. The teacher asks the students to create their own ostinato using the ingredient cards created as a class. This activity can be completed by individuals or in small groups. When the students complete their compositions, they must share the notation and perform them as an ostinato to accompany "Muffins." After each performance, the class discusses what they noticed about the composition, considers things the composers could change, and describes how the changes would make the composition different.

Musical Example 7.23. "Muffins," Composition Activity #1.

Muffins

Jill Reese

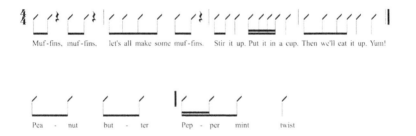

- o **Variation #1** (Winding it back): For students who are nonverbal, consider using any sort of vocable the student can successfully demonstrate as one of the sounds the students are using to create. Make a "sound muffin" rather than a traditional muffin. Have students use the type of sounds they explored during Exploration Activity #1 as ingredients for the sound muffin. The teacher and students can notate the ingredients using icons to represent the sounds.
- o **Variation #2** (Winding it back): For students with few composition experiences, consider composing collaboratively as a class. The teacher can allow the students to make choices and can discuss other possible choices and how that might change the way the ostinato sounds.
- o **Variation #3** (Winding it back): For students who struggle to read words, consider having students draw pictures of the ingredients on three-by-five cards. The students can arrange the pictures to match the ostinato they create.
- o **Variation #4** (Winding it back): For students who are struggling to think of ingredients, the teacher can have ingredients written ahead of time on three-by-five cards (either pictures of the ingredient, words, standard notation, or a combination depending on the previous

experience and needs of the students). The students can arrange the cards to create an ostinato.

- o **Variation #5** (Winding it back): For students who are not yet comfortable sharing their voices or who struggle to perform multiple parts simultaneously, consider using technology to facilitate the activity. The teacher can use technology such as the computer program Audacity (Audacity Team, 2014) to record the class performing the chant with the teacher scaffolding, and then the teacher can record each individual ostinato. Using the technology, the teacher can play the chant and ostinato simultaneously.
- o **Variation #6** (Winding it forward): For students who successfully complete the original activity, consider having them think of and notate their own ingredients (different from the ones contributed by the class).
- o **Variation #7** (Winding it forward): For students who successfully complete the original activity, consider challenging them to write two complementary ostinati.

Composition Activity #2:   Tonal composition. *Using their singing voices, students will be able to compose an introduction and coda for a familiar song.*

- During this activity, the students use their singing voices to create tonal patterns they will combine in various orders to compose an introduction and coda for the song "Bell Peter" (see Music Example 7.24). The goal is for students to create, revise, and document a four-beat phrase using tonic patterns as an introduction and coda. The teacher and students sing the familiar song "Bell Peter" while swinging their arms side to side on the macrobeat (dotted half note). The teacher has students echo various minor tonic patterns with their singing voices. The teacher shows the students the standard notation for a phrase (eight macrobeats long) that he or she will use as an introduction and coda for "Bell Peter." The teacher sings her composition as the introduction and coda; the students sing the song between the two. The teacher asks the students to describe the introduction and coda he or she composed. The students discover (1) the length is eight macrobeats, (2) the teacher used only the notes of the tonic chord, and (3) the introduction was the same as the coda. The teacher challenges the students to create their own introductions and codas for "Bell Peter" using the same characteristics. When the students complete their compositions, they must share the notation for and perform their introductions and codas for "Bell Peter." After each performance, the class discusses what they noticed about the composition, considers things the composers could change, and describes how the change would make the composition different.

Musical Example 7.24. "Bell Peter," Composition Activity #2.

The Bell Peter

Traditional

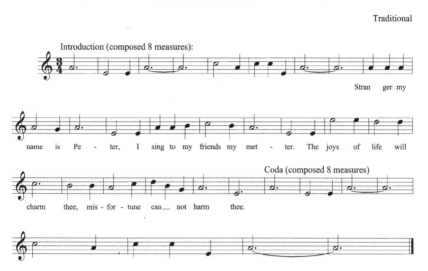

- Variation #1 (Winding it back): For students with few composition experiences, consider composing collaboratively as a class. The teacher encourages students to improvise various minor tonic patterns. The class discusses how to put them in order, other possible choices, and how the choices might change the way the composition sounds.
- Variation #2 (Winding it back): For students who struggle to read and write standard notation, consider having them use icons to represent pitch height and note length of their composition, or use a modified staff with only three lines as readiness for a full staff. (See Music Example 7.25.)

Musical Example 7.25. Composition Activity #2, Variation #2.

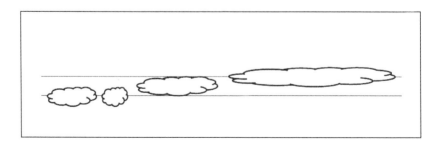

○ **Variation #3** (Winding it back): For students who struggle to think of tonic patterns to use, the teacher can model improvising tonic patterns, notate those patterns (using standard or iconic notation depending on the students' previous experiences), and then encourage the students to arrange those patterns to create their composition.

○ **Variation #4** (Winding it back): For students who struggle to create using multiple pitches, consider reducing the number of pitches they are using to two pitches. Limit the pitch content to the tonic root (A) and the dominant root (E), and encourage the students to compose by toggling between the two. (See Music Example 7.26.)

Musical Example 7.26. Composition Activity #2, Variation #4.

○ **Variation #5** (Winding it back): For students who struggle to record their compositions using notation, consider audio or video recording their introductions and conclusions. Students can return to the recording when they consider revising.

○ **Variation #6** (Winding forward): If students are successful composing the introduction and coda, the teacher could challenge the students to make the coda different from the introduction.

○ **Variation #7** (Winding it forward): If students are successful composing the introduction and coda using only the notes of a minor tonic chord, consider providing more options for an expanded composition (e.g., two beats tonic, two beats dominant, four beats tonic). Students could also expand to stepwise motion (neighboring and passing tones). (See Music Example 7.27.)

Musical Example 7.27. Composition Activity #2, Variation #7.

Composition Activity #3: Composing a variation. *Using their singing voices, students will be able to compose a variation of a familiar tune.*

• During this activity, the students use their singing voices to compose a variation on the song "Hop Old Squirrel" (see Music Example 7.28a). The goal is for students to consider options for changing the tonal content of a repeating pattern ("Hop old squirrel"), create two different variations on the song, describe how they varied the original tune, and describe the reasons they prefer one version to others. After students are familiar with the original song, the teacher will provide the students with notation paper that has three staves: notation of the original song on the top staff, space to write tonal patterns on the middle staff, and space to rewrite their final version of the song on the bottom staff. The teacher sings and shows notation for a variation he or she wrote (see Music Example 7.28b) and asks the students to describe what they notice is different from the original song. The teacher helps the students identify that the pitches for the "Hop old squirrel" pattern are different, and that the teacher used only the pitches of the song (B/*mi*, A/*re*, G/*do*). The teacher challenges the students to create two variations of the original tune by changing the pitches of the "Hop old squirrel" using only the pitches of the song (B/*mi*, A/*re*, G/*do*). When the students complete their compositions, they must share their notation and perform their two variations. After each performance, the composers describe how they varied the original song. After all variations have been performed, the students describe which variation was their favorite and provide support for their preference.

Musical Example 7.28a. "Hop Old Squirrel"

(a)

Hop Old Squirrel

Traditional

Musical Example 7.28b. "Hop Old Squirrel" and Variation.

- o **Variation #1** (Winding it back): If students are struggling to create using new pitch and rhythm content, consider varying the rhythm but remaining on the original pitch (*mi*). Students often benefit from removing the lyrics during this step. (See Music Example 7.29.)

Musical Example 7.29. Composition Activity #3, Variation #1.

- o **Variation #2** (Winding it back): If students are struggling to think of new patterns, consider working as a class to improvise new patterns (or if improvisation is still a challenge, the teacher could model improvising patterns and have students imitate the patterns with their voices) and write them as a group on three-by-five cards. The students could then rearrange the cards to compose a variation. (See Music Example 7.30.)

Musical Example 7.30. Composition Activity #3, Variation #2.

- o **Variation #3** (Winding it back): If the students are struggling to create new tonal patterns using their voices, the teacher might consider having students explore using individual tone bars of limited pitches (*do-re-mi* content from the original tune), then imitating with their voices the patterns they play on the tone bars.

○ **Variation #4** (Winding it forward): If the students are successful with the original activity, consider changing or adding options for tonal content. Students could be encouraged to explore notes beyond those in the original song (B-A-G). They could use notes of the tonic chord (*do-mi-sol*) in place of the original pattern or expand beyond the tonal content of the tune to the first six notes of the major scale (*do-re-mi-fa-sol-la*). (See Music Example 7.31.)

Musical Example 7.31. Composition Activity #3, Variation #4.

Hop Old Squirrel

Traditional

○ **Variation #5** (Winding it forward): If students are successful with the original activity, consider adding the option of varying both the rhythmic and the tonal content. (See Music Example 7.32.)

Musical Example 7.32. Composition Activity #3, Variation #5.

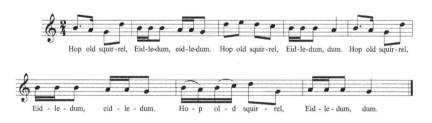

○ **Variation #6** (Winding it forward): If the students are successful with the original activity, consider challenging them to keep the "Hop old squirrel" pattern the same, but varying the "eidledum" patterns. (See Music Example 7.33.)

Musical Example 7.33. Composition Activity #3, Variation #6.

Composition Activity #4: Composing an original song. *Using their singing voices, students will be able to compose a new song based on the harmonic structure of a familiar song.*

- During this activity, the students use their singing voices to compose a new song based on the chord structure of "Hey Lolly, Lolly, Lo" (see Music Example 7.34). The goal is for students to improvise a melody using the harmonic structure of that song, notate their new song, then revise the song before sharing the final version. This song uses a sequence similar to Improvisation Activity #4, but it becomes composition because the students incorporate revision and document their final version. After following steps 1 to 3 of Improvisation Activity #4, the teacher demonstrates notating the new melody. The teacher asks students to notate their new melodies. After students notate their melodies, the teacher invites students

Musical Example 7.34. "Hey Lolly, Lolly, Lo."

Hey Lolly, Lolly, Lo

Traditional

to share the notation of and perform their in-progress creation for the class. After each performance, the class describes what they noticed about the composition, discusses options the composers have for revision, and experiments with how the change would make the composition different. The students consider the suggestions as they revise their composition in subsequent classes and then finalize their composition. The compositions can be performed by the class or, if appropriate, by instrumentalists in the district. The performances can be recorded, and the audio and notation can be posted on the website for the school district.

o **Variation #1** (Winding it back): For students who have little to no experience with notation, consider having them audio record their compositions. The teacher could then model notating the student's composition from the recording. Peers could then attempt to copy the notation of the various compositions to practice their notation skills.

o **Variation #2** (Winding it back): For students who are struggling to write a whole song independently, consider writing a song as a class and having individuals contribute parts of the song. Revision could also occur as a class.

o **Variation #2** (Winding it forward): If students are successful at composing a new tune based on the chord structure of a familiar song, consider asking them to write variations on their tunes or their peers' tunes. The original composer could compare his or her original composition with the variations and describe how the variations are different.

o **Variation #3** (Winding it forward): If students are successful at composing a new tune based on the chord structure of a familiar song, consider advancing to a song that has additional chord functions or is in a different tonality (this would require the students to have experience with many songs in that tonality). For example, if the students are successful with the song "Hey Lolly, Lolly, Lo" (which contains tonic and dominant functions), consider using a song like "Camptown Races" (which contains tonic, dominant, and subdominant functions) to challenge the students further, or a song in minor tonality like "Fishing."

CELEBRATING THE PROCESSES AND PRODUCTS OF VOCAL CREATIVITY

As soon as students being exploring, improvising, and composing, teachers must begin celebrating their divergent thinking and risk taking by sharing the process *and* products of their creativity. I emphasize both the process and the product because all too often in the arts, we highlight the product, when the richness of the learning happens during the creative process. Eisner (1998) suggests that celebrations of thinking, and celebrations of the creative processes central to learning, are often missing from classrooms. He suggests we celebrate thinking, learning, and creating in their many forms as a way of honoring students' differences and sharing the joy that accompanies personal growth.

Celebrations can be quiet and personal, such as sending a note home with individuals who took a step outside their comfort zone, took an especially innovative risk using their voice, or were leaders during group composition. Celebrations can be more public, such as including notation of classroom compositions in the school newsletter or posting audio of students' improvisations on the school website. Teachers can celebrate the compositions their students have created by informally publishing a CD and music yearbook that includes visual representation (iconic or standard notation) of students' compositions and narrative from the students describing their composition and revision process. The book can have compositions from students in each grade in the school and would be a great representation of how the compositional process evolves as students gain more experience. Celebrate the improvisations your students have created in class by including opportunities for improvisation in concerts and sharing video of the improvisation process. In the video, include short clips of students reflecting on the value of improvising and the things they have to think of when they are improvising. Celebrate the explorations your students have experienced by including a recording of students' vocal explorations on your website. Provide links to mp3s of a tune used for exploration (such as "City Line Avenue") and examples of students' vocal improvisations via video or audio clips. Along with the clips, include prompts such as "This student used her voice to create a new beep for her car. With an adult or another child, use your voice to create a special beep for your car." Inspired by the prompt, students and their families can extend the learning begun at school and continue to use their voices to create music at home. Provide a link for parents and students to download the Audacity software and encourage them to create songs together, record them, and share them with the teacher. Another way to extend creativity into the home and celebrate creativity at home is by sending a "Buddy Backpack" home with younger students. The Buddy Backpack contains a stuffed animal named Buddy, a journal to record Buddy's adventures, and an mp3 player (with earphones) that contains familiar songs from school but that can also record. Teachers can have one Buddy Backpack per class, and the Buddy Backpack can spend one week during the school year with a different student in each class. In the backpack, teachers provide directions for students to listen to the songs on the mp3 player and to teach an adult and the stuffed animal the songs; then, the students should sing and record with the adult a song that they know that is not already on the mp3 player; then, they create a song with Buddy and the adult about Buddy's adventures and record that on the mp3 player. This is just another way to extend musical creativity beyond the walls of the classroom and to celebrate communal creativity and the many different forms creating takes!

CONCLUSION

The activities described in this chapter are only some of the ways teachers can encourage students to use their voices to create musically. The variations suggested for winding the activities back and forward provide options for the teacher to individualize instruction and provide each student a safe environment for creative growth and taking chances. For some students—and even some teachers—generative musical creativity (especially with the voice) makes them feel especially vulnerable. This may be a symptom of the fact that the voice is a very personal musical instrument and that creativity provides a window into a person's independent musical knowledge. For these reasons, the most important strategy teachers can employ is to take risks alongside their students and to continue to grow as musicians through creativity, especially if this is a less developed side of their musicianship. Another strategy is to provide options within each activity (via winding it back and forward) to demonstrate that there are many different ways to be creative, and that they are all valid and honored. By providing frequent and varied opportunities to use the voice to explore, improvise, and compose early in the curriculum, teachers create an environment in which student growth will be exponential.

Vocal creativity is the most logical starting point to build musical creativity and musically independent thinking. By winding instruction back and forward to meet the individual needs of their students and providing a variety of ways to successfully participate in creative activities, teachers provide the opportunities and support students' need to build their musical creativity and express their musical thinking. By celebrating the students' creative products and the creative process, teachers lift up their students and advocate for the type of learning that is unique to music education.

REFERENCES

Audacity Team. (2014). Audacity®: Free audio editor and recorder (Version 2.0.5) [Computer program]. Retrieved from http://audacity.sourceforge.net/

Brophy, T. S. (2001). Developing improvisation in general music classes. *Music Educators Journal*, *88*(1), 34–41, 53.

Burnard, P. (2000). Examining experiential differences between improvisation and composition in children's music-making. *British Journal of Music Education*, *17*(3), 227–245.

Byo, S. J. (1999). Classroom teachers' and music specialists' perceived ability to implement the national standards for music education. *Journal of Research in Music Education*, *47*(2), 111–123.

Eisner, E. W. (1998). *The kind of schools we need: Personal essays*. Portsmouth, NH: Heinemann.

Gordon, E. E. (1989). Audiation, music learning theory, music aptitude, and creativity. In J. W. Richmond (Ed.), *Proceedings of the Suncoast Music Education Forum on Creativity* (pp. 75–81) Tampa, FL: University of South Florida.

Gordon, E. E. (2003). *Improvisation in the music classroom*. Chicago, IL: GIA Publications.

Kaschub, M. (1997). Exercising the musical imagination. *Music Educators Journal*, *84*(3), 26–32.

Kaschub, M., & Smith, J. (2009). *Minds on music: Composition for creativity and critical thinking*. Lanham, MD: Rowman & Littlefield Education.

Kratus, J. (1990). Structuring the music curriculum for creative learning. *Music Educators Journal*, *76*(9), 33–37.

Kratus, J. (1991). Growing with improvisation. *Music Educators Journal*, *78*(4), 35–40.

Kratus, J. (1996). A developmental approach to teaching music improvisation. *International Journal of Music Education*, *26*, 27–38.

Krudge, N. (2011). MadPad: Remix Your Life App (Version 1.1.0) [Software]. San Francisco, CA: Smule. Retrieved from https://itunes.apple.com/us/app/id456072329?mt=8

Louk, D. P. (2002). *National standards for music education: General music teachers' attitudes and practices* (Doctoral dissertation). Retrieved from Dissertation Abstracts International. (UMI No. ATT 3042585)

Orman, E. K. (2002). Comparison of the national standards for music education and elementary music specialists' use of class time. *Journal of Research in Music Education*, *50*(2), 155–164.

Partnership for 21st Century Skills. (n.d.). Framework for 21st century learning. Retrieved from http://www.p21.org/about-us/p21-framework

Reese, J. W. (2005). *Definitions of improvisation: Perspectives of three elementary general music teachers* (Master's thesis). Retrieved from ProQuest Dissertations and Theses database. (UMI No. 1440086)

Wiggins, J. (2005). Fostering revision and extension in student composing. *Music Educators Journal*, *91*(3), 35–42.

CHAPTER 8

Sequential Instruction for Older Beginners in Vocal and General Music

JOY ANDERSON, *Shenandoah Valley Children's Choir and Eastern Mennonite School*
EVAN BRUNO, *Chicago Children's Choir*

CHAPTER OVERVIEW

This chapter will focus on older beginners in the upper elementary and secondary general music classroom as well as choral rehearsal. Older beginners are defined as students whose musical skill levels are comparable to those of much younger learners but whose age and developmental level would cause music learning experiences appropriate for younger learners to be inappropriate and ineffective. This chapter will examine the following within the framework of this book's three principles (see chapter 1):

- Primarily intellectual understanding of musical concepts and an aurally internalized grasp of musical skills and concepts
- Examples of *winding* in the context of specific musical skills in the general music classroom:
  - Singing
  - Dancing
  - Playing instruments
  - Rhythmic and tonal reading and notating and the aural skills that form their basis

- Examples of winding in the context of the peculiar challenges of the choral classroom as distinct from the general music classroom:
  o Logistical and practical issues
  o Music learning issues
  o Performance issues
- Challenges of teaching older beginners

In an ideal world, intentional, sequential music education for every child would begin in early childhood. When this early beginning is provided, children can develop a deeply internalized grasp of tonal and rhythmic skills and concepts, as well as high levels of artistry and comfort with activities such as improvisation, solo singing, and movement. However, in many public schools, this is not possible. Hourigan (2015) states: "The obvious solution to this larger curricular problem is to find ways at *all* levels to include *all* students regardless of ability or background" (p. 93). When early music education is not possible, music educators face the challenges of engaging older students and helping them to develop these skills in ways and at levels that are still deep and substantive, but with fewer years to accomplish these goals, and in the case of ensemble classrooms, with the additional pressures of performance and competition obligations.

Both upper elementary/secondary general music classes and secondary-level choral ensembles frequently contain learners with vastly different skill, ability, and experience levels. Discussing these two situations together is useful because they share some common challenges. Unlike instrumental classrooms, which are often composed of players who at least *begin* somewhat together, learning to read music as they learn to play, these older-age general music classes and choral ensembles can frequently be the places where students with high levels of previously developed musicianship meet those who have far less skill, experience, and even motivation. The need for *winding forward* and *winding back* is tremendous in these situations. The inevitable, desirable, and enriching inclusion of students with special needs in our classrooms can offer further winding challenges.

In these situations, the aural and intellectual depth that can come from years of sequential skill building is not always possible. The temptation exists to default to teaching in the simplest, and most direct, but not always the most substantive ways, emphasizing activities such as identifying absolute note names or solfège on the staff without truly audiating intervals, identifying rhythmic note names without truly audiating rhythms, or even learning songs or preparing choral repertoire completely by rote and abandoning altogether the idea of teaching music reading and music fundamentals and the aural skills that should form their basis. If we are not very intentional, the desire to see and demonstrate immediate results in the form of correct "answers"—using correct terms, singing correct solfège syllables, and singing correct notes—and the pressures of preparing for performance and competition can actually discourage the careful development of the deep aural skills that are far more difficult to teach and less obvious to the observer or audience. Yet, the desires of older students and their teachers to obtain these more immediate results in the form of demonstrated knowledge or creditable performance must be taken seriously. It is neither practical nor musical to insist on basing an "older beginner" curriculum—especially one for a performing ensemble— *solely* on the ideal that is appropriate when beginning in early childhood or with beginning instrumentalists, starting with the most rhythmically and melodically simple material and very gradually increasing complexity and difficulty. Music educators who face the challenges of teaching older beginners and choral singers with very disparate skill levels must plan carefully to strike a balance between what can seem to be competing goals. On one side is incrementally developed rhythmic and tonal audiation, and on the other are musical and intellectual satisfaction and engagement from more immediately complex and sophisticated music and musical concepts.

The sequences and ideas that follow describe an attempt to strike this difficult balance between deliberate, experiential, and incremental aural and kinesthetic skill building and faster, more abstract and contextual introduction of vocabulary, symbols, and other music fundamentals. When this dual-direction approach is followed, the deep aural skills and the more straightforward musical understandings and, in the case of choral ensemble, the efficient and effective preparation of repertoire can "meet in the middle," and the result can be an older student whose musical needs for depth, engagement, and performance have been met. Moreover, this carefully sequenced aural skill development combined with immediate introduction of age-appropriate repertoire and concepts can partially address winding principles simply by its multilayered nature.

A word about the importance of sequence: success in winding forward or winding back for each student is based on knowing where each student falls in his or her learning process, which is, in turn, based on a clearly delineated pathway toward the goal of competence and expertise. Planning and teaching skills sequentially and incrementally provides this clear pathway and allows us to intentionally take a step backward on the path (winding back) when necessary or provide opportunities for more depth or acceleration along the path (winding forward) when a student demonstrates that need.

It will be useful to divide our discussion into several broad categories: first, the performance (music-making) skills, such as singing, instrument playing, moving, and creating, which can form the basis of the general
music curriculum; second, the aural and music literacy skills and theoretical understanding that should result from these performance skills; and
finally, the application of these ideas in the choral ensemble, a learning
environment with its own goals and challenges. The lesson components to
be included in an older beginner music classroom may be much the same
as the components of a music instructional program for younger students.
Just as young children must "begin at the beginning," so must older students with comparable skill and experience levels. The purpose of this
chapter is not to duplicate the information and ideas presented in other
chapters pertaining specifically to these lesson components and activities,
but rather to help educators adjust and modify those lesson components
and sequences for older beginner general music and choral ensemble classrooms. For this reason, only activities and sequences that may differ significantly for older beginners will be emphasized in this chapter.

MUSIC MAKING IN THE GENERAL
MUSIC CLASSROOM

Students in a music class should *make music* or respond to music (e.g.,
through movement) competently, meaningfully, expressively, artistically,
and with genuine, intrinsic satisfaction. Merely learning *about* music does
not build musicianship. Free from the obligation of preparing for public
performance, general music classes can offer students a variety of ways to
make and respond to music: singing, playing instruments, and moving in
creative and musical ways. The important goals of developing strong aural
and music literacy skills and a theoretical understanding of musical concepts are only meaningful as they support and further this fundamental
goal of making music competently and artistically.

Singing

The voice is our first, most accessible, and most intimate musical instrument.
For many students, however, it is also an instrument that is underused and
undertrained in music classes, and one that can present unfortunate social
challenges, especially for older students. These social challenges, along with
many music educators' own lack of training in and comfort with singing,
may be largely responsible for neglect of this skill in general music classes

for older students. Yet, when this skill is treated as a sequentially learnable one, singing can not only provide great enjoyment and satisfaction for students but also form a basis for music instruction that is artistic, flexible, and user-friendly, not to mention inexpensive! If an educator is fortunate, he or she may teach in an environment where singing is already culturally and socially acceptable and positive. In that instance, the task is simpler—to lead students to experience a progressively broader variety of repertoire and higher levels of singing competence. When a positive singing culture has not yet been established, however, singing should not be dismissed, as it so often is, as an unfeasible activity with older learners.

Bennett Reimer states (2003): "Music, I suggest, is perhaps our most effective mode for cultivating, extending, and refining the felt undergoings that are the basis for human consciousness and cognition" (p. 80). Singing is one of the most basic ways to make music. *Every* child and young person (and every adult, for that matter) can and should learn to sing well—that is, on pitch and with artistry and enjoyment. As with other musical skills and concepts, singing instruction and the creation of a positive classroom singing culture become positive and practicable curriculum components when approached through an effective sequence that can be *wound back* and *forward* when appropriate.

New and Reluctant Singers

It may be self-evident that the first step in teaching singing effectively in upper elementary and secondary classrooms is simply to encourage students to sing. To achieve this goal, music educators must create an environment where singing is personally safe, socially safe, and intrinsically valuable. The task of creating an environment where singing is "safe" for *all* students demands that the teacher accept that he or she cannot bestow self-esteem or social currency him- or herself, but can create and foster situations that encourage students to build genuine self-esteem and share genuine respect through the development of individual and group competence. Building this expertise on a foundation of substantive, quality repertoire from many genres will encourage students to discover the intrinsic value in singing.

A Possible Sequence for Building a Positive Classroom Singing Culture

A gentle and gradual progression into singing can help to initiate a culture in which singing is personally and socially "safe" and meaningful.

The first two steps toward this culture should happen simultaneously, and both involve comfort with the voice. First, students need to begin to use their *speaking* voices in musical ways. The speaking voice is safe because it is already used with such frequency, so using the voice in this way can begin to build a bridge toward singing. Rhythmic chanting in the context of echo patterning using neutral and rhythm syllables, rhythmic improvising, and rhythm reading (as described in this chapter and others) not only are important activities for rhythmic learning but also are only one step away from singing. Chanting rhymes and short poems, an important activity in early childhood and primary grade music, can also work in some classroom cultures if the rhyme lyrics are interesting, challenging, strange, funny, or disgusting. Rhymes in a variety of languages can also be appealing to older learners (Musical Example 8.1).

Musical Example 8.1

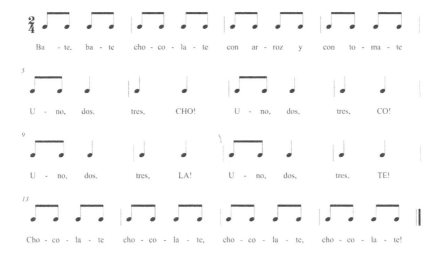

The rhyme in Musical Example 8.1 also involves an active game, which not only may make it more appealing but also can distract highly reluctant students and make them forget they are making music with their voices! Providing these musical speaking voice opportunities and accompanying activities can wind presinging instruction back to a place in the sequence that allows all students to participate in vocal music making.

During this presinging period, students need to *hear* singing voices of as many different types as possible. Hearing singing from a variety of genres and cultures is important, as well as hearing male and female, old and young voices, especially the full range of the male voice. When possible, of course, this exposure to singing should involve live performances, including the teacher's. Interesting, appealing recordings (audio and video) are also good options. Honest comments should be allowed and encouraged as part of creating a safe environment. At the same time, to keep discussions constructive and appropriate, conversations about others' singing should be guided toward issues of authenticity, culture, and meaning. Teaching students how to channel silly or inappropriate comments caused by embarrassment into constructive, relevant comments is an important winding step as we lead students toward competent and confident singing.

To be clear, these "listenings" do not have to be *only* listening—in fact, they should not be, in most cases. General music classes frequently include "listening lessons" based on orchestral or other instrumental music. Rhythm reading and movement activities, and those focused on form and other musical attributes, are often part of active music "listening" or "appreciation" curriculum components. Consider using a wide variety of *vocal* music for these types of activities as well. In addition to providing greater listening lesson variety, inclusion of vocal music recordings can offer meaningful and engaging opportunities for students to hear singing and, as much as possible, participate in the music making.

As students become more comfortable with the idea of singing and with using their own voices—even their speaking voices—to make music, the next step is to expand the range of those voices in musical ways. Vocal exploration should involve vocal pitch range, dynamics, tempo, poetic meaning, and other "presinging" attributes whose applications to later singing are obvious. Some vocal exploration activities appropriate for younger students are equally engaging for older students. Additionally, reading stories and longer poetry using the voice creatively (e.g., using different "voices" for different characters, or to create dramatic effect) can be meaningful (scary, funny, sad, or conveying other emotional content). Inviting students to invent vocal sound effects in the context of poetry, teacher-performed songs, and other activities can also provide opportunities for vocal exploration. Making use of these literary examples offers excellent opportunities for interdisciplinary experiences in drama, language arts, and other subjects as well.

When students have reached the level at which they are comfortable with varying vocal pitches in a speech or sound effect context, comfort with singing is very near. At this point, students can be invited to sing short, narrow-pitch-range, often repetitive bits of songs in the context of teacher singing or even carefully selected recordings. Song choice is especially important at this stage. Refrains of appealing and interesting folk songs are a good place to start. (Refrains are distinct from choruses, which are longer.) Good-quality, popular songs with singable refrains can also be worthwhile and appealing. Songs that tell stories, songs that carry emotional meaning, and again, songs that are funny or disgusting are good choices for classes containing reluctant singers. As with rhymes, mentioned earlier, songs in various languages offer challenge and interest as well. Folk songs and popular songs from other eras and cultures offer opportunities to explore even more interdisciplinary ideas. Songs from the past, sung in the context of conversations about meaning, can be powerful, engaging, and encouraging of a positive singing culture. Some examples of meaningful and engaging history songs with short refrains are "Johnny Has Gone for a Soldier" from the Revolutionary War; "Brother, Can You Spare a Dime" from the Depression era; and "Blowin' in the Wind," a Vietnam-era protest song by Bob Dylan.

Keep in mind, always, that singing will only become intrinsically valuable to students if the music itself holds some meaning and intrinsic value. Remember that quality does not depend on genre. Demonstrating our openness to a wide variety of good-quality, authentic songs by choosing the best we can find from many styles and genres will encourage our students to be open, curious, and musically adventurous. Just as winding principles demand that we assess and begin where each student's *skill level* lies, so we must assess where each student's *musical comfort zones* lie and build and expand from there when possible and appropriate. Worthwhile music exists in nearly every genre, and expanding our own musical horizons can demonstrate genuine care for our students, "honoring the individual needs" of each, as principle 1 suggests, and creating a singing culture of openness, curiosity, and respect.

As students' comfort with singing increases, the length and vocal range of singing excerpts should increase as well. Note: teachers of middle schoolers and young high schoolers need to be knowledgeable about and sensitive to issues of boys' changing voices. A number of excellent resources on boys' changing voices are available, including the DVD by Henry Leck (2001): *The Boy's Changing Voice: Take the High Road.* This introduction of expanding singing repertoire should be planned carefully and executed gradually. Educators must take the time to examine songs, their ranges, their potential for engagement and accessibility, and the possibilities they present as additions to a varied repertoire. As with the other musical skills described throughout this book, if students are not successful, wind back to the previous step in your carefully designed sequence, and spend a little more time there before moving on again.

Winding It Back

Simply following this sequence, continually assessing students' progress and responding accordingly, is a significant part of the winding process. Because all steps in the sequence are accomplished using worthwhile music, even those students who are already competent, confident singers will be musically enriched. Consider a further winding level, if students with more advanced skills and confidence are ready to move on while novice and reluctant singers still need more time at the speaking voice or vocal exploration levels. Spoken ostinati or other speaking-voice or vocal exploration patterns may be created and used to accompany more melodically complex songs, allowing part of the class to sing and another part to continue at the chanting or sound effect stage. This activity can be highly engaging and musically satisfying while addressing our three principles outlined in chapter 1 by authentically honoring individual needs, providing choices and multiple learning levels, and allowing all students to make music together in the ways most satisfying, successful, and safe for each.

MOVEMENT

The importance of movement in any music education experience cannot be overstated. Movement in the context of games and listening activities, dances of various types, and free and creative movement should play as significant a role in musical experiences for older learners as for younger ones. For carefully designed movement sequences and ideas, please refer to chapter 4. Caveats regarding the design of movement sequences for older learners include the following:

- Older students may exhibit more reluctance and initial awkwardness when invited to participate in free and creative movement than they will with structured movement and dance.
- Depending on the cultures in which older students have grown up, it may be likely that they have had more movement experiences in other (nonmusic class) contexts than younger students will have had. The types of experiences older students bring to class should inform educators' instructional and repertoire choices, as well as sequence design. As with singing repertoire, winding principles demand we assess and begin where students are and build from there, as far as is appropriate in each school setting.

• An instructional sequence and examples of folk dance use in the music classroom can be found in the appendix "Teaching Students to Dance" in the companion website.

PLAYING RECORDER

Many upper elementary and secondary music programs offer students the opportunity to learn to play the recorder. Along with the recorder's value as a legitimate and historic instrument, it also provides many students with their first experience on a melodic instrument. Recorder study can offer significant benefits to the music student. It can also offer great challenges because the fine motor skills necessary to finger the instrument, the breath control necessary to produce the correct pitch and good tone quality, and the music reading skills usually involved in learning to play can quickly create dramatically different skill levels. This can occur even among a fairly ability-homogeneous group of students that begins together. Add in class latecomers, students with different music experience backgrounds, and students with special needs, and the recorder classroom can present a significant winding challenge.

It is not necessary here to go into the minute rationale behind every recorder instructional sequence choice—only to reiterate the importance of sequential planning and teaching when prioritizing effective winding forward and winding back. A well-designed sequence will help each student to be successful and can help to lessen the wide skill divergence that is more likely to occur when a poorly considered sequence favors (without actually benefiting) students who can "figure it out themselves." In other words, a good sequence is more likely to aid the more challenged student without holding back the more able or experienced.

For example, one helpful guiding principle when designing a recorder sequence that encourages success for students is to introduce notes in order of ease of play (rather than simply in a scale order that might make logical sense). Many teachers introduce notes in the order of a descending scale. However, lower notes on the recorder are more difficult to play correctly, requiring greater breath control and introducing increasing challenge in covering more holes completely. The forked F fingering presents an additional challenge. Simply choosing to introduce the higher notes first does not hold back students for whom those breathing and fingering skills come easily, but it does help students who may find them more challenging, allowing those students to gain experience and confidence before tackling the lower notes.

Additionally, allowing adequate opportunity to develop playing technique through echo patterns and other aural recorder playing experiences *before* linking playing to music reading can both wind back for students whose lack of music reading skill could create difficulty and wind forward to provide students with high tonal and rhythmic ability and/or achievement to echo increasingly challenging patterns.

Once a sequence has been designed, the teacher needs to be prepared to wind back instruction—for the entire group, if that seems necessary, but more likely for one or more students whose motor skills, reading skill levels, lack of experience, or other factors make them unsuccessful at the level at which other students are functioning. At that point, two useful questions to ask ourselves as educators are:

- What *can* the student do?
- What are the fundamental goals for my students?

Consider the following sequence and the students who are participating in this recorder learning experience.

Lesson Example 8.1

Mr. Ochoa has established the following routine for introducing a new recorder skill:

1. He introduces the skill, inviting students to echo A to low E patterns.
2. He allows a brief individual practice time (less than a minute).
3. He invites volunteers to demonstrate the skill individually for the teacher and the class (a minute or less). He makes sure that one student from each previously established buddy pairing has demonstrated the skill competently.
4. Once these students have demonstrated the skill for the teacher, students pair with their buddies, and the students who have not yet demonstrated the skill do so for the buddy who has "passed" the skill (a minute or less).
5. Students report on their own and their buddies' success (eyes closed) with thumbs up, down, or sideways.
6. If a student or students are unsuccessful, the buddy tutors briefly, and Mr. Ochoa circulates through the class, helping as needed. During this time, students who were already successful try a previously explained winding forward option (e.g., incorporating the new interval with previously learned notes into improvised melodies).

7. With the class back together, Mr. Ochoa reviews low E on the staff, inviting students to read and play B, A, G, and low E (in preparation for a song they will learn). He allows a brief period of independent and buddy practice and review, circulating and assessing again, helping as needed.

8. Mr. Ochoa has placed a number of charts around the room, showing various combinations of B, A, G, and low E on the staff. He invites the buddy pairs to travel around the room, practicing each short melody and checking each other. Again, he circulates, assesses, and helps.

While this routine looks somewhat involved, it does not take much time to execute. Teaching students to follow this process initially took some time, but has saved time in the long run, and encourages accountability and collegiality and fosters expertise at each step. Of course, no system is perfect, and the class includes students whose motor skills or other factors cause them to need more time and help than the routine allows. At this point, the questions "What *can* the student do?" and "What are the fundamental goals for my students?" allow Mr. Ochoa to wind forward and back so that all students learn, demonstrate expertise, and make music together.

The majority of students, after the buddy assessment and tutorial, are on-level and ready for the next step. Most are now *experts* at

- playing low E and all previously learned notes;
- playing those notes in many combinations; and
- reading those notes from the staff.

When the class sings a number of songs in this tone set (from previous lessons), however, Mr Ochoa notices the following:

Annie's fine motor challenges make it very difficult for her to play most of the other notes, but she *can* play a B successfully and musically.

Kyle, David, and Shav have trouble moving quickly between the low E and the previously learned notes in all but the simplest combinations, but they *can* successfully play the low E and the previously learned notes slowly and in simple combinations.

Penny and Sarah are not yet consistently reading the notes successfully from the staff, but they *can* play the new and familiar notes in various combinations as aural patterns.

Andrew is easily overwhelmed by loud sounds, especially when they are all different, and Becca is easily distracted by those conflicting sounds, finding it difficult to hear and focus on her own recorder playing. Their routine has been modified from the beginning of the process. These two students and their buddies have followed the same process, playing very softly just outside the music room. (Mr. Ochoa has established with nearby classroom teachers that this is fine.) They have a small booklet containing the same staff notation as on the wall posters, and they work together through the booklet as the rest of the class circulates around the room. Mr. Ochoa checks their progress periodically. The class also has a few sets of sound-muffling headphones that Andrew uses sometimes when playing with the entire class.

The class will be working, next, on the song "Skin and Bones" (Musical Example 8.2).

Musical Example 8.2

Skin and Bones

The teacher's goals for all of the students are as follows:

- Make music artistically
- Use their *expertise* (what they *can* do) to contribute to the musical whole
- Learn a new skill or get a little better at a familiar one (gain expertise)

After the class reads from the staff (sings) "Skin and Bones" in rhythm syllables, in solfège, and then in absolute note names, the teacher invites students to ready their recorders. He invites all students to read (sing) the absolute note names slowly while fingering the correct notes on their recorders. Some students are successful. Others, as expected from previous assessment steps, are not ready to play all of the notes successfully. Mr. Ochoa invites students to practice silently and then to choose whether to play together or to finger only.

He then asks the class to either sing the notes or to play (their choice), but offers a third option, to play only the B when it comes in the song. Several students, including <u>Annie</u>, choose to do this. It sounds funny, and all the students laugh and enjoy the silly moment. Mr. Ochoa challenges <u>Annie</u> and the other B-note students to see if they can play the B musically enough that it doesn't stick out next time through. They become the "B-note team."

The teacher then designates other students (in seating sections) as the "A-note team," the "G-note team," and the "E-note team." The class plays the song again, but this time, each student plays only his or her assigned note. <u>Penny and Sarah</u>, who have successfully played the song by ear but

(216) *Winding It Back*

whose reading skills are lagging, must focus on the notation and track the notes to play at the correct time.

Mr. Ochoa introduces the ostinato in Musical Example 8.3 and invites all to read (sing) in absolute note names, fingering as they sing, and then to play it together.

Musical Example 8.3

Students are invited to choose whether to play the entire song melody or the ostinato the next time through. Several students, including Kyle, David, and Shav, who can play all the notes, including the new E, but have trouble with motor facility at tempo, choose the ostinato part. Andrew chooses to play with headphones on. Becca sits between her buddy and Andrew's buddy, helping her to focus on the part they all play together.

All students play again: some successfully on the song melody, some successfully on the B, some successfully on the ostinato, and a few successfully on another chosen note, just for fun and challenge—but all successfully, competently, and musically. *All* students have made music artistically; *all* students have demonstrated expertise by contributing to the musical whole; and *all* students have learned and improved. Through careful sequencing, assessment, and winding, our three principles have been addressed: individual learning needs of all students have been met, multiple access points and learning levels have been provided, and adequate conditions for simultaneous learning have been created.

AURAL AND MUSICAL LITERACY SKILLS AND MUSIC THEORY IN THE GENERAL MUSIC CLASSROOM

Edwin Gordon states (2003): "When students learn to audiate and perform music as a result of sequential music instruction, they develop a sense of ownership because they understand music" (p. x). Musical literacy, aural skills, and theoretical understanding of music should, ideally, work hand in hand. Too often, music reading and music theory lessons such as learning about notes on the staff, understanding rhythmic note values, and even analyzing chord progressions are treated by music educators as intellectual exercises, divorced from the sounds without which they ultimately have no meaning. It is not difficult to see how this type of visually and intellectually driven lesson can develop, especially when older learners are involved. Aural development takes time—more time than does rote memorization of "Every Good Boy Does Fine" or "Two eighth notes have the same value as one quarter note." When educators are presented with the challenge of teaching older beginners, the temptation is strong to neglect the all-important aural skills that should actually form the basis for music theory and music literacy instruction.

A clear picture of the planned learning sequence is important as educators make decisions about winding back for students whose previous experiences have not prepared them to perform as on-level students are ready to perform. Equally important is that music educators are clear in their own minds about their goals for each student. What do we really want each student to be able to perform and understand? For instance, how important is it that students name "eighth notes"? Is that more or less important than their ability to read and perform eighth notes accurately? And is either of those goals more or less important than students' ability to feel and perform the microbeat against the macrobeat and to distinguish, verbally and through movement, between duple and triple microbeats (simple vs. compound meter)?

This is not simply an academic question. The answer to this specific dilemma will determine whether we decide to differentiate our instruction, winding forward and back, to allow the older beginner time to develop the aural/kinesthetic macrobeat versus microbeat performance skill, or whether we will be content simply to "name" eighth notes and hope the student develops a deeper aural/kinesthetic grasp of macrobeat and microbeat as the class progresses. Of course, it follows that our answer to this question will ultimately affect assessment. Are we assessing whether or not each student can correctly identify eighth notes? Are we assessing whether or not each student can articulate that two eighth notes take up the same amount of time as one quarter note? Are we asking each student to articulate that paired eighth notes show two sounds on one beat? Are we asking students to read rhythmic patterns containing eighth notes, accurately, using a designated rhythm language? Ideally, the answer would be "yes" to all of these questions, but without clear priorities, we may end up focusing on and assessing more superficial goals than we intend, especially as we attempt to address the needs of a highly skill-diverse set of students.

If, as discussed in previous sections of this chapter, our fundamental goal is that students become *experts* at each skill we introduce, it is this basic goal of developing *expertise* that can help us to clarify our lesson planning and assessment priorities. With expertise as a goal, it becomes clear that it is preferable to have a student demonstrate mastery of a skill listed *earlier* in our rhythm sequence than for him or her simply to provide correct verbal or written responses to relatively superficial questions from a *more advanced* level of the sequence, even if the majority of the class is ready for those advanced concepts. To be intentional about our goals and priorities for our students, we must establish not only a clear sequence of rhythmic elements but also a clear picture of the increments necessary to develop a deeply internalized aural and kinesthetic grasp of each element or concept within the sequence. The clarification of these increments and sequences opens up possibilities for activities that can address the needs of on-level students and older beginners simultaneously, without resorting to rushed and superficial introduction of names and symbols that are meaningless without the internalization of fundamental skills. The following example is based on rhythm skills, but these ideas certainly relate as well to comparable melodic differentiation strategies.

Lesson Example 8.2

Ms. Lichty's seventh-grade general music class of twenty-four students is composed mostly of students who have had several years of sequential music instruction at the same school and at feeder elementary schools with compatible music curricula. The on-level students are comfortable reading, writing, improvising, and performing rhythmic material up to eighth-sixteenth patterns in triple microbeats (compound meter) in the instructor's rhythm sequence. For the sake of this discussion, we will stipulate that the class is using or preparing to use the following beat function rhythm syllables:

♩.	tah
♫♪.	tah-tu-teh
♩ ♪	tah—teh
♬♬♪.	tah-ki-tu-ki-teh-ki
♬♬♩	tah-ki-tu-ki-teh
♬♩.	tah-ki-tu-teh
♬♫	tah-ki-tu-teh-ki
♩♬♪	tah-tu-ki-teh-ki
♫♫	tah-tu-teh-ki
♫♫	tah-tu-ki-teh

Most students in the class have demonstrated their expertise in reading, writing, and performing rhythms up to the sixteenth notes and have had some experience chanting, echoing, and reading ♫♫. However:

Declan recently moved to the area from a school whose music program did not teach music reading or intentionally teach aural skills.

Sophie recently transferred in from the school's instrumental program and has some music reading skills, but little experience in compound meter and none in use of rhythm syllables.

Haruko and Raymond demonstrate relatively high tonal ability, but their rhythm aptitude is lower, and they are not as competent or confident as others in the class.

Frederick has been diagnosed with attention deficit hyperactivity disorder and is easily distracted and has trouble managing impulsivity.

Oliver demonstrates extremely high musical aptitude and has had many years of keyboard experience. His skill level is well above the rest of the students in the class, but he is uncomfortable with singing and expresses that the rhythm syllables the class uses are "too babyish" and "not what real musicians use."

Ms. Lichty has planned a series of lessons including segments focusing on the target rhythm patterns and based on the "Coffee" canon (Musical Example 8.4).

Musical Example 8.4

She is happy with her planned sequence and variety of activities and is confident that when students are assessed at the end of the set of lessons, they will be successful. The teacher executes the next several days' lessons, including the following rhythm-based lesson excerpts:

Day 1 Lesson Excerpt:

1. Ms. Lichty ("T" for teacher) chants a number of four-beat rhythm patterns in rhythm syllables, using 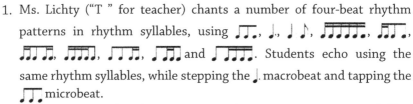. Students echo using the same rhythm syllables, while stepping the ♩. macrobeat and tapping the ♫ microbeat.

2. T chants more four-beat patterns, this time using a neutral "ba-ba-ba" syllable, inviting students to echo rhythms, but in rhythm syllables.

3. T leads the "rhythm ladder game": T leads students in chanting rhythms by pointing to rhythm elements on the rhythm ladder, which follows, in random order, for eight or more beats. Students read those rhythm elements aloud using rhythm syllables, as T points to each one.

   Rhythm ladder:

4. T adds other rhythms, one by one, to the ladder, inviting students to echo each rhythm element and chant it several times. The ladder game is played briefly after each addition:

5. T sings "Coffee" canon, inviting students to perform the macrobeat and microbeat together. She teaches the last phrase of the song by echo rote and invites students to sing that phrase, repeated as an ostinato, while she sings the entire song.

Day 2 Lesson Excerpt:

1. T reprises the final activity from the day before, inviting students to sing the final phrase as an ostinato.
2. T teaches the entire song by echo rote.
3. T reviews target rhythms aurally, first inviting students to echo rhythm syllables exactly and then inviting students to echo rhythm syllables from her neutral "ba-ba-ba" syllables.
4. Class reviews rhythms visually, playing the rhythm ladder game, beginning with the new rhythms from day 1, reviewing each briefly, and then adding the familiar rhythms.
5. T shows class a series of rhythm cards containing the following patterns from "Coffee" canon" (but in random order, not song order). The class reads each card using rhythm syllables:

Day 3 Lesson Excerpt:

1. T sings "Coffee Canon" while students perform the macrobeat and microbeat.
2. Students sing "Coffee Canon" while performing the macrobeat and microbeat.
3. T uses echo patterns and rhythm ladder game to briefly review rhythm elements.
4. T holds up (in random order) the "Coffee Canon" rhythm cards from day 2. Students read each in rhythm syllables.
5. T distributes an envelope to each student, each envelope containing a "rhythm puzzle"—all the rhythms of "Coffee Canon" (smaller versions of the cards). Students are invited to find private places in the room and place the rhythms in correct order to make the rhythm of "Coffee Canon." T circulates and checks rhythms.
6. T invites all students to sing "Coffee Canon" in rhythm syllables while pointing to rhythms.

Most students in the class are indeed successful. They are engaged throughout the activities, enjoy learning the new song, are able to demonstrate skills along the way, and are able to successfully complete the rhythm puzzle at the end of the third lesson excerpt.

However, Declan, who is new to the school, and Raymond, one of the students who struggles with rhythmic concepts, are uncomfortable with the movement activities and are not able to demonstrate the macrobeat at the slow tempo necessary with so many sixteenth-note rhythms, and they both seem overwhelmed at the idea of performing the macrobeat and microbeat simultaneously. Declan begins to act out in silly ways, and Raymond just steps or taps randomly and inaccurately and then stops participating entirely. Those students, along with Sophie, the former instrumental student, and Haruko, the other student with lower rhythmic aptitude, have trouble with the rhythm syllables. Oliver, the keyboardist with high aptitude, refuses to use the rhythm syllables at all. When Ms. Lichty chants rhythms on a neutral syllable and invites students to echo back in rhythm syllables, many of the new or struggling students are moderately successful in the large group but are unable to chant back individually with accuracy. Frederick does not participate with the group, but when redirected, he can echo back, both syllable to syllable and neutral to syllable, when invited to do so individually. When the time comes for the final assessment using the rhythm puzzle, Oliver finishes the rhythm in a matter of seconds and wastes the remainder of the time; Declan and Haruko surreptitiously look at others' work and attempt to copy it; Raymond makes a valiant attempt to successfully complete the rhythm alone but is not successful; and Frederick uses the rhythm puzzle cards to make a giant happy face on the floor.

Let us imagine, for a moment, that we are able to travel back in time with Ms. Lichty and her students. What might she do differently, so that every student in the class is fully engaged and fully successful? To answer that question, it will be necessary to go back to our resolution to base our goals, activities, and assessment on the notion of *expertise*. Consider the same lesson, adjusted to include many strategies to wind forward and back to challenge every student at an appropriate skill level, to offer students choices so that they will be encouraged to be more responsible for their own learning, and to incorporate more opportunities for small group and individual assessment *at each step* rather than waiting for one final assessment (Figure 8.1).

Using the assessment chart in Figure 8.2 (see p. 226), the teacher can easily keep track of which skills have been mastered, which are still in progress, and how close to mastery each student is at each point in the sequence.

Original Lesson Process	Winding Forward and Back
Day 1:	
1. Ms. Lichty ("T" for Teacher) chants a number of 4-beat rhythm patterns in rhythm syllables, using ♫♫, ♩, ♩ ♪, ♬♬♬, ♫♫ ♩, ♫♫ ♫♫, ♫♫♫♫, ♫♫ ♫♫, ♫♫♫♫, and ♩ ♫♫♫♫. Students echo using the same rhythm syllables, while stepping the ♩. macrobeat and tapping the ♫♫ microbeat.	• Before process step 1, T. chants patterns (no echoes yet) while introducing students to a movement repertoire (e.g. pat-clap-clap on ♫♫ microbeat; large arm-swings on macrobeat; alternating fingers snapping on sixteenth notes, etc.) S. copy movements and think of their own if desired. <u>Declan and Raymond</u> enjoy choosing their own movements from the menu, and even make up some of their own. • Students are then invited to echo T's 4-beat patterns while performing *movements of their choice or no movement at all* (rather than being required to step beat and tap microbeat). Again, <u>Declan and Raymond</u> are particularly happy with these choices. Their echo patterns are more accurate than if they had had to concentrate on more challenging beat/microbeat motions. • Students who have trouble speaking the rhythm syllables develop confidence and competence by "joining the tah-tu-teh team" and speaking only "tah-tu-teh" as an ostinato while T. chants rhythms. <u>Sophie</u> is glad to have this opportunity to get some easier rhythm syllables "on the tip of her tongue" before attempting all of them. <u>Declan</u>, <u>Haruko</u>, and <u>Raymond</u> are helped by this as well. • T. performs some patterns at a slower tempo and some at a faster tempo. <u>Sophie</u>, <u>Declan</u>, <u>Raymond</u>, and <u>Haruko</u> all feel more confident when allowed to practice oral patterns at a slower tempo. • T. invites students to improvise all together using any new or familiar triple microbeat rhythms. <u>Oliver</u> hears the word "improvise" and knowing it to be a "real" music word, is excited to try improvisation using numbers, but quickly (at first, grudgingly) finds the rhythm syllables to work better in this instance. T. compliments him on his musicianship in finding the most musical ways to accomplish a task. <u>The students challenged by the rhythm syllables</u> are happy that they can simply choose one or two rhythms at a time with which to improvise. • Students may choose whether to perform echoes alone or in small groups, and may choose a slow or fast tempo. <u>Haruko</u>, <u>Raymond</u>, and <u>Declan</u> continue to gain confidence through this flexibility.
2. T. chants more 4-beat patterns, this time using a neutral, "ba-ba-ba" syllable, inviting students to "echo" rhythms in rhythm syllables.	• As above, tempos and movement are varied • <u>Oliver</u> is invited to alternate echoing T's neutral syllable patterns with rhythm syllables or with the numbers he has learned in his piano lessons: "1 2 3, 4& 5& 6" etc.

Figure 8.1   Lesson Plan 8.2.

Original Lesson Process	Winding Forward and Back
3. Teacher leads the "rhythm ladder game": (T. points to rhythm elements on the rhythm ladder, below, in random order, for 8 or more beats. Students read those rhythm elements using rhythm syllables, as T. points to each one.) Rhythm ladder: ♩. ♫♩ ♩♪ ♬♬♬ ♬♩♩	• T. divides the class into 2 groups. One group is the "tah-tu-teh team" and chants that ostinato while other group follows T's finger, speaking those rhythms. Then the groups switch jobs. T. calls out, "Switch!" at random intervals. Oliver enjoys this challenge, and Frederick is able to focus more effectively because the random switching keeps him riveted to the task and the visual. • T. reminds S. to "embrace challenge, take risks, and expect mistakes"! All students benefit from the classroom culture encouraged by these reminders. • T. also reminds S. that since mistakes are to be expected, the first goal should be for the "tah"s to sound together, and then for the "tah-tu-teh"s to sound together. Haruko, Sophie, and Oliver particularly appreciate this intellectual explanation of what is happening aurally/orally, and this results in increased confidence and investment.
4. T. sings "Coffee Canon", inviting students to perform the microbeat. She teaches the last phrase of the song by echo-rote, and invites students to sing that phrase, repeated as an ostinato, while she sings the entire song.	· Oliver is invited to play the ostinato on the piano. He enjoys this but reminds Ms. Lichty that this part is "pretty easy." She tells him to wait until next lesson!
Day 2:	
1. T. reprises the final activity from the day before, inviting students to sing the final phrase as an ostinato.	· As above, Oliver is invited to play the ostinato on the piano – but he must also handsign the solfège at the same time. Others may join him by singing and handsigning the solfège, if they wish. If this continues to be "too easy" Oliver and others may create ostinati with their feet.
2. T. teaches the entire song by echo rote.	• Rather than simple echo-rote, T. sings entire song, asking students to listen and answer specific questions, e.g., "How many times do I sing the word 'coffee'?" "Do you hear any rhyming words?" "What syllable am I singing on the highest/lowest notes in the song?" Frederick's attention (along with other students') is focused by these questions. • T. invites students to create motions, individually or in small groups, to show "Coffee is not for me," "wake up," "nervous," "coffee cup," "They won't give coffee up." Students perform their motions for each other, and then perform them while T. sings the song again. Again, Frederick is able to focus well with this activity, and many other students enjoy being creative, and learn the words more effectively with this visual/kinesthetic element added.
3. T. reviews rhythms aurally, first inviting students to echo rhythm syllables exactly, and then inviting students to "echo" rhythm syllables from her neutral "ba-ba-ba" syllables.	• Ms. Lichty reminds students they may speak only the "tah" syllables if they wish. • Tempos are varied.

Figure 8.1 (Continued)

Original Lesson Process	Winding Forward and Back
4. Class reviews rhythms visually, playing the "rhythm ladder game," beginning with the new rhythms from Day 1, reviewing each briefly, and then adding the familiar rhythms.	· Again, tempos are varied, and students divide into the "rhythm reading group" and the "tah-tu-teh group," performing those parts with the random "Switch!" cue from Ms. Lichty. Increased focus and flexibility allow more students to read the rhythms successfully.
5. T. shows class a series of rhythm cards containing the following patterns from "Coffee Canon" (but in random order, not song order). The class reads each card using rhythm syllables: ♫ ♫ ♫ ♫ ♫ ♫ ♫ ♫♫♫♫ ♫♫♫♫♫ ♫♫♫♫ ♫♫♫♫♫♫ ♫♫♫♫ ♫ ♫ ♫ ♫ ♫♫ ♫ ♫♫ ♫	• After giving the class an opportunity to read all of the cards, Ms. Lichty places two of the cards on the board. She asks one student to choose one of the cards to read aloud. She asks <u>Raymond</u> to tell which card the student read. • This process is repeated, allowing <u>each of</u> the students Ms. Lichty has assessed to need some *winding back* to tell which of two cards was read. These students' success at this step increases their confidence and investment in the activity and also allows more confident students an opportunity to read individually.
Day 3:	
T. briefly chants triple microbeat patterns. S. echo. T. briefly chants patterns on neutral syllable. S. "echo" w/ rhythm syllables	• Nearly all students are able to perform this successfully after the previous two days of flexible choices. Those still struggling with rhythm syllables may still chant "tah" on the macrobeat.
Students sing "Coffee Canon" while tapping rhythm and stepping macrobeat. T. challenges S. to sing back correct rhythm syllables from T.'s singing of "Coffee Canon" motives. (e.g. T: "C-O-F-F-E-E"; S: "tah-tu-teh tah-tu-teh")	• Half of class performs macrobeat while singing while other half performs rhythm. They then switch jobs. Ms. Lichty invites students to choose one task or the other, OR to perform both together, stepping the macrobeat while tapping the rhythm. • The class performs these word-to-syllable "echoes" as a class and then T. invites volunteers to try individually.
T. invites S. to review a few of the rhythm cards from the previous lesson. Students read.	• T. places the cards on the board and numbers them. She tells students she will read one card, and they are to decide which card (or cards) she read and show her the number with fingers (eyes closed). Students focus, knowing this is an individual assessment, but feel safe with eyes closed, knowing only Ms. Lichty will see their answer.
T. distributes a "rhythm puzzle" envelope to each student, each envelope containing all the rhythms of "Coffee Canon," but mixed up. S. are asked to find private places in the room and place the rhythms in correct order to make the rhythm of "Coffee Canon."	• T. "buddies" several students. She assigns <u>Oliver</u> and <u>Frederick</u> as buddies and gives them the following tasks: ○ <u>Frederick</u> is to complete the rhythm puzzle correctly, and <u>Oliver</u> is to check him and tutor as needed. ○ Then, <u>Frederick</u> is to mix up the cards and <u>Oliver</u> is to read the resulting rhythms in numbers and in rhythm syllables. If that is too easy, <u>Frederick</u> is to clap to signal randomly that <u>Oliver</u> must switch from numbers to syllables and back again.

Figure 8.1 (Continued)

Student	Performs macrobeat motion	Performs microbeat motion	Performs macrobeat and microbeat simultaneously	Echoes rhythm syllables accurately	"Echoes" correct rhythms and syllables from T. neutral syll.	"Echoes" correct rhythms and syllables from T. song motives	Reads target rhythms accurately from ladder	Completes rhythm puzzle of "Coffee Canon" and reads rhythm.	Performs the following challenge (write in)
Raymond	✓	✓		✓			✓ at slow tempo	✓	
Haruko	✓	✓		✓	✓		✓ at slow tempo	✓	
Declan	✓	✓	✓	✓	✓	✓	✓	✓	
Sophie	✓	✓	✓	✓ at slow tempo	✓ at slow tempo		✓ at slow tempo	Completed correctly. Read with hesitations	
Oliver	✓	✓	✓	✓	✓	✓	✓	✓	Played ostinato on piano while handsigning in solfège; Alternated R.S. and numbers in altered rhythm
Frederick	✓	✓	✓	✓	✓		✓	✓	Altered rhythm for Oliver

Figure 8.2 Assessment chart 8.2.

Incorporating these winding strategies into the lesson may take slightly longer but should not greatly increase the time needed for the lesson. At the end of the set of the lessons incorporating winding forward and back strategies, Ms. Lichty knows far more than if she had followed the original set of lesson plans. Without differentiation strategies and frequent assessment opportunities, not only are students less engaged and less appropriately challenged, but also the teacher can likely document only which students could complete the final assessment and which could not. With only this information, she has no way to tell at which point each student began to be unsuccessful. In incorporating the strategies and frequent assessments, the teacher is able to observe and document the students' expertise and the limits of their expertise, and she is better able to plan the next lessons to address her students' strengths and challenges.

SEQUENTIAL INSTRUCTION IN THE CHORAL CLASSROOM

As in the general music classroom, sequence is of the utmost importance in the choral ensemble. Some choral ensembles are composed only of auditioned singers; yet even in these auditioned ensembles, students may come to the choral classroom with widely divergent skill and experience levels. The inclusion in a choral ensemble of both a student who has never experienced music reading or even singing and a student who has been studying private piano since the age of five can, without careful planning, create an environment that is both stressful for the novice and frustrating for the more advanced student. Ultimately, the goal of sequencing in the choral classroom should be for *all* students to attain expertise in music literacy (including the aural skills on which music literacy is ideally based) while also performing, and performing well, beautiful music that is of the highest quality, is rich in cultural authenticity, and contributes to the healthy vocal development of each singer.

Many of the ideas regarding general music, presented in previous sections of this chapter, are equally applicable in the choral classroom. Novice and reluctant singers are frequently present in choral ensembles, and many of the techniques presented to encourage these students to sing in the general music classroom can be valuable in a choral setting as well. Aural skill and musical literacy scaffolding techniques used in singing portions of the general music curriculum may be transferred directly or adapted to choral rehearsals. For this reason, specific sequences will not be laid out in this section. However, these two musical learning situations (general music and choral ensembles) are undeniably different, so we will now turn our attention to these differences.

While the humane and caring development of our students' individual musicianship is certainly a high priority, another primary goal of the choral rehearsal is to prepare for and execute a quality performance. A one-size-fits-all approach to developing individual and collective musicianship not only fails to serve the needs of all choral singers but also can greatly diminish the quality of their performances if too much time is spent attempting to bring all students to the same level of musicianship at the same time. Careful winding forward and back, weaving together thoughtfully sequenced literacy skills and meticulously planned repertoire preparation, can lead to an effective, enriching, and positive choral environment; quality performances; and music literacy and aural skills appropriate for each singer.

This section of the chapter will address winding issues peculiar to the choral rehearsal, specifically those situations and priorities that are distinct from the general music classroom. These different situations and priorities include logistical/practical issues, music learning issues, and performance issues. Each of these categories of concern may be positively influenced by careful winding forward and back to (1) honor individual learning needs of all students, (2) provide multiple access points and learning levels, and (3) create adequate conditions for simultaneous learning.

Logistical/Practical Issues

The choral ensemble classroom is a different place from an elementary or secondary general music classroom. Seating is nearly always in rows—numerous rows—that make seeing every student well very difficult and that make moving among students nearly impossible. This traditional seating structure works well as an environment for part singing and creation of a collective musical product. This seating arrangement features all singers facing the conductor and an imaginary audience, with students organized by part or in some other musically intentional order, and with singers close enough together to hear each other well while still projecting sound toward that imaginary (and future) audience. However, while very good reasons exist for this fairly universal choral seating arrangement, the structure can be problematic for directors committed to teaching each student well and as an individual.

Similarly, the single visual focus (dry-erase board, interactive board, chart, poster) frequently used in a general music classroom usually gives way in the choral classroom to multiple individual octavos—with each octavo containing multiple pages and multiple parts on each page.

Teaching developing choral singers how to read these octavos competently is an important part of choral teaching. Yet these octavos can prove a major stumbling block to singers challenged by inexperience, focus issues, reading difficulties, or any number of special needs.

The sheer number of students in choral ensembles can present additional challenges not always present in general music classrooms since high enrollment in choral ensembles (seen to focus on performance) is rightly considered more appropriate—even desirable—than high enrollment in general music classes (seen to focus on academic instruction). The task of winding forward and back to meet individual student needs can seem much more daunting in a choral ensemble of one hundred and fifty students than in a general music class of twenty.

What can choral directors do to create learning and music-making environments most conducive to individual *and* collective success? First, we need to feel free not to be bound by traditional structures, materials, and routines when they are unnecessary or do not serve our purposes well. As mentioned earlier, traditional choral rows are intended to serve specific purposes—focusing sound, allowing the conductor to be seen by all, organizing parts—and when those purposes are important during the choral rehearsal, it makes sense for that traditional setup to be used. However, not every moment of our choral rehearsals is spent in activities that require the traditional choral seating plan. Sectionals, group work on parts or special projects, many types of movement, and other important activities (including those designed to wind forward and back) within our rehearsals can work much better in other seating arrangements. Directors should be as creative and intentional in their room organization as they are in their instructional and musical choices. Chairs around the room's perimeter with large space in the middle of the room, multiple small circles, rows facing each other, and even no chairs at all can create learning and music-making spaces more workable and more conducive to effective teaching, assessment, and winding. Many choral rooms are built with terraced floors, but directors should not allow that permanent structure to dictate chair placement. Even in choral rooms with permanently fixed chairs, directors can find ways for their singers to move, regroup, and free themselves from a single, traditional choral seating arrangement.

Comparable creativity and flexibility can help us to be more effective and more intentional in using octavos and other visuals. When directors are clear in their own minds about the primary purposes of each rehearsal activity, deliberate choices for visuals become clearer as well. For example, if an ensemble containing a high percentage of novice choral singers is learning how to read octavos, certainly, those singers need to see actual octavos. However, each singer does not necessarily need to focus his or her own attention primarily on his or her own octavo. In fact, it can be more effective at this stage to use a document camera to project the octavo image on a single screen so that the director can point out various parts of the score and increase the chances that singers look at the places the director intends. Singers can then look at their individual octavos and find the place to begin singing, mark their scores, or identify a specific musical marking. (It is important to note that this technique and others mentioned later cannot legally and should not ethically be used to avoid purchase of multiple octavos.)

If the rehearsal goal for the ensemble or a learning goal for an individual student can best be served by using a visual other than the actual score, directors should feel free to create and use this alternative visual. For instance, if the director's goal is to scaffold instruction to lead students to read a specific melody from the score, creating a visual that isolates that particular melody and projecting it centrally or distributing individual copies can provide a transitional step toward actual melodic reading from the score. This technique can be especially helpful for students with many types of special needs. Scores themselves may also be modified and made more useful to specific students through use of erasable highlighters, enlargements with a copier, and other means.

But perhaps the musical goal does not involve music literacy at all. In that case, it may be that use of a score is not the best way to accomplish that goal. Many types of music, especially many non-Western pieces, are most authentically taught and learned aurally/orally, and even music that is appropriately learned through the use of traditional notation can be taught best aurally to students who learn best that way. Most students can and should learn to read music, but music reading does not have to be the goal for every piece in every rehearsal, and individual score reading does not have to be the only way students read when they do read. Rote teaching, modified scores, and centrally projected notation can be perfectly appropriate and legitimate ways to teach a choral piece, as well as effective ways to wind back for students not yet ready for traditional choral score reading.

Large numbers in a choral ensemble can be effectively managed, in part, by careful and intentional grouping. Just as thoughtful buddy pairing in a general music class can encourage peer tutoring and assessment, collegiality, and collaborative learning, so the creation of carefully chosen small groups can facilitate routines for project-based learning and other types of group learning and music making. Small groups are no panacea, of course. Realistically, winding forward and back will require more work and more creativity when it involves more people, but organizing students into different types of groups for different purposes can provide one way to address individual needs more effectively. It bears mentioning that winding for some students may entail *not* requiring them to work in groups at all.

Music Learning Challenges

Choral ensembles in school settings do not exist for the single purpose of preparing for public performance, nor do they exist for the sole purpose of developing their members' aural and music literacy skills or individual musicianship. If school ensembles did exist for a single purpose—whatever that purpose was—our jobs as choral directors would be easier, or at least more straightforward. Should we choose repertoire based on its value in teaching musical skills? Should a music learning sequence drive our repertoire choices? Or should our repertoire drive our aural skill and literacy sequences? Is it even possible or desirable to teach these skills sequentially in a choral setting? Should each of our rehearsals include a dedicated time for sight-reading and music theory learning, or should that learning come completely from our repertoire and happen "incidentally" as each concept presents itself? These and other questions are both important and ultimately not definitively answerable. Excellent choral conductors, each with his or her students' best interests at heart, will answer these questions differently. Whatever our answers to these questions, however, it is certain that we all desire both meaningful, satisfying musical experiences and strong, independent musicianship for all of our students.

The "meet in the middle" idea mentioned in this chapter's introduction, focused on aural skill development versus intellectual musical understanding, can also be a useful idea when reconciling the related but sometimes competing goals of creditable performance and personal musicianship. If each goal or priority is set up as its own distinct learning sequence, we can establish the clear, sequential, incremental pathways that facilitate winding forward and back; eventually, we will see these distinct pathways converge in a young musician who understands and audiates well and performs well, as part of a group that performs well together.

Lesson Example 8.3

Mr. Douglas's freshman mixed choir is preparing six pieces. The ensemble contains some experienced choral singers, some with moderate experience, and some with no experience at all. The class also includes several students with diagnosed special needs. The choir meets three times per week, for one hour.

Mr. Douglas is committed to leading the choir to excellent performances and top scores at competitions, and its members to the highest and deepest levels of musicianship each can reach in the time available.

Mr. Douglas takes time at the beginning of the year to get to know his singers through conversations with them, through discussions with other teachers and their parents about them, and by acquainting himself with the Individualized Education Programs (IEPs) and 504 plans of the students who have them. He conducts some preliminary formal and informal assessments (in consultation with some of the students' special education teachers) to gain a clearer idea of students' musical literacy and aural skill levels. He chooses repertoire to serve a variety of purposes:

- To create an appealing, high-quality, and well-rounded program
- To meet the appropriate level of challenge for the greatest cross-section of his students, including a wide range of difficulty so that each student's skill level is addressed intentionally by at least one piece
- To allow for a variety of teaching approaches: accessible melodic and rhythmic reading, scaffolded reading at a more challenging level, and various methods of rote learning
- To make connections with as many students as possible by honoring their cultural backgrounds

He outlines a learning sequence for each piece of repertoire based on the most accessible attributes or the most authentic ways to teach each piece. He plans and anticipates ways to wind forward and back in each teaching sequence based on the information he has gathered about each student, knowing that this information base will grow throughout the year, requiring flexibility and responsiveness.

In addition to the learning sequence for each individual piece of repertoire, Mr. Douglas also outlines separate musical literacy sequences for rhythmic skills, melodic skills, and harmonic and partwork skills. To meet the needs of the novice choral singers, he also lays out a sequence for learning to read from a choral score. Several students are not yet singing on pitch, so for those students, Mr. Douglas also outlines a sequence (including opportunities for vocal exploration that function as part of the warm-up for all students), with specific milestones, to help them develop singing skill and confidence.

Each of these sequences is planned and written down, along with ideas and tools for individual and group assessment and specific plans for winding forward and back. Throughout the year, these plans, assessments, and tools evolve, but Mr. Douglas's initial work and planning keep the daily work of meeting so many students' needs from becoming unmanageable. Mr. Douglas makes several discoveries as the year progresses:

- Students are excited when a skill or concept learned in their dedicated melodic, rhythmic, or harmonic lessons appears in a piece of repertoire. Similarly, they find it satisfying when a concept only partially understood or "heard" in repertoire preparation arises in a rhythmic, melodic, or harmonic skills lesson and they are finally ready to internalize and audiate it.

- Because Mr. Douglas has spent time planning repertoire-based sequences and sequences based on melodic, harmonic, and rhythmic skills (and other skills), he is more easily able to wind forward and back to serve different students' needs simultaneously. For instance, one piece of repertoire has a very easy-to-read rhythm but a more challenging melody. While he chose the piece partly for the accessible rhythmic material, he knows several students actually have the skill to hear and read the melodic material. He presents this opportunity, and this challenge supplements the work those students are doing in their sequential melodic lessons.

- The process of sequential learning itself promotes confidence and a sense of accomplishment in individual students and in the group as a whole. Additionally, students discover that while one sequence may be challenging to them—even frustrating—another may come more easily.

Performance Challenges

It is unfortunate that directors often see musical excellence and the inclusion in ensembles of students with special needs and challenges as mutually exclusive or at least as competing priorities. Directors are only human, and they care about scores at "festival," invitations to sing at prestigious venues, and the respect and admiration of their peers and communities. It is important, however, that we do not allow these strong incentives to pull us away from what should be our true mission and to exclude certain students in the name of "musical excellence." The truth is, if musical "excellence"—pristine tuning, mature tone quality, perfect rhythmic precision—were honestly our first priority, we would be leading or singing in professional ensembles, not teaching children and youth. In embracing our role as teachers and directors of *developing* musicians, we can find the balance we seek between the laudable desire to create the most beautiful, excellent sound we can and the passionate advocacy for each one of our students to become his or her best musical self. In this mission, we return to our central question of *expertise*. Hammel and Hourigan (2011) state: "The key to participation by a student with special needs is that it must be meaningful. Each student should make a contribution to the ensemble" (p. 161).

We need to ask ourselves: What *can* each student do, and how *can* each student contribute to the musical excellence of the group?

Lesson Example 8.4

Michael is an eager choral student who has moderate tonal ability combined with very little singing experience. He is also experiencing a voice change. Michael's director, Mr. Richardson, considers the piece they are working on and asks himself: Can Michael sing every note in this piece on pitch? Can he sing one note on pitch? Two? All the notes between F and C? When Mr. Richardson knows the answers to these questions, he can provide authentic opportunities for Michael and each student not only to learn and improve but also to genuinely contribute to the musical excellence of the group. Perhaps "Piece A" will be the piece of repertoire Michael will use to practice singing with the fullest range of his voice, making mistakes, taking risks, and improving, but for "Piece B," Mr. Richardson, knowing Michael has a confident, in-tune range of a fifth, will write a harmony part that will add depth to the existing composed harmony and melody, allowing him to sing perfectly in tune. If this were not possible because the rules of the school district's choral competition require pieces to be performed as written, then Mr. Richardson may encourage Michael to embrace his place in his musical journey toward singing competence and to make those mistakes and take those risks. Perhaps Michael will indicate he wishes only to sing the parts of the song he can sing in tune. He and Mr. Richardson can plan the places in the piece that incorporate the notes Michael sings consistently in tune, marking them and expanding those markings as his singing skill develops. This is only one illustration of the type of winding that can happen when we emphasize what students *can* do rather than what they *cannot* do.

Lesson Example 8.5

Mrs. Frasier has planned choreography to accompany a piece in her seventh-grade girls' chorus's spring concert. The movement involves colorful streamers and various types of movement. All of the singers are involved in the movement in some way. Christine uses a wheelchair and has limited use of her hands and arms. She uses a joystick to control her wheelchair independently. Because at her old school Christine was expected to sit to the side and not participate in movement activities with her chorus, she assumes this is what she will be doing and moves out of the way when the singers begin to practice this piece. Mrs.

Frasier, however, does not want Christine to miss out on this opportunity or to feel left out, and more important, she does not want her chorus to miss out on the unique contribution Christine can make to the group and its performance. Together, Mrs. Frasier, Christine, and the other chorus members brainstorm and experiment with all of the things Christine *can* do, and they discover that Christine is such a competent "driver" (as well as an excellent singer) that she can spin her chair, causing her streamers to make an amazing, beautiful effect that no one else could have created. The girls and Mrs. Frasier modify the choreography so that Christine is in the center of the stage and the other girls move as spokes in the wheel. The singing and movement at the performance exemplify musical excellence, and Christine is authentically and genuinely part of that.

CONCLUSION

The upper elementary and secondary general music classroom and the choral ensemble offer opportunities for all students to make music artistically, to develop strong aural skills, to move in authentic and creative ways, and to learn to read and understand music. While these classrooms present music educators and choral conductors with significant differentiation challenges, they also offer wonderful opportunities to bring together highly experienced and skilled students with those whose musical journeys are just beginning. Intentional planning, winding forward and back, careful assessment, flexibility, and creativity can create musical communities that allow all students to achieve their full musical potential and that encourage the creation and performance of beautiful and meaningful music.

REFERENCES

Gordon, E. E. (2003). *Learning sequences in music*. Chicago, IL: GIA.

Hammel, A., & Hourigan, R. M. (2011). *Teaching music to students with special needs: A label-free approach*. New York, NY: Oxford University Press.

Hourigan, R. M. (2015). Universal design for learning: Understandings for students with learning differences in the 21st century. In C. M. Conway (Ed.), *Designing musicianship focused curriculum and assessment* (pp. 89–112). Chicago, IL: GIA.

Leck, H. (2001). The Boy's Changing Voice. Milwaukee, WI: Hal Leonard

Reimer, B. (2003). *A philosophy of music education*. Upper Saddle River, NJ: Prentice-Hall.

CHAPTER 9

Combining Pitches into Scale Types

Extending Tonal Knowledge

ROBERTA Y. HICKOX, *Halifax Area School District,*
Halifax, Pennsylvania
ALICE M. HAMMEL, *James Madison University*

CHAPTER OVERVIEW

As students achieve competency at earlier levels in our sequences, we may begin to prepare them for more advanced concepts. *Winding back* (*and forward*) musical skills can become more complicated as the differences in individual competencies widen. By carefully delineating each step in a sequence and assessing individual students, the winding process may continue, allowing all learners to access the content in ways that honor individual learning needs. This chapter introduces the concept of winding through:

- scale work (pentatonic, diatonic, modal);
- interval study;
- partwork (resting tone, drone, ostinato, canon, partner songs); and
- harmony (chord root melody, tonic/dominant in major and minor).

Further assessment documents and procedures are introduced to continue to meet the needs of every student in a music class or ensemble.

A s teachers, we long to move beyond "the basics" to provide a more advanced set of musical awareness skills for our students. Once students have demonstrated their ability to perform rhythmic, melodic, harmonic, improvisatory, and creative movement at a fundamental level, we may begin to prepare them for a more expansive understanding of music. This is a place in our curricula, however, where we can continue to leave some students behind unless we continue to wind back our learning sequences to meet their needs. It is also a place in our curricula where we have the opportunity to wind forward material for students who are, and perhaps have been, waiting for their learning to begin.

SCALES

Once students have been prepared through experiencing a wide variety of melodic songs, chants, and vocal exploration activities (as delineated in chapters 2, 3, and 5), they are ready to continue in their melodic skill development. A recommended next step is to begin the study of scales. At this point, students are already familiar with various pitches and their placement within melodies they know. The pitches contained in a given melody can now be organized into scale types. The study of scales allows students access to a deeper comprehension of pitches and how they relate to each other in a more global sense. It also extends tonal knowledge into more vertical audiation and an understanding of harmony (Gordon, 2012).

Many of us learned major scales as a rote learning exercise without any audiation practice or theoretical understanding; some of us learned scales as a series of intervals in a particular order as a theory exercise. When scales are introduced in a sequential manner by comparing a new sound/ scale type to a familiar sound/scale type, as we recommend, it is likely that students' understanding of scales will include the audiation background to identify the scale and the expertise in manipulating pitches within the scale, as well as the theoretical information about the order of intervals.

When audiation is used as the basis for scale comprehension, scales are first introduced as a collection of pitches (a tone set) in an ascending and descending order. Students' audiation is already prepared for the study of *do* pentatonic as the first scale type, because the pitches contained in *do* pentatonic (*do, re, mi, sol, la*) are already well known (see chapters 3 and 5 for detailed information regarding the background students will have prior to this instruction). From a student perspective, the study of scale types can begin as early as second grade, or whenever all the pitches contained in *do* pentatonic have been audiated and manipulated as described in Figure 9.1 (Choksy, 1974). Students should be able to do the activities listed in

Figure 9.1 with independence and relative ease before formal presentation of scale study begins.

Student name	Sings a variety of *do* pentatonic songs	Sings a variety of *do* pentatonic songs in solfège	Reads a variety of *do* pentatonic songs in solfège, from various staff placements	Decodes solfège of known songs and patterns that include *do, re, mi, sol,* and *la*	Uses solfège (*do, re, mi, sol,* and *la*) abstractly, in tone ladders and tone sets
Jonathon	X	X	X		
Maribeth	X	X	X		
Isaiah	X	X	X		
Anibel	X	X			
Quin	X				
Tanner	X	X	X	X	X
Hsui-Hui	X	X	X		X

Figure 9.1 Readiness requirements for the study of *do* pentatonic.

Do **Pentatonic**

When a student is able to demonstrate the use of *do, re, mi, sol,* and *la* out of the context of known songs and patterns, his or her audiation skills contain these solfège syllables in many combinations, increasing the likelihood that he or she audiates the sound of a scale in addition to the individual sounds of pitches. The procedure for introducing the scale type *do* pentatonic is outlined as follows:

1. Students sing the song "Great Big House" (Musical Example 9.1) using text.
2. Students sing "Great Big House" in solfège.

Musical Example 9.1

Great Big House

Traditional

Great   big   house   in   New   Or - leans,   For - ty   sto - ries   high - ,

Ev' - ry   room   that   I've   been   in,   Filled   with   chic - ken   pie.

3. Students sing and identify the resting tone as *do*.
4. Students sing and list all the pitches used in the song as a tone set; the teacher writes the pitches from lowest to highest, leaving a space for the missing solfège (*drm sl*).
5. The teacher circles the resting tone in the tone set.
6. Students count the number of different solfège pitches used, deriving "five" as the answer.
7. The teacher names the scale "*do* pentatonic" because *do* is the resting tone and "penta" (the Greek word for "five") indicates that there are five different solfège pitches.

To determine if students understand the meaning of the term "*do* pentatonic," the teacher may ask questions such as:

- What if the song ended on *re*? Would it be labeled *do* pentatonic? (No)
- Would the *do* need to be changed or the "pentatonic"? (The *do*)
- Why? (*Re* is the resting tone so the song would be "*re* pentatonic")
- What if the song had the tone set *drm s*—would it be labeled *do* pentatonic? (No)
- Would the *do* need to be changed or the "pentatonic"? (The "pentatonic")
- Why? (There are only four different pitches used so the song would not be "*do* pentatonic" but "*do* tetratonic")

After following the same procedure with other *do* pentatonic songs (singing a song in solfège, deriving the pitches used and ordering them in a tone set, deriving and circling the tone set, and naming the scale "*do* pentatonic" or "other"), students will be asked to compare the sound of a *do* pentatonic song with a different song. Let's use "Hot Cross Buns" as an example:

1. Students sing "Hot Cross Buns" using text (Musical Example 9.2).

Musical Example 9.2

Hot Cross Buns

Traditional

Hot   cross buns,   Hot cross buns,   One a pen-ny, two a pen-ny, Hot cross buns.

2. The teacher tells the students, "Compare the sound of 'Hot Cross Buns' with the sound of 'Great Big House.' Does 'Hot Cross Buns' sound like a *do* pentatonic song? [No] Does it have too many pitches? [No] Too few pitches? [Yes] What is the resting tone? [*Do*]."

3. Students sing and list all the solfège for "Hot Cross Buns" and circle the resting tone (*drm*).
4. The teacher asks the students, "Is 'Hot Cross Buns' a *do* pentatonic song? [No] Why or why not? [It only has three different pitches]."

In a different lesson, students may compare the sound of a different song with that of a known *do* pentatonic song to ascertain if they can hear scale type by categorizing it as "*do* pentatonic" or "other":

1. Students sing "Lucy Locket" using text (Musical Example 9.3).

Musical Example 9.3

Lucy Locket

Traditional

Lu - cy Lock - et lost her pock - et. Kit - ty Fi - sher found it.

Not a pen - ny was there in it, on - ly rib - bons round it.

2. The teacher tells the students, "Compare the sound of 'Lucy Locket' with the sound of 'Great Big House'—does 'Lucy Locket' sound like a *do* pentatonic song? [No] Does it have too many sounds? [No] Too few sounds? [Yes] What is the resting tone? [*mi*]."
3. Students sing and list all the solfège for "Lucy Locket" and circle the resting tone. The teacher asks, "Is 'Lucy Locket' a *do* pentatonic song? [No] Why or why not? [It only has three different pitches]."

Winding It Back—*Do* Pentatonic

In almost every classroom or ensemble, there will be students who become confused and "lost" as their peers move forward into more complicated melodic material. Because a teacher may have employed a winding it back paradigm from the beginning, it will already be apparent that some students are not ready to move forward with the class. For these students, winding back questioning and allowing students to level themselves in melodic exercises will allow them to continue to learn at their own pace, without embarrassment or a feeling that they are being remediated. The simultaneous learning offered through winding allows each student to be challenged at his or her own level: the content from winding back serves as a review for some students and honors the individual learning needs of others. A further advantage to this paradigm is that when students have always experienced music through the lens of winding (back and forward), they are aware that everyone is learning together, and different concepts can be mastered simultaneously.

A winding example for *do* pentatonic is discussed in the following vignette.

WINDING IT BACK BY SINGING FEWER PITCHES

As the students are singing "Great Big House" in solfège, Nelson needs to audiate and sing the *mi* to *sol* portion for assessment, rather than the entire song. He is still working on singing that minor third in tune and recognizing it in a song. We often allow students to work in pairs or small groups to find melodic elements or segments and present them to the class. This detective work is considered fun and can lead to a rousing round of handbell sight-singing (see the appendix "Solfège Games" on the companion website), with Nelson and a partner singing the *mi* and *sol* pitches as they are found in "Great Big House." Another small group may work with only the *mi, re,* and *do* pitches, while others work with the complete *do* pentatonic scale, providing simultaneous learning experiences for all students.

Deriving Scale Type for *La*-Centered Songs

Not all songs are centered on *do*. Students may know a number of songs that are centered on *la*, making *la* pentatonic the next logical scale type to be explored, due to the abundance of developmentally appropriate songs using that scale type. Before beginning formal instruction in *la* pentatonic as a part of scale study, the students should be able to do the activities listed in Figure 9.2.

Student name	Sings a variety of *la* pentatonic songs	Sings a variety of *la* pentatonic songs in solfège	Reads a variety of *la* pentatonic songs in solfège, from various staff placements	Decodes solfège of known songs and patterns that include *la, do, re, mi,* and *sol*	Uses solfège (*la, do, re, mi,* and *sol*) abstractly, in tone ladders and tone sets
Jeremiah	X	X	X	X	X
Steven	X	X			
Kaden	X	X	X		X
Hannah	X	X			

Figure 9.2 Readiness requirements for the study of *la* pentatonic.

The procedure for introducing *la* pentatonic might look like this:

1. Students sing a variety of songs and categorize them as "*do* pentatonic" or "other" and sing the resting tone.
2. Students sing the song "The Gallows Pole" using text (Musical Example 9.4).

Musical Example 9.4

The Gallows Pole

Traditional

Hang - man, hang - man, slack your rope, slack it for a - while.

Think I see my fa - ther com - ing, Ri - din' ma - ny a mile.

3. Students sing "The Gallows Pole" in solfège.
4. Students sing and identify the resting tone as *la*.
5. Students sing and list all the pitches used in the song as a tone set; the teacher writes the pitches from lowest to highest, leaving a space for the missing solfège (*l, drm s*).
6. The teacher circles the resting tone in the tone set.
7. Students count the number of different solfège pitches used, deriving "five" as the answer.
8. Students name the scale "*la* pentatonic" because *do* is the resting tone and "penta" (the Greek word for "five") indicates that there are five different solfège pitches.

This sequence is summarized in Figure 9.3 in a generic chart of steps that can be modified for use in identifying scale types.

Steps to identifying scale type	Date of mastery
Sing a variety of songs and name them as a known scale type or "other". Sing the resting tone.	
Sing a selected song in the new scale type with text.	
Sing the song in solfège.	
Sing and identify the resting tone in solfège.	

Figure 9.3   Steps for identifying scale types.

Steps to identifying scale type	Date of mastery
Sing and list all the pitches used in the song as a tone set; the teacher writes the pitches from lowest to highest, leaving a space for any missing solfège. Circle the resting tone in the tone set.	
Count the number of different solfège pitches used.	
Name the scale, with resting tone first, then the number of different solfège pitches (bi = 2 pitches, tri = 3 pitches, tetra = 4 pitches, penta = 5 pitches, hexa = 6 pitches). Tonic scales do not include fa; chordal scales include *fa*.	

Figure 9.3   (Continued)

To determine if students understand the meaning of the term "*la* penta-tonic," the teacher may ask questions such as:

- What if the song ended on *re*? Would it be labeled *la* pentatonic? (No)
- Would the *la* need to be changed or the "pentatonic"? (The *la*)
- Why? (*Re* is the resting tone so the song would be "*re* pentatonic")
- What if the song had the tone set *l, drm*—would it be labeled *la* pentatonic? (No)
- Would the *la* need to be changed or the "pentatonic"? (The "pentatonic")
- Why? (There are only four different pitches used so the song would be "*la* tetratonic")

Alternation between choral responses and individual student responses to these questions can be effective.

After using the same procedure with other *la* pentatonic songs (singing a song in solfège, deriving the pitches used and ordering them in a tone set, deriving and circling the tone set, and naming the scale "*la* pentatonic" or "other"), students may be asked to compare the sound of a *la* pentatonic song with a different song. Let's use "Rocky Mountain" as an example.

1. Students sing "Rocky Mountain" using text (Musical Example 9.5).

Musical Example 9.5

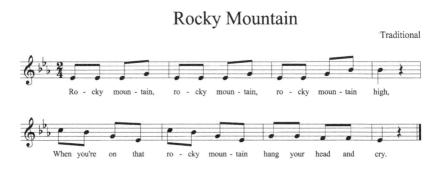

Rocky Mountain

Traditional

Ro - cky moun - tain, ro - cky moun - tain, ro - cky moun - tain high,

When you're on that ro - cky moun - tain hang your head and cry.

2. The teacher tells the students, "Compare the sound of 'Rocky Mountain' with the sound of 'Great Big House.' Does 'Rocky Mountain' sound like a *la* pentatonic song? [No] Why or why not? [The resting tone is *la*]." (See Figure 9.4.)

3. Students sing several songs using text, sing the resting tone, and categorize each as *do* pentatonic or *la* pentatonic:

'Liza Jane—verse	*do* pentatonic
Canoe Song	*la* pentatonic
Land of the Silver Birch	*la* pentatonic
Bow Wow Wow	*do* pentatonic
My Good Old Man	*la* pentatonic
Ida Red	*do* pentatonic

4. Students sing and list all the solfège for each of the previous songs and circle the resting tone.

5. Students explain why their answers were correct or incorrect.

Comparing two scale types	Date of mastery
Sing the text of two songs, singing the resting tone after each.	
Derive if the two songs have the same/different scale type.	
Cite evidence to support the same/different scale type.	
Sing song #1 in solfège, write down each solfège syllable, and circle the resting tone.	
Name the scale type for song #1.	
Sing song #2 in solfège, write down each solfège syllable, and circle the resting tone.	
Name the scale type for song #2.	
Review evidence previously cited to correct errors or confirm conclusions.	

Figure 9.4   Comparing scale types.

Winding It Back—*La* Pentatonic

In the study of scales, students are again reminded that we learn what is by what is not. By repeatedly and systematically learning to audiate and perform a *do* or *la* resting tone, students are asked to perform one task. If a student who needs winding is only asked to respond to one of the questions posed to the class, and if the question is always the same, it can serve as a point of assessment for that student. It is often helpful to use a question card or picture of the choice the student will be asked to make. We have given students this card before class or before the activity to allow for wait time before the question (which is always the same: e.g., "Is it *do* or *la* centered?") is asked. Teachers sometimes underestimate the power of wait time and options in response when winding back instruction for students.

Further Studies in Pentatonic (*Re* and *Sol*)

In chapter 9 of our companion website, you will find a continued and extensive discussion of procedures for other pentatonic tonal areas. This includes combining pitches into scale types, tracking progress for pentatonic scales, readiness requirements for *re* and *sol* pentatonic, and utilizing songs in a variety of scales to continue the dialogue begun here.

Diatonic Major

After developing an understanding of the sound and construction of several pentatonic scales, students have the readiness for work with diatonic major. A chart for tracking student readiness for diatonic scales can be found in chapter 9 of the companion website. The procedure for introducing diatonic major can look like this:

1. Students sing a variety of songs and categorize them as "*do* pentatonic" or "other" and sing the resting tone.
2. Students sing "The Swan" using text (Musical Example 9.6).

Musical Example 9.6

The Swan

Traditional

Sweet -ly the swan sings, Do - dee - a - doh, do - dee - a - doh, do - dee - a - doh.

3. Students sing the resting tone of "The Swan" and label it as "*do* pentatonic" or "other."
4. Students sing "The Swan" in solfège. The teacher asks, "Is 'The Swan' a *do* pentatonic song? [No] Other? [Yes] Why? [Contains too many pitches]."

5. Students sing and list all the solfège for "The Swan" and circle the resting tone. The teacher notes, "When the tone set of a song includes *ti* and the resting tone is *do*, the scale type is 'diatonic major.'"
6. Students sing several songs using text, sing the resting tone, and name the scale type:

Come, Follow	diatonic major
Dance Josey	*do* pentatonic (extended)
Let Us Chase the Squirrel	*do* tetratonic
We Love Cold Water	diatonic major

The notation for these songs can be found in the alphabetical collection of song notation in the companion website.

7. Students sing and list all solfège for each of the previous songs and circle the resting tone.
8. Students explain why their answers were correct or incorrect.

In a similar manner, natural minor will be compared to *la* pentatonic, so that students hear the difference in the scales before visually deriving that they are different. We have found that *la*-based minor is preferable to *do*-based minor for teaching scales and intervals. The rationale is that it is the most natural step to take from diatonic major and requires the fewest alterations. In our experience, students are able to audiate and theoretically understand *la*-based minor in a more meaningful way and at an earlier age. For additional discussion of tonal syllable systems, see "Selecting Rhythm and Tonal Syllables" in chapter 10 of the companion website. Before formal instruction in *la* minor (natural minor), students should be able to do the activities listed in Figure 9.5.

Student name	Sing a variety of natural minor songs	Sing a variety of natural minor songs in solfège	Read a variety of natural minor songs in solfège, from various staff placements	Decode solfège of known songs and patterns that include *la, ti, do, re, mi, fa,* and *sol*	Use solfège (*la, ti, do, re, mi, fa,* and *sol*) abstractly, in tone ladders and tone sets
Carissa	X				
Haley	X				
Evan	X	X			

Figure 9.5 Readiness requirements for the study of natural minor.

By referring to the chart in Figure 9.5, one can apply the steps to the introduction of natural minor. Students categorize a variety of songs as "*la* pentatonic," "diatonic major," or "other" to establish understanding of same and different scale types; sing a natural minor song such as "Sweet William" (Musical Example 9.7); derive the tone set and resting tone to confirm their audiation as "other"; and then name the new scale type "natural minor." Because instruction is presented sequentially, there are multiple access points for individual students: the lesson objective has most students on step 5 naming diatonic major, some are singing "The Swan" in solfège and labeling "*do* pentatonic" or "other," and some are challenged to additionally identify the scale type of "Come, Follow."

Musical Example 9.7

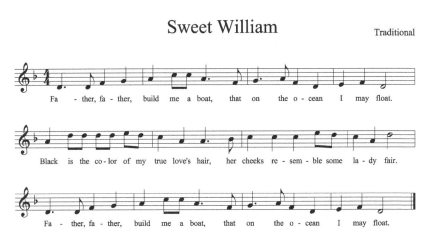

Additional songs such as those listed to follow can be used to reinforce audiation of natural minor:

Hey, Ho	natural minor
Frère Jacques	*do* hexachordal (extended)
Merry Minstrels	diatonic major
Zudio	*la* tetratonic
When Johnny Comes Marching Home	natural minor

Winding It Back—Diatonic Major and Natural Minor

Every one of us has what is considered an uneven profile regarding our knowledge and competence in various skills and understandings. This uneven profile (asynchronous development) is almost always exacerbated in students with special needs and for students who struggle in discrete areas of music (and other areas of education). Because of this, we sometimes work to increase a relative area of strength instead of ameliorate or assess a relative challenge. One way to do this is to ask the student to work in a different area of skill, as described in the next vignette.

RHYTHMIC IMPROVISATION

Julia uses a ventilator to assist with her breathing. She is not able to participate in melodic work through vocalizations. She is, however, very adept in the areas of rhythm and improvisation. Her teacher is just beginning natural minor with the seventh-grade choir and wants to be sure Julia is always participating in meaningful ways. She chooses to ask Julia to create a rhythmic improvisation to perform to "Sweet William." Julia chooses several rhythm instruments and performs a different rhythmic improvisation each time the choir sings "Sweet William." Her teacher is able to assess the current rhythmic elements and phrases with a checklist and is delighted to see Julia continuing to utilize more rhythmic ideas and unusual sounds when improvising.

Preparation for Harmonic Minor

The harmonic minor scale is then compared to both the *la* pentatonic and the natural minor scale. Students should be able to do the activities listed in Figure 9.6.

Student name	Sings a variety of harmonic minor songs	Sings a variety of harmonic minor songs in solfège	Reads a variety of harmonic minor songs in solfège, from various staff placements	Decodes solfège of known songs and patterns that include *la, ti, do, re, mi, fa,* and *si*	Uses solfège (*la, ti, do, re, mi, fa,* and *si*) abstractly, in tone ladders and tone sets
Zachary	X				
Spencer	X	X			
Makayla	X				

Figure 9.6   Readiness requirements for the study of harmonic minor.

An instructional sequence for introducing harmonic minor can be found in chapter 9 of the companion website.

Dorian and Mixolydian Scale Work

Our companion website includes a thorough discussion and strategies for teaching Dorian and Mixolydian scales. The website also provides specific repertoire and sequences for teaching these important scales. See "Readiness Requirements for the Study of Dorian," "Readiness Requirements for the Study of Mixolydian," and a chart for tracking progress of diatonic scales in multiple tonalities in chapter 9 of the companion website.

EXTENDING MELODIC UNDERSTANDING THROUGH THE STUDY OF INTERVALS

Melody is "measured" in intervals, the distance between two pitches. Successful study of intervals will yield an increased ability to understand the complexities of melody (horizontal audiation) and harmony (vertical audiation), as well as the theoretical knowledge to compose and arrange in a purposeful way. At its simplest level, melody contains steps and skips. Beginning as early as first grade, students can learn to identify simple intervals by progressing through a sequence.

In the sequence we are describing in this chapter, students begin their melodic study as they sing songs with very limited tone sets (*sol* and *mi* only, for example) within a lesson that includes more expansive tone sets and varied scales. When given the choice between "the high pitch" and "the low pitch," students are able to sing the songs, substituting the words "high" and "low" for the text of the song. To this adapted vocabulary, the students add body solfa to indicate where the "high" and "low" sounds might go on their bodies (shoulders and waist, respectively). They are then able to sing the song with the text "high" and "low" and kinesthetically demonstrate with body solfa. Because adequate conditions for simultaneous learning have been established, some students may be adding body solfa, while others are challenged to substitute "high" and "low" for the text of the song. The distance or "interval" between "high" and "low" can then be named a "skip." Students later learn to show a skip with hand signs and to sing the skip in these songs as *sol* and *mi*. When the pitch *do* is introduced, students will be able to identify all the skips among the known pitches: *sol-mi, mi-sol, mi-do,* and *do-mi.* A more detailed description and examples of this sequence can be found in chapter 3.

By incorporating several different songs with a slightly expanded tone set (*la* is added to *sol* and *mi*), students experience that the pitch *la* can be shown with hands above the head to indicate that it is a "step" higher than *sol.* When the pitch *re* is introduced to expand the tone set to *drm sl,* known steps now include *sol-la, la-sol, mi-re, re-mi, do-re,* and *re-do.*

Do Pentatonic Intervals

Before a formal introduction of *do* pentatonic intervals, students must know several *do* pentatonic songs that include skips and steps (*do, re, mi, so,* and *la*) and be able to sing those songs in solfège. The ability to decode neutral syllables or sounds of known songs and patterns into solfège is necessary for students to accurately audiate intervals. Students must also be able to use solfège abstractly, out of the context of known songs, through the use of tools such as a tone ladder and tone set.

One way to begin this study is to ask students to listen and watch as the teacher demonstrates singing *do* pentatonic intervals while pointing to the tone ladder. Students echo, singing *do* pentatonic intervals while reading from the tone ladder, as in Musical Example 9.8.

Musical Example 9.8 *Do* pentatonic intervals.

Students listen and watch as the teacher demonstrates singing *do* pentatonic intervals from the same starting pitch while pointing to the tone ladder. Students echo, singing from the same starting pitch while reading from tone ladder, as in Musical Example 9.9.

Musical Example 9.9 *Do* pentatonic intervals from the same starting pitch.

As with all sequences, each step is an assessment for the subsequent step. If at any point the students are experiencing great difficulty performing a particular step of the sequence, the teacher should wind it back to the preceding step to shore up any problems there before moving ahead on another lesson.

DO PENTATONIC INTERVALS

The third-grade music class was studying *do* pentatonic intervals. Emma was struggling: she could perform all the *do* pentatonic songs that her class had been singing for several years and could sing the *do* pentatonic intervals as they ascended and descended the scale, but was not yet able to sing those same *do* pentatonic intervals from the same starting pitch. Emma's music teacher helped Emma wind it back by asking Emma to echo each interval after the class sang it. This challenged the class, which was accustomed to singing the intervals one after the other without pause, and enabled Emma to have additional time to audiate the intervals from the same pitch. Simultaneous learning that served individual learning needs was achieved within the same lesson segment.

If *fa* is introduced next in the melodic sequence, students may explore intervals in the *do* pentachordal scale. A *do* pentachord interval sequence, titled "Intervals in *Do* Pentachord," can be found in chapter 9 of the companion website. The addition of *ti* completes the pitches needed for examination of diatonic major intervals.

Diatonic Major Intervals

Before beginning instruction regarding diatonic major intervals, students must know several songs in diatonic major that include skips and steps (*do, re, mi, fa, so, la, ti,* and *do'*) and be able to sing those songs in solfège. The ability to decode neutral syllables or sounds of known songs and patterns into solfège is necessary for students to accurately audiate intervals. Students must also be able to use solfège abstractly, out of the context of known songs, through the use of tools such as a tone ladder and tone set.

1. Students sing only the known major seconds while the teacher points to the tone ladder (Musical Example 9.10).

Musical Example 9.10 Known major seconds in diatonic major.

2. Students derive that *la-ti* is also a major second.
3. Students derive that *ti-do'* sounds different than a major second and that *ti-do'* sounds closer together (is a smaller step) than a major second. Students derive that the *ti-do'* interval is a minor second.
4. Students listen and watch as the teacher demonstrates singing diatonic major intervals while pointing to the tone ladder. Students echo, singing diatonic intervals while reading from the tone ladder, as in Musical Example 9.11.

Musical Example 9.11 Diatonic major intervals.

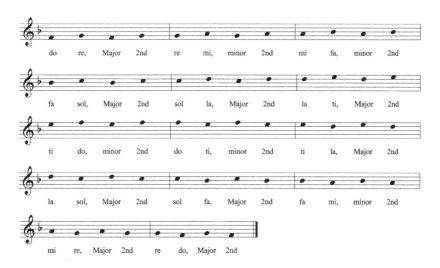

5. Students listen and watch as the teacher demonstrates singing diatonic major intervals from the same starting pitch while pointing to the tone ladder. Students echo, singing diatonic major intervals from the same starting pitch while reading from the tone ladder, as in Musical Example 9.12.

Musical Example 9.12 Diatonic major intervals from the same starting pitch.

Larger Intervals

Students will demonstrate, identify, and name intervals larger than minor seconds, major seconds, and minor thirds in much the same manner, first by listening to the teacher demonstrate and name the interval while referring to the tone ladder, then by echoing the singing. The recommended order to present larger intervals is as follows:

> major third
> perfect octave
> perfect fifth
> perfect fourth
> major sixth
> minor sixth
> major seventh
> minor seventh

PARTWORK: VERTICAL STACKING OF MELODY AND RHYTHM AS AN EXTENSION OF TONAL STUDIES

The study of partwork (performing more than one musical task at a time) begins very early in formal music education. Students are asked to speak a rhyme and show the macrobeat, sing a song and show the melodic contour of a phrase, tap a rhythmic ostinato while singing a song, and play a drone on a barred percussion instrument while singing a song on a daily basis in music class at the elementary level. The sequential introduction of part-work can be extremely helpful to all students, as each step in the sequence functions as an assessment for the subsequent step. A template for track-ing student readiness for partwork can be found in chapter 9 of the com- ⓟ panion website.

Winding It Back—Partwork

When a student is struggling to perform a partwork task, the teacher can wind back the partwork sequence to strengthen the skill before a student is asked to move ahead in the sequence. The types of partwork presented in this chapter include resting tone, drone, rhythmic ostinato, melodic ostinato, canon, root melody, tonic/dominant patterning leading to tonic/ dominant chords, and vocal chording.

WINDING IT BACK WITH PARTWORK

Vinny is having difficulty patting the macrobeat in one hand and the rhythm in the other hand while singing a song. His teacher asks Vinny to pat the macrobeat and microbeats instead (this step in the sequence is often less difficult than beat and rhythm combined). He is successful in this partwork experience. During the next music class, the teacher asks Vinny to pat the rhythm with one hand only while performing the melody. Vinny is able to do that. She then asks Vinny to pat the rhythm and the microbeats while audiating the melody. It takes two weeks for Vinny to accomplish this step. Once he is success-fully audiating, he is then able to sing and pat the beat and the rhythm simultaneously.

The Importance of Independence
When Performing Partwork

In all instances of partwork, students must be able to sing the given song entirely without the aid of the teacher. If the teacher's help is required in any way (showing motions to help students remember text, using hand signs to help students perform the melody correctly, joining in the song to help the students, etc.), the students are not ready to add partwork. The teacher may wish to use a different and better-known song to add partwork or to work on the chosen song until the students can sing without him or her.

Audiating the Resting Tone

By alternating the singing of a known song with the singing of the resting tone, the ability of students to sing in tune will increase greatly, as each pitch is compared to the resting tone the students are audiating. To follow is a sequence for teaching resting tone:

1. Students sing several songs with a pronounced resting tone. The teacher notes, "The final pitch of a song is called the 'resting tone.'"
2. Students sing a song using text, stopping on the teacher's clap. The teacher sings the resting tone (after a brief, unmetered breath, during which students audiate the pattern).
3. Students sing using text and identify whether the teacher is singing the resting tone or the text.

In a subsequent lesson, the teacher and students first review the previous step, with the students singing the text and the teacher singing the resting tone, which allows the teacher to assess group progress. They then switch jobs: students sing the resting tone (after an audiation breath) when the teacher stops singing the text. In the following lesson, the students will be asked to perform both jobs: singing using text, then switching to singing the resting tone at the teacher's clap (after an audiation breath).

In other lessons, students will do the following:

- Sing the resting tone (after an audiation breath) when the teacher stops singing on neutral syllable
- Sing the resting tone (after an audiation breath) when the teacher stops singing the text to songs previously unknown by the students
- Sing the resting tone (after an audiation breath) when the teacher stops improvising in solfège
- Sing the resting tone (after an audiation breath) when the teacher stops improvising on a neutral syllable
- Sing the resting tone (after an audiation breath) when the teacher stops improvising on the recorder or piano

---

WINDING BACK THE RESTING TONE

Cameron's class was practicing the concept of resting tone. Cameron needed more time audiating the resting tone, so the teacher sang a familiar song and had several students take turns singing the resting tone each time she stopped singing. When it was Cameron's turn, the teacher was careful to stop very frequently (at least every two beats) so that Cameron could remember the resting tone and sing it successfully, thus building his audiation.

The teacher honors the student's individual needs when he or she winds back a lesson segment, and this occurs ideally while the other students are also meaningfully engaged in learning. By allowing those other students to sing the resting tone first, the teacher challenged them while also allowing Cameron additional time to audiate. The resting tone lesson segments will not need to be in consecutive lessons but will need to be presented in a sequential order.

Extending the Singing of the Resting Tone into a Drone

By extending the singing of the resting tone into a drone, students must maintain their audiation of the resting tone for a more extended time period, further increasing their ability to sing with accurate intonation. To follow is a sequence for teaching drone:

1. Students sing using text; the teacher sings the resting tone as a drone using text.
2. Students identify that the teacher sang only one pitch but sang all the words to the song. They also identify that the teacher's only pitch was the resting tone of the song, *do*.
3. The teacher says, "We will define 'drone' as 'holding out the resting tone.'"

In a subsequent lesson, the teacher and students may switch jobs: students sing the drone using text ("stuck on a note"); the teacher sings the melody using text. To wind it back, students can sing the resting tone on the macrobeat pulse as an interim step before singing the drone.

The following lesson segments can be presented in subsequent lessons (see Figure 9.7):

- Half of the class sings the melody using text; half sings the drone using text. Then they switch jobs.

- The class switches jobs during the song at the teacher's signal.
- A small group of students sings the melody using text; a small group of students sings the drone using text.
- Individual students sing the melody using text; individual students sing the drone using text.

Curricular goal	Date of mastery
Student sings the text in a large group while the teacher sings the resting tone as a drone with text.	
Student sings the resting tone as a drone with text in a large group while the teacher sings the text.	
Student sings the text in a small group while the teacher sings the resting tone as a drone with text.	
Student sings the resting tone as a drone with text in a small group while the teacher sings the text.	
Student sings the resting tone pulse while another student sings the text.	
Student sings the text while another student sings the resting tone pulse.	

Figure 9.7   Assessment of drone.

These lesson segments need not be presented in consecutive lessons but must be presented in sequential order for the teacher to be able to wind it back. Within any lesson, small groups of students can be asked to sing particular tasks in sequential order, with one group's work serving as a challenge for their particular learning level and review for the next group's work (e.g., group 1 sings the text while the teacher sings the resting tone as a drone; individuals in group 2 are asked to sing the resting tone pulse with a partner singing the text).

Adding a Rhythmic Ostinato

Performing a rhythmic ostinato can be seen as an extension of beat keeping. A procedure for introducing rhythmic ostinato might look like this:

1. Students sing a song using text and patsch the beat.
2. Students sing a song using text and clap the beat.
3. Students sing a song using text and keep the beat in an alternating pattern (patsch, clap, patsch, clap, etc.).

4. The teacher notes, "When a pattern is stubbornly repeated, it's called an 'ostinato.'"
5. Students create a different two-beat ostinato by choosing other places on their bodies to keep the beat (head/shoulders, legs/chest, etc.).

Additional rhythmic ostinati can be extracted from rhythm patterns in the song itself. An example in the song "Great Big House" is as follows:

1. Students sing "Great Big House" using text (see Musical Example 9.1).
2. Students sing "Great Big House"; the teacher repeatedly taps the rhythm of phrase 2 ("forty stories high—") by clapping the eighth notes and patching the quarter notes.
3. Students derive that the teacher was not showing the macrobeats, the microbeats, or the rhythm of the song.
4. Students derive that the teacher was showing a pattern that stubbornly repeated; therefore, the teacher was showing an ostinato.
5. Students derive that the teacher's pattern started and ended at the same time as their song.
6. Students derive that the teacher's pattern matched the rhythm of phrase 2 ("forty stories high—").
7. Students sing "Great Big House" using text; the teacher taps the rhythm of phrase 2 by clapping the eighth notes and patching the quarter notes.

In a subsequent lesson, the teacher and students may switch jobs: students will perform the rhythm of phrase 2 of "Great Big House" as an ostinato, clapping the eighth notes and patching the quarter notes as the teacher sings using text.

The following lesson segments will be presented in subsequent lessons:

• Half of the class sings the melody using text; half performs the rhythmic ostinato. Then they switch jobs.
• The class switches jobs during the song at the teacher's signal.
• A small group of students sings the melody using text; a small group of students performs the rhythmic ostinato.
• Individual students sing the melody using text; individual students perform the rhythmic ostinato.

These lesson segments need not be presented in consecutive lessons but must be presented in sequential order for the teacher to be able to wind it back. Again, small groups or individuals can be given different tasks that are challenging to their individual learning levels, with these tasks being presented in a sequential order within the lesson segment (e.g., group 1 sings the ostinato with the teacher singing the text and switches jobs at the teacher's signal; group 2 is separated into pairs who sing the text while another pair performs the rhythmic ostinato).

Adding a Melodic Ostinato

In the same fashion, a melodic ostinato sequence can benefit all students. As with all partwork, students must first be able to perform the song (e.g., "Rocky Mountain" in Musical Example 9.5) without the aid of the teacher. The teacher can then accompany the song by singing the melodic ostinato; students identify that the teacher sang a stubbornly repeated pattern from the song, called an ostinato. The teacher and students exchange jobs, with the students performing the ostinato and the teacher performing the song. The size of the groups performing each job can vary, with fewer students singing the ostinato/song for additional challenge and more students singing the ostinato/song for additional support. Melodic ostinato is described in Musical Example 9.13.

Musical Example 9.13 "Rocky Mountain" ostinato.

hang   your   head   and   cry

Winding It Forward—Melodic Ostinati

It is ideal that all students have an opportunity to be assessed alone when performing partwork. However, it is not the expectation that all students achieve all steps in all sequences, as this would not serve their interests. Instead, consider these steps as additional challenge for those students with high music aptitude or those who have achieved all previous steps:

Students sing a melodic ostinato while the teacher

- sings a new melody on a neutral syllable,
- sings a new melody on text,
- improvises on a neutral syllable or in solfège, or
- improvises on a recorder or piano.

Students who are not yet ready for winding forward activities may continue to work on partwork activities in small groups at the level that currently challenges them (e.g., group 1 is divided into two groups who sing the melody with text or the melodic ostinato; the individuals in group 2 are assigned various winding forward activities that are performed simultaneously for added challenge).

Singing in Canon

There has been little research on the appropriate order for introducing partwork activities. With that in mind, canon can be introduced at approximately the same grade level as ostinato, as long as the students are able to sing several songs to be used in canon completely without the aid of the teacher. The following vignette examines an introductory sequence and winding ideas for canon.

WINDING A CANON

While Amir's class sang "Bounce High" (Musical Example 9.14) independently of Mrs. Frantz, she sang "Bounce High" in canon after two beats. The class was able to derive that Mrs. Frantz had sung the same song, starting and ending after the class. Mrs. Frantz named this "canon." In the next lesson, Mrs. Frantz sang "Great Big House" in canon with the class, and the class identified "canon." Next, Mrs. Frantz asked the class to sing after her in canon; Amir and his classmates were successful after reminding each other to start at the beginning of the song instead of continuing the song after Mrs. Frantz's entrance. In subsequent lessons and with a variety of songs, the class continued to practice singing in canon, first with half the class singing in canon with the other half, then with small groups of four to five students. As the size of the groups decreased, Mrs. Frantz recognized that Amir had not thoroughly audiated the canon, but had been following the singing and cues of other students. To wind it back, Mrs. Frantz had Amir sing in a group of five students, placing him in the middle of the five but with space between him and his neighbors. Amir's group sang first with another group singing in canon: Amir felt supported because he sat in the middle of the group and could hear himself singing accurately because of the additional space surrounding him. After several other small groups had performed the canon, Amir's group performed again with Amir sitting adjacent to the canon group. Amir was successful, and Mrs. Frantz made a note in her lesson plan to have Amir sing in the canon group in the next lesson.

Musical Example 9.14

Bounce High

Traditional

Bounce high, bounce low, bounce the ball to Shi - loh.

Once again, it is not the intention that every student completes each partwork sequence. Most students will be asked to perform in small groups in canon with the teacher at this time, while some students will need the additional challenge of singing alone and other students will need to sing in larger groups to learn successfully.

Introduction of Partner Songs

Because the students have learned a wide variety of songs in pentatonic, there will be many choices of songs to sing in canon. Two songs that are pentatonic and are the same length can be sung simultaneously, creating the first experience of partner songs. A sequence for introducing partner songs is as follows:

1. Students sing "Lucy Locket" using text (see Musical Example 9.3).
2. Students sing "Lucky Locket" using text while the teacher sings "Great Big House" (see Musical Example 9.1).
3. Students derive that the teacher was singing, but was singing a different song that started and ended at the same time as their own song.
4. Students derive that the teacher was singing the song "Great Big House."
5. The teacher notes, "When two different songs sound good when sung at the same time, they are called 'partner songs'" (see Figure 9.8 for a partner song example).
6. Students sing the partner song "Great Big House" while the teacher sings "Lucy Locket."
7. Students sing "Lucy Locket" while the teacher sings the partner song "Great Big House," switching at the teacher's signal (raises hand, shows a sign, taps a wood block).

Activity (i.e. canon, rhythmic ostinato or partner songs)	Sings song without help	Sings the song while another part occurs (i.e. ostinato, drone, canon)	Describes and identifies the other part	Performs the other part	Performs the other part while the song occurs	Performs the song and the other part simultaneously (i.e. tapping/ playing the ostinato, hand signing in canon)
Jonah						
Becca						
Simon						
Jaidyn						

Figure 9.8 Template for tracking progress in partwork activities.

Additional partner song combinations can be created from two songs in the same mode with identical chord changes (e.g., "Skip to My Lou" and "Paw Paw Patch").

Tonic and Dominant Harmonic Functions

When students begin to learn repertoire beyond the pentatonic scale types, tonic and dominant harmonic functions are implied. A simplified bass line called a "root melody" or the "chord roots" can then be introduced as a bridge to the study of tonic and dominant harmony. A sequence for introducing root melody is as follows:

1. Students sing "Paw Paw Patch" using text while the teacher sings the root melody in major (*do* and *sol* only) on a neutral syllable (Musical Example 9.15).
2. Students identify that the teacher sang something different than the students.
3. Students sing "Paw Paw Patch" while the teacher sings the root melody in major on a neutral syllable and identify whether the teacher is singing the melody or something different.
4. Students identify that the teacher sang only two pitches—one was a higher sound and one was a lower sound.
5. The teacher notes, "When a tune has only two pitches, complements the melody, and has no words, we call that a 'root melody.'"

Musical Example 9.15 (a) "Paw Paw Patch" and (b) root melody.

6. Students sing using text while the teacher sings the root melody in major in solfège (*do* and *sol*) and shows hand signs.
7. Students sing the root melody in major in solfège with hand signs while the teacher sings using text.

This root melody sequence can be wound forward to challenge students, as in the following vignette.

WINDING IT FORWARD WITH THE CHORD ROOT MELODY

The third-grade class had recently learned to accompany Ms. Hoffman's song with their performance of the chord root melody. To extend their harmonic audiation, Ms. Hoffman divided the class into two halves; group 1 sang "Paw Paw Patch," and group 2 sang the chord root melody in solfège with hand signs. When Ms. Hoffman played the triangle, the groups switched jobs (melody or chord root melody). The class enjoyed the demands inherent in audiating melody and chord root melody simultaneously. Ms. Hoffman recognized that Sylvie, Eliza, and Walid craved additional challenge, so in the next lesson the students sang the chord root melody in solfège, showing the *sol* hand sign in the right hand and the *do* hand sign in the left hand, while Ms. Hoffman sang "Paw Paw Patch." The activity repeated, with the students "playing" the *sol* with one finger on the right hand (as on an "air piano") and the *do* with one finger on the left hand. Finally, the students "played" the chord root melody and sang "Paw Paw Patch." Ms. Hoffman demonstrated how to play the chord root melody on the piano while singing "Paw Paw Patch"; Sylvie, Eliza, and Walid sang and played as well. Throughout the remainder of the marking period, two to three students volunteered to sing and play each lesson.

Tonic/Dominant sequence	Date of mastery
Sing a repertoire of songs including tonic and dominant functions, with text and chord root melodies	
Echo tonic and dominant tonal patterns, neutral syllable to neutral syllable	
Echo tonic and dominant tonal patterns, solfège syllable to solfège syllable	
Name tonal patterns that contain only *do, mi,* and *sol* as "tonic" (Musical example 9.19)	
Name tonic patterns and echo other patterns (dominant) when the teacher performs tonic and dominant patterns	
Improvise a series of tonic patterns, separated by the teacher's performance of intermittent dominant patterns to maintain intonation	
Improvise a tonic pattern different than the teacher's tonic pattern	
Name tonal patterns that contain only *sol, ti, re,* and *fa* as "dominant" (Musical example 9.20)	
Name dominant patterns and echo other patterns (tonic) when the teacher performs tonic and dominant patterns	
Improvise a series of dominant patterns, separated by the teacher's performance of intermittent tonic patterns to maintain intonation	
Improvise a dominant pattern different than the teacher's dominant pattern	
Improvise a series of tonic and dominant patterns, alternating according to a given pattern (TTDT, TDTDT, etc.) (Musical example 9.21)	
Improvise a series of tonic and dominant patterns, alternating according to a given pattern (TTDT, TDTDT, etc.) and applying a given rhythm pattern (strumming effect)	
Sing with assigned voice leading in a vocal chording sequence	
Sing with assigned voice leading in a vocal chording sequence, applying a given rhythm pattern	
Improvise a melody, accompanied by the class's vocal chording	

Figure 9.9 Tracking progress in a tonic/dominant sequence.

Musical Example 9.16 Tonic pitches in major.

Musical Example 9.17 Dominant pitches in major.

Musical Example 9.18 Rhythm pattern for tonic/dominant improvisation.

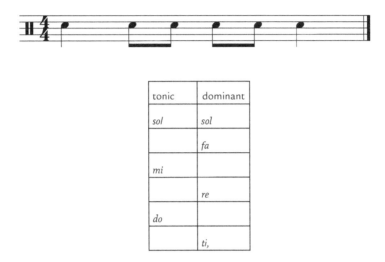

tonic	dominant
sol	*sol*
	fa
mi	
	re
do	
	ti,

Figure 9.10   Vocal chording sequence.

It has been our experience that most students are very motivated to work their way completely through this chord root melody sequence to perform alone, singing the text and playing the root melody on the piano.

The work of Dr. Christopher D. Azzara and Dr. Richard F. Grunow in harmonic improvisation has greatly influenced this next sequence (Azzara & Grunow, 1996). As students add chord root melodies to known songs in major, they begin to audiate tonic and dominant harmonic functions. The chart in Figure 9.9 can be used to track class progress in a sequence for introducing tonic and dominant harmonic functions.

Figure 9.10 provides a vocal chording sequence appropriate for students who are prepared for this level of independence. Musical Example 9.16 shows tonic pitches in major, Musical Example 9.17 shows dominant pitches in major, and Musical Example 9.18 shows a rhythm for use in improvisation using the tonic and dominant functions.

Charts for tracking progress of tonic/dominant function and subdominant function in multiple tonalities can be found in   chapter 9 of the companion website. In addition, instructional sequences for introducing tonic/dominant and subdominant in minor can be found in chapter 9 of ⓘ the companion website.

Form

An examination of form through folk dance, creative movement, singing games, songs, and art music can be found in the appendix in the compan- ⓘ ion website. The companion website also contains notation for songs cited in this book, as well as folk song sources for song material.

CONCLUSION

Successful teaching of the melodic learning process requires a thorough knowledge of the subject matter; the use of a variety of aural, kinesthetic, and visual teaching strategies; and a great deal of time and effort as we develop sequences to delineate the learning process for all students. It is our responsibility to ensure that the diverse learning needs of our students are consistently met and to provide the best music instruction possible. Through use of practical examples and ideas outlined in this chapter and in ⓘ chapter 9 of the companion website, you may begin to approach the melodic learning process with new strategies to enhance the success of your music instruction. The most successful strategies will be the strategies you develop with your specific students in mind. From the study of melody through the combination of pitches into scales and their measurement through inter- vals, teachers are led to organize their instruction into logical and sequen- tial steps so that these sequences can be used to wind back instruction for students.

Students who sometimes struggle to achieve melodic competencies are often unable to continue to increase their skills as their classmates move on to more difficult concepts. It is almost impossible for them to "catch up" at another access point because they missed some critical step earlier in the sequence. By adopting the philosophy that it is our responsibility to teach every student in our classrooms and to implement individualized instruc- tion and assessment strategies, we are accepting the challenge inherent in this statement. Through winding back and winding forward our skills and objectives, we will be able to teach and assess every student at each point in their knowledge acquisition. In doing so, we are finally teaching to the individual needs of our students.

REFERENCES

Azzara, C. D., & Grunow, R. F. (2006). *Developing musicianship through improvisation, Books 1-3*. Chicago, IL: GIA.

Choksy, L. (1974). *The Kodaly method I: Comprehensive music education*. Upper Saddle River, NJ: Prentice-Hall.

Gordon, E. E. (2012). *Learning sequences in music: A contemporary music learning theory*. Chicago, IL: GIA.

Hammel, A. M., & Hourigan, R. (2011). *Teaching music to students with special needs: A label-free approach*. New York, NY: Oxford University Press.

CHAPTER 10

Moving, Chanting, and Singing for All Students in Instrumental Music

SUSAN A. HARVEY, *Midwestern State University*
DAVID A. STRINGHAM, *James Madison University*

CHAPTER OVERVIEW

Moving, chanting, and singing are means by which teachers can help all students at a variety of developmental levels sequentially develop comprehensive musicianship skills in instrumental music contexts. These skills can be applied to preparing repertoire for performance, as well as generative creativity in music. This chapter will do the following:

- Describe techniques for helping students develop musicianship by learning tonal and rhythm content through singing and chanting, in a sound-before-sight and sound-before-syllable approach
- Transfer this content to their instrument to develop executive skills
- Apply singing, chanting, and moving activities to instrumental music rehearsals

Moving, chanting, and singing activities may be wound forward and back so that all students learn daily.

MR. MINCY INTRODUCES $\frac{6}{8}$

Pat plays third trumpet in the West Sometown Middle School Concert Band. He and his peers have just performed their first concert of the year, and they arrive the next day to begin preparing for their next concert. Their teacher, Mr. Mincy, steps onto the podium, raises his hand for silence, and leads them through their warm-up routine. Students engage in breathing exercises, count through a series of unfamiliar eighth- and sixteenth-note rhythms, and play their B-flat major scale in whole notes, half notes, and a rhythm pattern used in their state for performing scales at solo festival auditions. Then, they open their folders to find their new pieces. One is an arrangement of "The Washington Post March." Instead of the $\frac{4}{4}$ time signature, to which Pat and his peers are accustomed, they see " $\frac{6}{8}$." Mr. Mincy goes to the blackboard and begins an explanation of counting in $\frac{6}{8}$. Now, instead of counting to four in each measure, students should count to six. Instead of a quarter note getting a beat, now an eighth note gets a beat. Instead of four beats per measure, there are now six. To make sure students understand, Mr. Mincy leads them through several counting exercises. Students dutifully count to six and tap their feet as instructed, but many seem confused and uncomfortable. The ensemble then proceeds to read the beginning of "The Washington Post March." Pat tries his best to count to six in his head but finds himself seeing the opening notes and thinking "1, 2 & . . ." Students spend the next 15 minutes of class becoming increasingly frustrated, as does Mr. Mincy, who is exasperated, but he remains patient and reminds students, "You're not counting."

Many of us who have taught beginning instrumental music ensembles can connect with the story in the previous vignette. Beginning instrumental music instruction often emphasizes associating written notation with fingerings and durations to produce a concert in a reasonably short amount of time. This approach promotes preparing a concert performance but can seem at odds with the *winding it back* framework articulated by Hammel and Hourigan in chapter 1.

JEAN

Jean began playing clarinet in fourth grade. She studied with a private teacher and performed in All-District Band every year of middle and high school. Jean loved music and performance so much that she decided to major in music education. As a college freshman, she failed first-semester ear training and sight-singing. By second semester, she was discouraged and changed her major. Jean could not match pitch with her voice and therefore could not sight-sing. As a clarinet player, Jean was never asked to sing in class or listen for harmonic function. She was taught to play expressively and to balance within the ensemble. Although Jean was talented, her potential for musical understanding was never reached. She could not audiate melodic passages prior to playing and became frustrated when asked to demonstrate skills she had not experienced prior to college.

Many teachers can think of a classmate or former student whose experiences are similar to Jean's. Instrumental music instruction at all levels often focuses on learning to perform notated music on an instrument. This approach sets a single group-level goal (e.g., perform "Procession of the Cyborgs"), which may alienate students who find this objective too easy or difficult. Further, opportunities to sequentially develop musicianship skills, such as moving, chanting, singing, and creating music, are often absent in instrumental music settings that prioritize performance from notation. Consistently engaging in sequential chanting, singing, movement, and creative activities offers students multiple access points and learning levels. Students apply these skills not only when performing on their instrument but also when creating their own music through arranging, composition, and improvisation (Gordon, 2012; Green, 2014; Woody and Lehmann, 2010). When students become fluent with rhythm and tonal syllable systems, many teaching strategies can be wound back and forward to simultaneously challenge students at all levels of musicianship, addressing each student's individual learning needs. These strategies are also valuable for practice at home, to help students experience success, increase their motivation, and improve their self-esteem.

To ensure students develop musicianship skills in the secondary instrumental classroom, we suggest instruction that honors students' general music backgrounds and builds on knowledge of rhythm and tonal syllable systems to help students understand how notes relate to one another (see chapters 5 and 6). Learning to group individual notes in meaningful ways and anticipate musical events can inform multiple ways for students to listen to, perform, create, and read music. These systems also provide frameworks to wind instruction forward and back, helping teachers provide adequate conditions for simultaneous learning. There are many considerations associated with choosing tonal and rhythm syllables. Comparison charts, detailed descriptions, musical examples, and teaching demonstrations to help teachers choose systems most appropriate for their students can be found in "Selecting Rhythm and Tonal Syllables" in chapter 10 of the companion website.

Mr. Mincy's students described in the first vignette will benefit from a variety of teaching strategies to become independent decision makers. All students can develop musicianship by using rhythm syllables, moving in meter (i.e., small and large beats) while chanting rhythms, reading rhythms in a variety of forms (e.g., independent of pitch, in melodic contexts), and performing rhythm duets. Jean, in the second vignette, would develop musicianship by using tonal syllable systems (e.g., solfège, numbers) to help her audiate and sing melodies, resting tones (i.e., tonal centers), bass lines, and other material in multiple tonalities (e.g., major, minor, Dorian, Locrian); read melodies and tonal patterns in a variety of forms (e.g., independent of rhythm, in melodic contexts); and sing and play chamber music. In this chapter, we describe teaching strategies and activities for helping students demonstrate musicianship, executive skills, and music performance. Through multiple means of engagement, representation, action, and expression, or universal design for learning (UDL; Center for Applied Special Technology, 2011), students show their understanding in a variety of ways (e.g., beat demonstration; rhythm syllable expression; visual, aural, or kinesthetic strategies) to create individualized experiences that honor their individual learning needs, principle 1. By winding instruction forward and back and applying UDL principles in an instrumental music learning environment, any student may demonstrate skills within an ensemble. These opportunities allow for students to demonstrate skills at multiple access points, principle 2, and provide an environment for simultaneous learning in the classroom setting, principle 3 (see chapter 1).

ESTABLISHING FOUNDATIONS OF RHYTHM THROUGH MOVEMENT
Steady Beat

As stated in earlier chapters (chapters 1 through 4), establishing a sense of steady beat is fundamental. If a student cannot feel a steady beat, he or she will neither be able to perform at a steady tempo nor understand concepts of beat division. Activities to develop a sense of steady beat include patting the thighs or other body parts, tapping the feet or heels, stepping in place, swaying to a steady beat, snapping fingers, or echoing verbally. By including some of these activities in rehearsal, students learn basic beat and rhythm skills and have practice opportunities within the ensemble. These activities provide many access points for students at a variety of learning levels.

Students may be comfortable with some of these activities more than others; each student needs to find a natural way to demonstrate steady beat. For example, Conway, Marshall, and Hartz (2014) describe a variety of flow activities (e.g., painting broad brushstrokes on an imaginary canvas, tracing the sun's path), weight activities (e.g., externalizing style and volume contrasts), and elasticity-of-time activities (e.g., conducting a ritardando or accelerando, stepping accurately to large beats getting faster or slower) intended to help instrumental music students develop beat competency.

Grunow, Gordon, and Azzara (2001, p. 281) suggest a sequence of activities for beginning instrumentalists to develop "physical coordination and rhythm readiness" using large beats only (in duple meter, large beat = one hundred; in triple meter, large beat = seventy-two). These activities could be assessed using a chart similar to that in Figure 10.1.

	Duple	Triple
*Move both arms in the same direction (up and down) while sitting with elbows resting on a desk or tabletop		
*Move both arms in the opposite direction (one arm is up while the other is down) while sitting with elbows resting on a desk or tabletop		
*Swing both arms in the same direction (front and back) while standing		
*Sway the upper part of the body from side to side while sitting		
*Move both feet (heels only—up and down) in the same direction while sitting		
*Move both feet (heels only) in the opposite direction (one is up while the other is down) while sitting		
*Move both arms and both feet together in the same direction while sitting		
*Stand and rock in place. With both feet on the floor, shift the weight from one foot to the other with knees bending. The weight should be on the heel of one foot when the weight is on the toes of the other		

Figure 10.1   Large beat movement assessment chart.

In the previous sequence, a teacher can wind instruction forward or back by inviting students to self-level where they feel comfortable, and advance in the sequence from that point. For example, a student who struggles with gross motor skills may not accurately demonstrate a more advanced skill (e.g., moving feet independently in opposite directions). He or she might practice an easier skill (e.g., moving both feet in the same direction to a steady beat) until prepared to advance in the sequence. Winding instruction forward or back to meet students' needs aligns with the three principles guiding this book: honoring each student, providing multiple access points for learning, and providing conditions for simultaneous learning.

Beat Divisions

Once steady beat is established, all students need to feel divisions of the beat. Students demonstrate beat and beat divisions in many different ways; it is important for each student to find comfortable combinations for demonstrating rhythm through movement. For example, Grunow et al. (2001, p. 281) suggest that students do the following:

1. Stand and rock in place to [large beats]. Tap thighs with both arms and hands to duple [small beats] and with only hands to triple [small beats].
2. Sit and move both feet (heels) in the same direction to [large beats] and both arms and hands to duple [small beats] and only hands to triple [small beats].

Other possible combinations appear in Figure 10.2.

	Duple	Triple
*Students (individuals or sections) play either large beat or small beat on their instrument while someone else performs the other.		
*Students tap a large beat on one thigh with one hand and tap small beats on the other thigh with one hand.		
*Students step large beats in place while clapping small beats.		
*Maintaining large beat in dominant hand and small beat in nondominant hand, switch hands (large beat nondominant and small beat in dominant)		
*Alternate hands every eight, four, or two beats		
*Alternate hands every three, five, or seven beats		
*Step large beat and tap the small beat with two fingers (e.g., pointer and middle) in opposite palm		

Figure 10.2 Large and small beat movement assessment chart.

All teachers have students who perform rhythm and beat competencies at different difficulty levels. The creative movement activities described in chapter 4 may be useful in these situations.

Chanting Basic Rhythms

As students demonstrate large beats and small beats in duple and triple meter, they also learn to chant rhythm patterns on neutral syllables and rhythm syllables. We suggest a sequence for introducing these patterns later, in "Moving, Chanting, and Singing to Develop Musicianship."

ESTABLISHING FOUNDATIONS OF TONALITY THROUGH SINGING IN INSTRUMENTAL MUSIC
Resting Tones

Just as moving to and internalizing a sense of steady beat and beat division help students develop a sense of meter, beginning to audiate tonal centers, or resting tones, helps students begin to develop a concept of tonality (please see chapters 3, 5, and 9 to learn more about helping students audiate and sing resting tones.

Melodies and Bass Lines

Students learn to sing complete melodies and bass lines on a neutral syllable. Longer melodies can be taught in phrases as needed. Learning bass lines with melodies is important to help students hear tonal centers, audiate harmonic progressions (providing context for more structured activities described later), and begin developing the musical vocabulary they can use to create their own music. Students may sing bass lines to music in their method books, melodies taught in class by ear, and music they are learning. With daily practice, students begin to audiate harmonic function to melodies in major, minor, and other tonalities (e.g., Dorian, Mixolydian). This encourages students to audiate bass lines and harmonies while playing a single line. Singing bass lines can be wound back for students who need to hear tonal centers (e.g., they would only sing tonic). To wind this forward, students could start to sing harmonies after learning to sing bass lines. All students could participate at the same time, yet be challenged appropriately. With the addition of instruments, students again would self-level when playing melodies, bass lines, and harmonies previously sung.

Foundations for Generative Creativity

Learning to sing melodies and bass lines helps students develop a vocabulary they can use in creating their own music. For example, given an antecedent phrase from a familiar tune, students improvise a consequent phrase in response. "Green Bushes," in Musical Example 10.1, is from a folk tune in the second movement of Vaughan Williams's *Folk Song Suite*.[1] In this example, the original melody appears in four-measure antecedent phrases, followed by sample improvised consequent phrases. This task could be wound back by asking students to improvise rhythms on chord roots or inner voices, or wound forward by asking students to improvise antecedent phrases or pairs of antecedent and consequent phrases (see Azzara & Grunow, 2006, for a variety of sequential improvisation activities of this nature). Students could also be asked to compose four-measure consequent phrases.

Musical Example 10.1 Original antecedent phrases and improvised consequent phrases for "Green Bushes."
"Green Bushes" from *Folk Song Suite* (Ralph Vaughan Williams), published by Boosey and Hawkes.

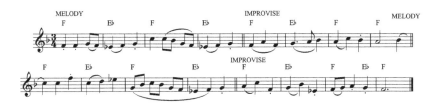

MOVING, CHANTING, AND SINGING TO DEVELOP MUSICIANSHIP IN INSTRUMENTAL MUSIC

We have used activities similar to the following to help our students develop their musicianship. "Selecting Rhythm and Tonal Syllables," found in chapter 10 of the companion website, includes examples of rhythmic and tonal syllable systems, as well as hierarchies through which these systems can be sequenced.

Neutral to Neutral (Babble)
Chanting

Before introducing any rhythm syllable system, a neutral-to-neutral (babble[2]) approach is a basic means for students to access and experience rhythm. Once a foundation is established, a syllable system may be added.

To begin this process, the teacher musically chants a four-beat pattern on a neutral syllable (e.g., "bah" or "doo"). Students respond by musically chanting the same four-beat pattern on a neutral syllable, as a group or individually, beginning on the following large beat (see Musical Example 10.2).

Musical Example 10.2 Four-beat pattern on a neutral syllable.

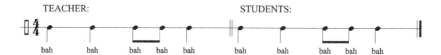

After students echo, the teacher expressively chants another rhythmic pattern in time. This pattern can be the same pattern as the first if students need another attempt, a more advanced rhythm if students are successful, or an easier pattern if students need more preparation for the pattern they are performing incorrectly. In this way, a teacher can wind instruction back or forward in "real time." By chanting with a neutral syllable, students internalize how small and large beats interact in a given meter, without focusing on learning syllables or repeating numbers. Students learn to internalize pulse and subdivision and maintain large and small beat movement while listening and chanting. Movement, as well as chanting, is assessed individually (movement through observation and chanting by calling on students to perform alone) or in groups. Students echo teacher-modeled patterns and can be invited to improvise four-beat patterns on a neutral syllable. Students chant improvisations as a group or individually. Improvising in a group alleviates the anxiety some students have about sharing their own creations, which is especially common if these are unfamiliar activities. Teachers are responsible for creating a safe environment where individual students share improvisations. Sharing individually allows a means for individual student assessment; however, developing a culture in which students are comfortable improvising individually may take time. Figure 10.3 suggests ideas for creating a safe environment for improvisation.

1. Let volunteers improvise first.
2. Encourage all students.
3. Always provide positive feedback.
4. Be excited to hear each student, even if his or her improvisation is simple or poorly executed.
5. Assign parameters if they help students feel safe (e.g., improvise using only large and small beats).
6. Give a student advance notice so they may prepare to improvise (e.g., at the beginning of class, a day or two in advance).
7. Listen to students alone prior to having them perform in front of the class.
8. Model improvising for your students.
9. Encourage students to write down ideas to incorporate in their improvisation.
10. Help students articulate attributes that make some improvisations more successful than others.

Figure 10.3   Creating a safe environment for improvisation.

As students become comfortable improvising, teachers informally assess each student. Assessment criteria could include listening for steady tempo, playing large and small beats in time, articulation (e.g., tonguing on wind instruments, bow technique on string instruments, correct wrist movement on percussion instruments), and performing with characteristic tone on their instrument.

A nonthreatening improvisation assessment technique is for students to stand in a circle facing the outside. As students improvise as a group, the teacher walks around the outside of the circle to assess each student. Students perform improvisations at the same time, but students can hear themselves because they are facing out. At the end of class or the activity, the teacher places a check in columns for students who demonstrated large and small beats. Comments can be made in regard to other music skills (e.g., posture, technique, breath support, tone). The teacher may not assess each student every day, especially in large ensembles. Assessing in nonthreatening ways allows students to experience success, develop self-esteem and self-worth, and preserve their dignity.

Using a checklist (see Figure 10.4) and taking notes allows the teacher to assess formatively and plan instruction that meets all students' needs. For example, when students improvise, they self-level, winding it forward or back to meet their personal comfort level. Students may perform rhythms with which they are comfortable to increase their chance of success. Some students challenge themselves by winding it forward using the most challenging rhythms they know or experimenting with familiar and/ or unfamiliar rhythms. Other students continue to reinforce beat or beat division, developing fundamental skills. Again, the teacher documents student abilities and plans accordingly.

Name	Executive Skills									
	Correct Hand Position	Date Observed	Correct Instrument Position	Date Observed	Correct Playing Posture	Date Observed	Correct Embouchure	Date Observed	Correct Articulations	Date Observed
Kotter	✓	12-Sep	✓		✓	12-Sep	✓	14-Sep	✓	23-Sep
Indigo	✓	12-Sep	✓		✓	12-Sep	✓	14-Sep	✓	24-Sep
Ralph	✓	12-Sep	✓		✓	12-Sep				
Nathan	✓	12-Sep	✓		✓	12-Sep	✓	16-Sep	✓	23-Sep
Veronica	✓	12-Sep	✓		✓	12-Sep	✓	16-Sep	✓	23-Sep
Lesley	✓	12-Sep	✓		✓	12-Sep	✓	14-Sep	✓	24-Aug

Figure 10.4 Assessment Checklist for Executive Skills.

Assessment allows the teacher to recognize students' strengths and areas for continued development. For example, the assessment shown in Figure 10.4 may suggest that Ralph may need instruction wound back for embouchure and articulation while Nathan needs instruction wound forward with the addition of lip slurs based on embouchure. By listening to students' improvisations, the teacher might notice that Kotter tends to rush when playing macrobeats or that Lesley is comfortable performing syncopations, and the teacher could wind rhythm instruction back or forward, respectively. Instruction can be planned to address each student's individual learning needs (principle 1).

After assessing students, the teacher may provide accommodations by limiting functions for certain students (e.g., large and small beats) and/or allowing other students the opportunity to incorporate other functions they may feel comfortable improvising. Improvisation allows many students to respond based on their level of readiness and comfort. Students may challenge themselves and try new rhythm or tonal patterns. Through this self-leveling process, students demonstrate readiness for more advanced rhythm functions.

Singing

Similar strategies are applied to singing. Students who sing learn to hear patterns of pitches and intervals, including complete melodies, which are applied to performing on an instrument. A teacher begins a pattern sequence with two or more pitches from the selected tonal hierarchy (see Musical Example 10.3). The teacher sings a tonal pattern using a neutral syllable (e.g., "bum" or "bah"). Before students respond, the teacher pauses and encourages them to take a deep breath before performing the pattern. This pause and subsequent breath encourage students to audiate and perform each pattern, rather than simply imitate it. The teacher cues this deep breath, and students echo the pattern on a neutral syllable. For students to have a kinesthetic experience with intervals and begin foreshadowing labels, incorporate Curwen-Glover hand signs with tonal patterns (see body solfa in chapter 3, Table 3.1, and hand signs in chapter 5 of the companion website).

Musical Example 10.3 Tonal patterns for neutral syllable echoes.

Patterns are composed of two or more notes, depending on students' music achievement. Some hierarchies may promote learning patterns based on tonal functions, while others are based on intervals (see chapter 9). All students start by learning simple intervals (e.g., a minor third) or harmonic functions (e.g., I and V7 in major tonality) in the selected hierarchy to establish a foundation. More complex intervals, harmonic functions, and tonalities are added as students demonstrate the ability to audiate and sing patterns of increasing difficulty. This concept may be wound back to the comparative high/low before pitch matching occurs (see chapters 3, 5, and 9 for pitch-matching strategies).

While learning to echo tonal patterns, students can be invited to improvise similar tonal patterns on a neutral syllable. As with rhythm improvisation discussed earlier, students improvise individually or in a group. Student responses vary; some sound like tonal babble, suggesting that the student is not audiating intervals or functions within the hierarchy. Other student improvisations reveal that they are grouping pitches by intervals or harmonic functions, in spite of not learning tonal syllables.

Syllable to Syllable
Chanting

To teach students rhythm syllables, the teacher chants a pattern using the selected rhythm system and students respond chanting the same pattern (see Musical Example 10.4). These patterns are the same ones used to teach neutral-to-neutral echoes as described earlier. Through a process similar to language development, students become fluent with verbal syllables and associate them with rhythms they previously learned. Asking students to improvise a different four-beat pattern in response to the teacher, using the same rhythm functions and syllables, reinforces fluency (see Musical Example 10.5 for an example). As students become comfortable chanting these rhythms with syllables, more advanced rhythm syllables from the selected hierarchy are introduced. For more information on rhythm syllables, please see "Selecting Rhythm and Tonal Syllables" ⓑ in chapter 10 on the companion website.

Musical Example 10.4 Rhythm pattern with syllables for syllable-to-syllable echoes.

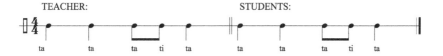

Musical Example 10.5 Sample four-beat improvisation using large and small beats.

As students externalize (through movement and chanting) large beats, small beats, and more advanced rhythm functions (e.g., subdivisions), they begin to internalize these elements of meter. Often, teachers use amplified metronomes in rehearsal. Instead, by engaging students in movement and learning rhythm patterns, students learn to maintain internal pulse themselves, without relying on external aural stimuli. The teacher does not need to keep time by clapping, tapping, or using a metronome. If students change the tempo, the teacher stops the ensemble, asks students to chant one or more patterns in the desired tempo, and then restarts the music at that tempo. No direction needs to be given regarding what students performed incorrectly; students hear they are not playing in time, re-establish the tempo by chanting, and are ready to continue rehearsing.

Singing

Once students sing patterns successfully using a neutral syllable, pitches are named using solfège, numbers, function, or tonality (e.g., tonic, dominant, major, minor). The teacher sings the same pattern used when singing with a neutral syllable, but replaces the neutral syllable with solfège or numbers (see Musical Example 10.6). Students associate these new syllables with patterns they already know.

Musical Example 10.6 Echoing tonal patterns with syllables.

After students successfully sing patterns using solfège or numbers, more complex patterns with additional functions or intervals are learned (first at the neutral syllable level as described earlier). For example, in an interval-based hierarchy, a teacher beginning with *sol-mi* would add *la* after students successfully sing *sol-mi* patterns. Different combinations of *sol, mi,* and *la* are sung until students are ready to add the next new note.

Students improvise patterns composed of the same pitches in response to their teacher. For example, students learning major tonic patterns composed of *do, mi,* and *sol* could respond by creating a new pattern of the same function, as in Musical Example 10.7.

Musical Example 10.7 Sample student tonic tonal pattern in major tonality.

Winding It Back and Forward

Students in instrumental ensembles sing at varying skill levels. Some are singing for the first time and learning to match pitch with their voices. Some are unable to match pitch, but make aural discriminations (e.g., differentiate between high and low, identify same and different). For these students learning to sing, concepts may need to be wound back to demonstrate differences and allow them to participate in vocal exploration exercises (please see appendix). Once students match pitch, they learn to sing patterns based on the selected tonal hierarchy. To facilitate assessment, teachers create a checklist (see Figure 10.6) for each pattern, interval, or tonal function that reflects the selected hierarchy (see chapters 5 and 9).

More advanced students read Curwen-Glover hand signs, with half the class following one hand and the other half following the other. Students learn to sing intervals that may be challenging to tune when performing, including minor seconds (e.g., *mi* and *fa*). When students experience challenging intervals through singing, they learn to center each pitch and balance them in the ensemble by matching volume. The interval produces a color that sounds different from the dissonance initially sung. Singing challenging intervals in tonal contexts focuses student attention on pitch and encourages students to transfer skills to improve intonation in instrumental performance.

Singing and chanting patterns are wound forward by challenging students to provide syllables for a pattern the teacher chants or sings using a neutral syllable (e.g., "bah"). Students respond by chanting with rhythm syllables or singing with tonal syllables (solfège or numbers; see Musical Example 10.8). More advanced students enjoy the challenge of improvising patterns with syllables in response, containing the same (or different) intervals or functions implied by the teacher pattern. This is a challenge for students depending on their choices with regard to tonal and rhythmic functions, intervals, or tempo.

Musical Example 10.8 Neutral-to-syllable rhythm pattern echo.

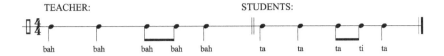

Neutral-to-Instrument Chanting and Singing

To begin neutral-to-instrument transfers, students perform rhythmic and melodic patterns on an instrument after hearing their teacher chant a rhythm pattern using a neutral syllable (e.g., "bah"). Students respond by performing the pattern on an instrument on a given pitch. We encourage beginning students to start performing rhythm patterns as soon as they can play one note. A student's ability to perform patterns on a wind instrument is based on the ability to articulate patterns on their instrument (tonguing) and employ appropriate technique (e.g., fingering). For example, students may chant sixteenth-note patterns but not yet have psychomotor skills to play them on an instrument. By teaching students to play patterns aurally, students develop muscle memory with tonal understanding before seeing patterns in notation. Students focus on listening, including tone, intonation, musicality, and blend, when chanting and singing instead of reading notation. Often, musicality is one of the last skills students add to their performance, often focusing on notes and rhythms first; however, by chanting and singing musically prior to performing, students transfer that musicality to their playing.

Students begin playing tonal patterns once they can play two notes on an instrument. Students develop psychomotor skills without the distraction of considering on which line or space a pitch is notated. Once students play simple patterns successfully, more complex patterns and new notes are added. Without focusing on reading patterns, students focus on tone and coordination involved in changing notes. For example, flute students need considerable coordination to move between C and D in the staff. If students isolate the two notes by echoing a melodic pattern performed by their teacher (see Musical Example 10.9), they listen to the pitches and try to match what they audiate and sing.

Implementing an aural approach allows teachers to wind back instruction to help students who do not understand placement of notes on a staff to demonstrate other skills (e.g., correct fingering, tone production, articulation). Inviting a more advanced student to lead tonal echoes for the class or encouraging students to learn to perform these patterns on a secondary instrument can wind pattern activities forward.

Musical Example 10.9 Sample melodic patterns for aural echoing.

If students first visually process notated combinations of the two notes, they focus attention on deciphering which note is on the line and which is on the space. The fingering becomes primary, and listening is no longer a focal point. As students develop coordination, new notes can be added. For example, after students successfully play combinations of *mi, re,* and *do,* the teacher then sings different combinations of the three notes (see Musical Example 10.10).

Musical Example 10.10 Sample melodic patterns in G major.

As students progress, melodic patterns advance to imply harmonic progression. A convenient source of such patterns is melodic material from songs with tonic and dominant chords or tonic, dominant, and subdominant chords. "Common Tunes for Instrumental Education," found in chapter 10 of the companion website, includes lists of titles categorized by harmonic content.

Neutral-to-instrument techniques apply to melodies and bass lines that students learn to sing on neutral syllables. See Musical Example 10.11 for an example of teaching the beginning of "Twinkle, Twinkle, Little Star" using short melodic patterns.

Musical Example 10.11 Melodic patterns from "Twinkle, Twinkle, Little Star."

Learning to play melodies by ear on an instrument helps students strengthen the connection between sounds they audiate and those produced on their instrument, and reinforces musical vocabulary they are learning to sing and audiate. Students learn to play melodies and bass lines from any repertoire, including ensemble music, folk tunes (see companion website), holiday music, music for specific occasions (e.g., "Happy Birthday"), and music they listen to on the radio. Students self-level when given opportunities to identify songs they wish to learn. They try to match instrument sounds with an aural image they are audiating, often finding new notes on their instruments. For example, if a teacher assigns students to learn to play a melody of their choice by ear, one student may learn "Down by the Station" because he or she is comfortable with the range and it reinforces a fingering that challenges him or her. Another student may select a melody in minor tonality because the sound of that tonality intrigues him or her. A more advanced student may choose to learn a melody in major tonality and then learn it in minor tonality, or learn a tune in triple meter and then learn to play it in duple meter. Through these activities, students can demonstrate skills at different individual levels (principle 2) and learn tunes in multiple tonalities and meters simultaneously within a classroom (principle 3).

More complex activities allow for winding instruction forward, giving students opportunities to think like improvisers, composers, and arrangers as they manipulate musical elements such as tonality and meter. For some students, the teacher needs to wind back the concept of selecting a melody to learn by ear. The teacher guides the student to select a song that uses few notes (e.g., "Mary Had a Little Lamb") and helps the student find the beginning pitch. The student may need to break the melody into smaller pieces (e.g., be asked to sing the first two measures before trying to play the first two measures) or be guided toward important structural pitches to play (e.g., *mi* and *do*). The teacher may break the concept down further by having the student indicate through movement the melodic contour of the phrase, with or without Curwen-Glover hand signs. All students can learn in the instrumental classroom. By winding it forward and back, teachers provide opportunities for simultaneous learning for all students within the same classroom (principle 3).

When students learn to audiate melodies and perform them on their instruments, they often make up fingerings. The teacher becomes a facilitator, teaching students better fingerings for notes learned on their own. Once a student learns a song, encourage that student to teach other students the melody. Students teach themselves to play other melodies they know or want to learn (e.g., movie themes, pop music they heard on the radio).

Instrument to Instrument

Teachers play an instrument and have students respond by playing rhythm or tonal patterns. Students learn, from their teacher's modeling, how to shape a rhythmic or melodic phrase, articulate, release notes, and match note length. Teachers play patterns on different instruments. This allows each student to imitate tone, fingering, instrument position, posture, breathing, and articulation on his or her instrument.

Demonstrating all instruments provides a visual model for students learning executive skills (e.g., posture, hand position, instrument position, bow technique, mallet position, mallet technique). When a teacher models an instrument, students observe and often change notes based on watching the teacher. By rotating instruments, students have to listen because a visual is not always present. The teacher also can block fingerings with a stand or lead patterns from the rear of the class.

Melodic patterns can be taught in four-beat patterns, without pauses or audiation breaths between the teacher model and student response. When the teacher plays a melodic pattern, the student responds and plays the pattern back without pause. This reinforces student ability to maintain beat while performing. The teacher continues to play melodic patterns, alternating four beats with students playing back the pattern. The pause sometimes turns into an extra beat instead of unmetered processing time. Students are more successful if melodic echoes begin with stepwise patterns when playing patterns. To teach melodic patterns, the beginning pitch is given to students. The teacher plays a four-note pattern (see Musical Example 10.12 for an example). Students start on the same pitch and play the pattern.

Musical Example 10.12 Four-note melodic pattern.

do   do   re   mi

After students echo, the teacher begins the next pattern on the last pitch played (in this example, *mi* [concert D]). Students know where to begin the next pattern, using the same fingering they last played. If students do not end on the correct pitch, the teacher repeats the pitch for four beats so that students determine which pitch they are supposed to be performing. Within the melodic pattern, rhythm can be appropriate to student abilities (e.g., large and small beats for beginning students).

Melodic patterns can be wound back and forward. For example, a student struggling to learn a four-note melodic pattern might be asked to identify the first and/or last note. A student who quickly grasps the melodic pattern can be challenged to learn it in another key (e.g., "Make E-flat *do*, and figure out the pattern in Musical Example 10.12").

To wind this pattern back, the teacher teaches the melody in smaller chunks as melodic patterns, which are later connected to perform a phrase or the entire melody. Learning to echo a teacher's model (with good intonation, characteristic tone, good executive skills, and expressive performance) helps students focus on these skills without the distraction of reading notation.

Improvising melodic patterns, inspired by patterns provided by a teacher, is an example of winding it forward. Parameters for these improvisations can vary from few (e.g., "Improvise a four-beat melodic pattern in response to my four-beat melodic pattern") to many (e.g., "Improvise a four-beat melodic pattern that starts on *mi*, ends on *do*, and uses only large beats"). See Musical Example 10.13 for examples of what students may improvise in response to these two prompts. These improvised patterns could be echoed by the class and/or transcribed and used as future melodic patterns in the classroom. A checklist such as the one in Figure 10.5 could be used to assess students' responses.

Musical Example 10.13 Sample student improvisations in response to four-beat melodic pattern.

Playing melodic patterns without notation allows students to demonstrate scalewise and chordal patterns. When students audiate patterns and know fingerings, they more easily apply them when reading them in notated music. Some students have excellent tonal audiation but may not have skills to read notation. These students can demonstrate aural skills and learn to hear bass lines, melodies, countermelodies, and harmonies and to improvise, compose, and arrange.

Name	Tonal Improvise Sing sol-mi	Date Observed	Tonal Improvise Sing sol-la	Date Observed	Tonal Improvise Sing mi-la	Date Observed	Tonal Improvise Play sol-mi	Date Observed	Tonal Improvise Play sol-la	Date Observed	Tonal Improvise Sing mi-la	Date Observed
Kotter	×	9/17	×	9/25								
Indigo	×	9/17										
Ralph	×	9/19	×	9/25								
Nathan												
Veronica	×	9/19	×	9/27								
Lesley	×	9/20										

Figure 10.5   Assessment Checklist for Tonal Pattern Improvisation

VISUAL PRESENTATION

When students first experience rhythms and melodic patterning aurally, through babbling, singing, chanting, and playing by ear, subsequent visual presentations of music notation are easier to understand. Students' aural skills are ahead of their reading skills—as they should be.

As students begin interacting with notation representing a tonal or rhythm system, each pattern can be added to a tonal or rhythm bank on a bulletin board. Students can keep a tonal or rhythm bank handout in their music folder as a reference at school and home. Students notate each new pattern as they learn it and write syllables under patterns in their bank as needed (Musical Example 10.14). To wind this back, some students may need a sheet with one familiar pattern they already perform well and one new pattern in either duple or triple. The rhythm syllables may be written in for the student. To wind this forward, some students may have all possible combinations of sixteenth notes in both duple and triple.

Musical Example 10.14 Sample rhythm elements.

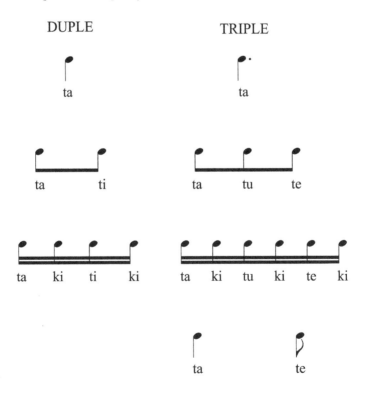

DUPLE   TRIPLE

ta   ta

ta   ti   ta   tu   te

ta   ki   ti   ki   ta   ki   tu   ki   te   ki

ta   te

TONAL AND MELODIC PATTERN PRESENTATION

Students who learn a vocabulary of tonal and melodic patterns by ear and on their instruments and who understand solfège or numbers associated with those patterns are ready to read and comprehend notation. The notion of "reading music" is often confusing to students without this readiness, and students often resort to simply associating notation they read with fingerings on their instrument. As Grunow (2005) notes:

> Reading language requires more than merely saying words with the correct pronunciation; [similarly,] reading music requires more than "counting" rhythms and relating note names to fingerings on an instrument. Reading involves comprehension. . . . Students who are taught to decode notation by "counting" rhythms and by associating note names with fingerings or keys on a musical instrument are not reading with comprehension. To portray such behaviors as anything beyond "lower level" skills would be an exaggeration. (pp. 186–187)

To facilitate students' comprehension of notation, present students with familiar tonal or melodic patterns in a variety of forms (e.g., flashcards held by the teacher, notation that students may already have in their folder, rhythm and tonal ladders [see chapters 5 and 6], excerpts a teacher has notated with notation software, and projects using technology). It is helpful for the teacher to reinforce the connection between what students already audiate and play and what they are now seeing in notation. For example, students should identify and sing *do* on the staff (or the resting tone for that tonality); melodic (in a rhythmic context) and tonal (not in a rhythmic context) patterns may be echoed by students as described in the syllable-to-syllable section earlier, but this time with notation. Students may need reminders to attend to the notation rather than sing and play by ear.

Once students read familiar patterns in notation, the teacher interjects unfamiliar material to create new excerpts for students to read. For example, a student who can sing, play by ear, and read "Amazing Grace" in concert F major might be asked to read one of the melodies in Musical Example 10.15. These examples can easily be wound back or forward for each student; reading could be wound back with simpler rhythms or limited range, or wound forward by creating examples in another clef, key, and/or meter. The three examples in Musical Example 10.15 are easy, moderate, and advanced difficulty, respectively. Examples like this could be transposed to different clefs and different keys for various instruments; students could be given excerpts of varying difficulty without feeling singled out.

Musical Example 10.15 Melodies of varying difficulty for reading, based on "Amazing Grace."

In addition to notating familiar tonal and melodic patterns, students can compose patterns. This activity extends to writing complete melodies to use as reading exercises similar to Musical Example 10.15. Composition can be wound back or forward for each student; in many cases, students will self-level by writing music they can audiate. An example of winding it back would be asking a student who struggles with writing a new melody to write tonal patterns for each chord in the harmony implied by the melody (see Musical Example 10.16 for an example using tonic, dominant, and subdominant harmonies); a more advanced student could be challenged with composing in a different meter or tonality.

Musical Example 10.16 Tonal patterns for tonic, dominant, and subdominant harmonies.

RHYTHM CARDS

Rhythm cards (see Figure 10.6) are effective for developing student rhythm reading skills (see Chapter 6). Once students experience rhythms kinesthetically and verbally, they are prepared for visual presentation. See Figure 10.7 and Musical Example 10.17 for strategies to incorporate reading rhythm cards and performing rhythm duets in an instrumental rehearsal.

---

* Students chant rhythm while moving to large and small beats.
* Students play rhythm on the same pitch.
* Half of the students sing or play the rhythm on one pitch; the other half sing or play the rhythm on a different pitch. The teacher can assign pitches to create consonant or dissonant intervals that are more or less challenging to tune.
* Students sing or play the rhythm on three or more pitches to create chords, and work on balance, blend, and intonation of those chords. To wind this activity forward, build chords that are more challenging to tune (e.g., seventh chords, minor chords).

Figure 10.6 Rhythm Card Strategies

---

* Half of the students chant one rhythm, half chant the other.
* Half of the students sing or play one rhythm, half sing or play the other. To wind this activity forward or back, assign more consonant or dissonant intervals that are more or less challenging to tune.
* Half of the students perform one rhythm on a triad; half perform another rhythm on a different triad. This prepares students for polytonality they may encounter in more advanced repertoire (e.g., Ives, *Variations on America*; Persichetti, *Pageant*; Schuman, *George Washington Bridge*; Zdechlik, *Chorale and Shaker Dance*).
* One student (or group of students) performs an assigned rhythm, while other student(s) improvise a rhythm pattern of the same length with same or different functions.
* Students compose a rhythm duet to be performed by their peers.

Figure 10.7 Rhythm Duet Strategies

Musical Example 10.17 Rhythm duet.

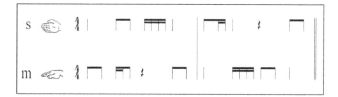

When performing a rhythm card or rhythm duet, students self-level if given a choice of notes to play. An example: Orchestra students choose from the notes A, C-sharp, or E to perform a rhythm card. Some violinists choose the A string because the A string may be the first string on which students learned to play and are most comfortable, the A string is an open string that allows them to focus on bowing, or it provides the root of the chord that the student is most comfortable performing. Other students may choose to play C-sharp, because the third of the chord sounds different or exciting or offers a challenge of finger placement beyond performing on an open string.

Self-leveling opportunities enable students to challenge themselves, to practice what they need, or to feel safe in what they do well. Another self-leveling activity is to allow students a choice of two rhythms to play as a rhythm duet. One rhythm would be easier when compared to the second and more challenging rhythm. Students who like or want a challenge may select the harder of the two rhythms. Students who need the easier rhythm may select the easier rhythm.

CHANTING AND SINGING TO ENHANCE EXECUTIVE SKILLS IN INSTRUMENTAL MUSIC ARTICULATIONS

Chanting and singing also promote other performance objectives, such as articulation. For example, students echo neutral syllable patterns selected to reinforce articulation for their instrument (e.g., "doh" for low brass; "too" for flutes; "tee" for single-reed instruments, trumpets, and horns). All students chant at the same time with different syllables (see Musical Example 10.18). This develops student articulations for attacks, tongue placement, and physical motions inherent to playing a particular instrument. After chanting articulation syllables, students echo patterns on their instruments; students also can use these articulation syllables to improvise rhythms.

Musical Example 10.18 Instrument-specific neutral-to-neutral rhythm pattern echo.

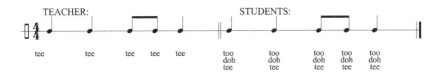

Music Style and Phrasing

Students develop musical style by imitating teacher models of tonal and rhythm patterns that suggest varied styles. Styles include, but are not limited to, march, staccato (separated), legato (connected), and swing. Teacher models also demonstrate common musical phrasing. Students learn that music has constant direction, with ebb and flow of phrases (i.e., adding crescendos and decrescendos). Students improvise to explore varied interpretations of a particular phrase (e.g., experiment with dynamics and articulations) or practice a new style (e.g., "What would a variation on 'London Bridge' sound like if played in a swing style?"). To wind this back, students may focus on playing in one style (e.g., legato), on one pitch (e.g., concert F), to practice performing in a legato style. To wind this forward, students could add expressive elements to improvisation on scalewise patterns and leaps, alternate between legato and staccato styles every four measures, or trade solos by common phrase lengths (e.g., four measures, eight measures).

Tone Development

During rhythmic echoing with instruments, students try to match their teacher's tone and pitch. By modeling patterns on each instrument, the teacher allows students opportunities to hear a characteristic tone on every instrument. Aural presentation of instrument tone through echoing allows students to focus on developing tone without the distraction of reading. Teacher modeling can be wound forward to include more advanced skills (e.g., vibrato, growling, more challenging bowing techniques on string instruments) and other musical styles (e.g., learning to play lead alto in a big band, fiddling), and is important at all levels of instruction.

Intonation

Singing allows students to experience balance and blend in the ensemble without concentrating on executive skills associated with performing on their instruments. When students play instruments, balance, blend, and intonation skills transfer from singing. Students who learn to sing in a tonal context start adjusting intonation before instrument-specific intonation tendencies are taught. (See Bernhard, 2002, for a review of the literature on this topic.) When playing duets, students start hearing intervals that have been sung. When singing a major chord, students learn to automatically adjust the third and fifth. The same applies to performing on instruments. When students perform in an ensemble, they start adjusting the intonation to match what they sing. More advanced students can play rhythmic echoes on pitches of chords that are used in a piece of repertoire. For example, students can perform rhythmic echoes on pitches of a V7 chord and be given additional responsibility to tune the chord, perform with a specific articulation, or perform with appropriate style.

If students learn Curwen-Glover hand signs with solfège, a teacher can display a hand sign for students to play. When playing from hand signs, students anticipate pitches, know how to play each note that is signed, and compare the pitch they perform with the one anticipated based on the teacher's visual model. This activity can be wound forward by dividing the class into two groups and using hand signs (one hand for each half of the class). Teachers can model hand signs that suggest a variety of intervals at varying levels of difficulty, encouraging students to learn at different levels simultaneously (principle 3).

New Notes and Tonal Centers

Instrumentalists also learn new notes and new tonal centers (keys) through singing and echoing melodic patterns. For example, orchestra students who have learned the notes G, A, B, and C (i.e., *do, re, mi,* and *fa* in G major) can learn a new note before seeing the notation. The teacher shows the new fingering for D. The students have been singing melodic patterns with C and D to prepare for the new note. The students sing the note D. The teacher plays D, and then students play D. The new note (D) is then introduced in melodic patterning sequences. Students use their aural skills to hear when the new note occurs in the melodic sequence and they demonstrate understanding of the note by echo playing melodic patterns. The patterns could start on *do* (G), then ascend scalewise to *fa* (C). Patterns could then go between *fa* and *sol* (C and D) so that students practice the new fingering and/or bowing while adjusting intonation.

New tonal centers can be taught to students aurally. For example, in beginning band, students typically learn concert B-flat and then concert E-flat. Once the note concert A-flat is taught, the teacher starts a melodic echo on concert E-flat. When playing a scalewise sequence, students expect to hear combinations of *do, re, mi, fa,* and *sol.* Since E-flat is the new tonal center, students will expect to hear concert A-flat as *fa* and will aurally recognize that concert A-flat must be played to match the expected sequence. If an A is performed (see Musical Example 10.19), students hear that it is incorrect.

Musical Example 10.19 Melodic patterns in E-flat major.

Winding Executive Skills Back and Forward

Some students are able to demonstrate alternating between two notes at a slow tempo. More advanced students may play scalewise patterns, scales in thirds, and arpeggiated chords at fast tempos and with complex rhythms. Students who are developing a skill, such as the flute player learning to go between C and D, may develop the skill practicing "Hot Cross Buns" in the key of B-flat. The student knows the tune from singing in class. If the student needs to wind it back further, the student may play an adapted melody (with only C and B-flat) while one or more other students play the entire melody. Another option is to transpose "Hot Cross Buns" to a different key that allows the student to play the entire melody while avoiding the challenge of fingering D to C (see Musical Example 10.20). At the same time a student is learning "Hot Cross Buns," a more advanced student is learning "Alouette," increasing tempo and learning it in a new key (principle 3).

Musical Example 10.20 Examples of winding it back for "Hot Cross Buns."

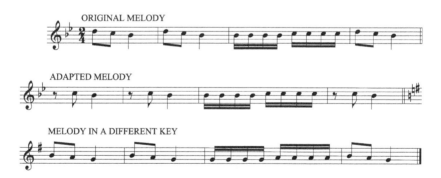

APPLYING SINGING AND CHANTING TO PERFORMANCE
Putting It All Together: Look, Listen, Perform

Look, Listen, Perform (LLP; Harvey, 2010) is a process for teaching students to read and play music. LLP is used to teach beginning students using any method book, and for advanced students learning complex music. LLP includes practice strategies that are taught in class and transferred to students' home practice. *Look* refers to strategies (see Figure 10.8) to observe notation.

Key Signature	Melodic Patterns
Time Signature	Rhythmic Patterns
Accidentals	Repeats, Endings, D.S., Coda
Unusual Fingerings	
Fingering Patterns (e.g., scalewise, arpeggiated, chordal)	

Figure 10.8   *Look Strategies.*

Listen refers to strategies that guide students to audiate, sing, and develop psychomotor skills before performing on an instrument (see Figure 10.9). Strategies are used depending on student abilities. Some strategies require critical thinking skills to wind concepts forward.

* Teacher sings melody on tonal syllables; students visually follow notation while listening to melody and phrasing
* Teacher and students sing while using Curwen-Glover hand signs
* Teacher sings while students listen and practice fingerings
* Students sing while using Curwen-Glover hand signs (teacher establishes context and starts students)
* Students sing written pitch names while practicing fingerings
* Students sing written pitch names while using Curwen-Glover hand signs
* Students blow air through their instrument while practicing fingerings (but not playing)
* Students chant rhythm while moving to large and small beats
* Students chant rhythm while practicing fingerings on their instrument
* Students silently audiate melody while using Curwen hand signs
* Students silently audiate melody while practicing fingerings on their instrument

Figure 10.9   *Listen* Strategies.

Perform is the last step in the process. Students perform the exercise, etude, or melodic passage. The lists of *Look* and *Listen* strategies demonstrate many ways students prepare to play their instrument. Some strategies are easy, while others are advanced. These strategies are designed for use in the classroom to teach students a variety of ways to learn to audiate and perform music. When students learn to play from a method book or learn new music, the teacher selects three or four listening strategies from Figure 10.9 before students perform the exercise. The next song in the book can use different strategies or focus on areas in which students are developing or need to be challenged. Teachers can implement a variety of strategies to challenge all students and invite students to share ideas for more or less challenging activities they may have discovered in their own practice. The next vignette is a sample teaching sequence Mr. Mincy uses to apply these strategies to "Procession of the Cyborgs"[3] (melody in Musical Example 10.21).

MR. MINCY'S TEACHING SEQUENCE FOR "PROCESSION OF THE CYBORGS"

As Mr. Mincy's students begin work on this piece, they find the melody in their part (trumpets and horns, mm. 5–12; flutes, clarinets, and alto saxophones, mm. 13–20; low brass and low woodwinds, mm. 29–36). Mr. Mincy sings the melody with solfège beginning on *re* (concert C) while students listen and finger their instruments.

Next, he asks students playing first clarinet to identify the note in their part that does not match what was sung. (The correct answer is measure 16, the fourth measure of the tune, in which first clarinets play a concert G in harmony with the concert D notated in the melody.) Mr. Mincy sings the melody, then the first clarinet part, so all students hear the difference.

Mr. Mincy sings the melody again, reminding all students to listen for phrasing and reminding students playing first clarinet to audiate a different note in measure 16. Students listen and finger along, then sing using solfège. Depending on their success, Mr. Mincy may choose to sing the passage again with students.

Once students have experienced success singing the passage with solfège, they sing it on note names (written pitches) and finger along on their instruments. Mr. Mincy concludes work on this section by inviting students to play the entire melody and congratulates them on their improved intonation and phrasing.

Musical Example 10.21 Melody from "Procession of the Cyborgs."

"Procession of the Cyborgs" challenges students because it is written in Dorian tonality. Students begin singing on the resting tone, *re*. Once students learn the melody, they are told where the harmony part begins. A similar sequence to the one used to teach the melody (see the previous vignette and Musical Example 10.21) can be used to teach harmony. As students learn the harmony, strategies in Figure 10.10 can be used to wind instruction back and forward.

Winding It Back
- Students sing while fingering.
- Teacher sings while students practice fingerings.
- Individual students receive adapted parts in which they always play the melody.
- Students are asked to highlight and play only notes they are currently able to play.

Winding It Forward
- Half the students sing the melody and the other half sing the harmony (then, have groups switch parts).
- Students play the melody while the teacher plays the harmony (then, switch parts).
- Half the students play the melody and the other half plays the harmony (then, have groups switch parts).
- Students play their part and adjust the balance.

Figure 10.10   Strategies for Winding Harmonic Instruction Back and Forward

In this approach, students are asked to engage in each activity by doing something different or listening to something new. Students who develop skills aurally contribute more meaningfully to the ensemble; in turn, the ensemble becomes more successful as a whole. Most important, students become independent musical decision makers who utilize these skills in informed lifelong pursuit of musical activities.

Written Pitches

To learn note names, students sing using written pitches (letter names) for their instrument. When singing a flat or sharp, such as B-flat, students sing "flat" instead of singing "B-flat." Singing "B-flat" is two syllables and changes the rhythm. Similarly, students sing "sharp" when they have a sharped note (e.g., F-sharp, C-sharp) to avoid changing the rhythm. Another system may be used if the teacher prefers not to sing "flat" or "sharp." Students sing "ess" at the end of the note letter (e.g., "bess" for B-flat, "ess" for E-flat, "ahss" for A-flat). If notes have a sharp, "-eese" is added to the letter to create new syllables (e.g., "geese" for G-sharp, "feese" for F-sharp, "eese" for E-sharp).

Written pitch names may be taught from the first note students learn to play on their instruments. Students read melodic patterns, melody fragments, and melodies while singing pitch names for their instrument. See Musical Example 10.22 for an example of this activity using the first four measures of "Lightly Row" (notated in Bb major). Students playing B-flat instruments sing note names in C major, students playing E-flat instruments sing note names in G major, and students playing F instruments sing note names in F major. To wind this forward, students use Curwen-Glover hand signs to show tonal context for the pitch while singing written pitch names. Students also finger the note on their instrument while

singing note names. Singing written pitches and learning note names reinforces note-reading skills. Learning pitch names helps students (1) learn
note names, (2) avoid referring to a note with a fingering (e.g., showing a
fingering for a B-flat without knowing the note is called B-flat), and (3) realize that *do* is a different note when the tonal center changes.

Musical Example 10.22 Four measures of "Lightly Row" with transposed written pitches.

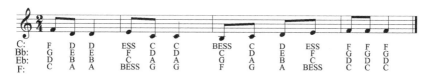

Chording

Chording (Hammel and Harvey, 2009) is one method for students to learn
harmonic function. When students know five successive diatonic notes,
they can use those notes to sing and play a tonic triad. In chording, students first learn to perform the tonic triad (see Musical Example 10.23),
then add other chord functions (e.g., dominant, subdominant). Students
can begin chording using a sequence in Figures 10.11 and 10.12.

---

1. With solfège syllables from Figure 10.12 on the board, the teacher models singing notes
   from the chords (see Figure 10.14) while pointing to corresponding syllables.
2. Students sing these notes while the teacher accompanies (e.g., piano, guitar) to provide
   harmonic context.
3. Students apply their knowledge of the teacher's selected tonal system to determine
   which notes in a given key will produce these pitches on their instruments.
4. Students perform these notes on their instrument while the teacher accompanies to
   provide harmonic context.

Figure 10.11 Introducing Chording

Musical Example 10.23 Series of tonic patterns for chording.

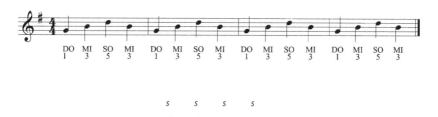

Figure 10.12 Visual Representation of Chording

Students add bass lines to chording using the sequence of pitches outlined in Musical Example 10.24 (in B-flat major for wind and percussion instruments) and the teaching sequence in Figure 10.13.

Musical Example 10.24 Series of pitches for chording.

DO MI SO MI   DO MI SO MI   SO FA RE TI   DO MI SO MI

1. With solfège syllables from Figure 10.14 on the board, the teacher models singing the chords while pointing to corresponding syllables.
2. Students learn the bass line (i.e., *do-do-sol-do*) for this progression.
3. Divide students into two groups; one group sings the bass line while the other sings chord tones as modeled by the teacher; then switch parts.
4. Repeat Step 3 with students performing on their instruments.

Figure 10.13　Adding Bass Lines to Chording

Creating Chorales

Skills learned in chording activities extend to students creating their own chorales. Students can first choose among chord tones to create a chorale of only tonic chords, using only whole notes. While the teacher encourages students to play different chord tones during the chorale, students will self-level (see Figure 10.14) when selecting pitches, choosing notes they consider easiest, most challenging, or most interesting in their harmonic function. By experiencing all parts, students learn to feel and hear how pitches function when playing the root, third, or fifth of a chord. Students transfer this skill to performing music with others when making adjustments in pitch based on the part of the chord they are playing.

After students become comfortable with a chorale of tonic chords, adding a dominant chord (V7), and subsequently a subdominant chord (IV), allows even beginners with limited range to self-level, playing notes in the chord and improving their ability to hear and understand harmonic function.[4] Students begin by singing the chord notes in a I-I-V7-I chord progression (see Figure 10.14). Students may need to learn fingerings for low *ti*.

To further understand harmonic function, students learn chord resolutions in the chord progression I-I-V7-I. Students sing possible resolutions starting on *do* (i.e., *do-do-low ti-do, do-do-re-do*). Once students sing both resolutions, half the class sings *do-do-low ti-do* and the other half sings *do-do-re-do*. The teacher assists by modeling Curwen-Glover hand signs as needed. When

Figure 10.14 Voice-leading resolutions for tonic and dominant harmony in major tonality.

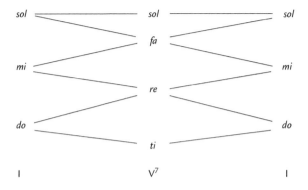

students can sing the resolutions in tune, they play each on their instrument, and then half the class plays one resolution while the other half plays the other resolution. This creates harmony on the V7 chord because *ti* and *re* are played at the same time. Students sing then play all possible resolutions starting from each pitch in the chord (i.e., *do, mi, sol*) and then add a subdominant chord to create a I-IV-V7-I progression (see Figure 10.15). Students can choose a starting pitch from the tonic chord and make resolution choices. Students enjoy performing *fa*, the seventh, once they realize that note adds color to the chord.

As resolutions are taught, students create chorales as part of their daily warm-up. Students create a chorale using a series of tonic chords, first by singing, then by playing. Students play a whole note for each chord. Students select a starting chord tone to perform and are given the option to change on each chord. Some students self-level and choose to sing and play the bass line; others choose chord resolutions. On the board would be information similar to that in Figure 10.15.

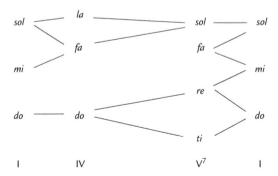

Figure 10.15 Voice leading resolutions for tonic, dominant, and subdominant progression in major tonality.

Arrows can be added to Figure 10.15 to help students visualize all possible resolutions. The teacher may play piano with the chords, to reinforce harmonic function, while students sing or play instruments.

IMPROVISING MELODIES AND ACCOMPANIMENTS

Students may improvise vocally on a neutral syllable ("bah") while the rest of the students sing an assigned part. For example, students sing or play pitches with an assigned group to create the following pattern:

Group 1:	sol	sol	sol	sol
Group 2:	mi	mi	re	mi
Group 3:	do	do	ti	do
Chord:	I	I	V	I

While the students sing or play their assigned part, another student vocally improvises on a neutral syllable (e.g., "bah") or on an instrument. Students learn that dissonance creates color, and if their improvisation sounds dissonant, they can resolve dissonance by using passing tones. This is an opportunity to improvise freely. Eventually, a blues progression can be introduced for musicians to chord and improvise.

Students can also learn to improvise harmonies. This activity might begin with a song with tonic and dominant chord functions (e.g., "Skip to My Lou," in Musical Example 10.25).

Musical Example 10.25 Melody and chord changes for "Skip to My Lou."

Students can create their own accompaniments based on chord resolutions. Their part can be sung or played. One student can perform the melody while others harmonize.

Another example is to use the following chord progression:

Group 1:	*sol*	*la*	*sol*	*sol*
Group 2:	*mi*	*fa*	*mi*	*re*
Group 3:	*do*	*do*	*do*	*ti,*
Group 4:	*do*	*fa,*	*do*	*sol,*
Chord:	I	IV	I	V

Once students can chord, another student can learn by ear the melody to a familiar song that uses this chord progression, such as "The Lion Sleeps Tonight." This activity can also be taught in minor tonality. For example, "Zum Gali Gali" (see companion website) can be harmonized with a minor triad, with students chording on *la, do,* and *mi.* Students learn the melody by ear, play it on their instruments, and compose their own arrangement after learning to sing the song. In creating their arrangements, students may choose to move among chord tones in the minor tonic harmony. To wind this activity back, give parameters to meet student needs and allow students to demonstrate their learning at multiple levels (principle 2). This may include, but is not limited to, suggesting easier and more challenging note choices, giving students a chording pattern, or selecting part of the melody to play (e.g., *la-la-ti-do*) as an ostinato.

Beyond these activities, once students learn to hear rhythm, tonal, and melodic patterns and internalize harmonic function, they will arrange melodies they know by ear (e.g., themes from *Star Wars*). Some will write compositions for full band to perform in concerts. Students often compose music inspired by other people (e.g., family member, friend, historical figure), literature, movies, events, or experiences. By starting with chanting and singing and sequencing further instruction, students self-level, understand harmonic function, improvise, arrange, and compose. For more ideas about incorporating creative activities, please see chapters 4 and 7.

APPLYING HARMONIC STRATEGIES TO ENSEMBLE MUSIC

Students learn from early experiences how to listen for chord progressions and chord resolutions. In Musical Example 10.26, a melody (trumpet), bass line (tuba), and inner voice (alto saxophone) from "Gallant March"[5] are presented. A sequence for teaching harmonic function for "Gallant March" is in Figure 10.16.

Musical Example 10.26 Melody, bass line, and inner voice from "Gallant March."

Sequence for Teaching Harmony for *Gallant March*.

1. The teacher first teaches the bass line selecting from strategies noted earlier. For this example, the teacher sings the bass line while demonstrating Curwen-Glover hand signs.

2. After hearing the bass line at least two times, students sing and hand sign with the teacher or the teacher demonstrates the hand signs while students use hand signs and sing.

3. Students aurally discover which notes on their instrument are *do* and *fa*.

4. Students play the bass line with the teacher modeling the hand signs. Students also play the bass line without teacher modeling hand signs.

5. When students can play the bass line, the teacher adds a new part, the E♭ alto saxophone. Students sing the bass line and the teacher sings the new part. The teacher asks if the new part was the same or different from their part. Both parts are sung again. The teacher also sings the E♭ part separate from the bass line but with the appropriate hand signs. Students sing the E♭ part.

6. Once students know the new part, they add their instruments. Divide students into two groups, one plays the bass line and the other plays the E♭ part. Another choice is the students play the bass line and the teacher plays the E♭ part. The groups can be switched so everyone experiences both parts.

7. The melody is added in the same format the other parts were taught. While students are learning the parts, they are also listening for balance within the ensemble, which assists with harmonic understanding.

Figure 10.16 Four-note melodic pattern.

MORE IDEAS FOR WINDING IT FORWARD
Transposition

Once students learn and understand that tonal centers can change, students can learn to transpose melodies by ear using patterns, melodies, and bass lines they have learned. For example, students first perform "Mary Had a Little Lamb" in the key originally presented. When given a different starting pitch, students begin on that note and rely on their ear to know when a note is missed. Students work toward performing the melody in a new key.

Student Leaders

Some students who move quickly through tonal or rhythmic concepts are also capable of leading patterns for the class to echo. In this role, students must maintain tonal or rhythmic context, remember the last pattern played, be prepared to start the next pattern in time, anticipate rhythm and melodic direction to perform, and have technical facility to model patterns on their instrument.

Returning to Mr. Mincy and Jean

Mr. Mincy (in the first and third vignettes), Jean (in the second vignette), and all students will develop musicianship skills by using the strategies in this chapter. These strategies help students to develop their sense of meter (beats and beat divisions in multiple meters) and tonality (simple harmonic functions in multiple tonalities), to audiate and perform melodies and bass lines, and to feel the inherent musical flow of phrases and melodic passages. On the companion website, we outline thirteen weeks of sequenced instructional strategies—with opportunities to wind instruction back and forward—that Mr. Mincy might use to prepare, present, and perform "The Washington Post March."

CONCLUSION

Teaching students to move, chant, sing, and create in instrumental music offers numerous benefits to all aspects of musicianship. We have successfully used these strategies with instrumental ensembles at all levels; even a few minutes of moving, chanting, singing, and creating each day helps students develop aural skills, technique, expression, and increased comprehension of music. Contextualizing these activities in tonal and rhythm hierarchies not only supports sequential musical development but also provides a practical framework for teachers to wind activities back and forward. If educating all students is our goal, then it is critical to have a repertoire of strategies that allow teachers to create simultaneous learning environments (principle 3) in which individual students' learning needs are honored (principle 1). Teaching in this way allows all students multiple access points for developing personal musicianship to the fullest extent possible through their instrumental music education (principle 2).

NOTES

1. *Folk Song Suite* (Ralph Vaughan Williams), published by Boosey and Hawkes.
2. "During the tonal babble stage, children attempt to sing with speaking voice quality. Relationships among sounds they make have little or nothing in common with context established by the culture.... In the rhythm babble stage, children make different sounds and erratic movements. These sounds and movements are not in consistent tempo, they are close together, and contextually unnatural to adult culture" (Gordon, 2013, p. 6).
3. "Procession of the Cyborgs" (Mark Williams), published by Alfred Music Publishing.
4. Depending on students' range on their instruments, a teacher may choose to teach the dominant chord in first inversion to make simpler the voice leading between *do* and *ti* in the lowest voice. Similarly, a subdominant chord could be introduced in second inversion, leaving the lowest voice on *do*. Regardless of the voicing a teacher might select, the harmonic objective is for students to learn to hear and perform tonic, dominant, and subdominant functions.
5. "Gallant March" (Michael Sweeney), published by Hal Leonard Corporation.

REFERENCES

Azzara, C. D., & Grunow, R. F. (2006). *Developing musicianship through improvisation.* Chicago, IL: GIA.

Bernhard, H. C. (2002). Singing in instrumental music education: Research and implications. *Update: Applications of Research in Music Education, 22,* 28–35.

Center for Applied Special Technology. (2011). *Universal Design for Learning guidelines version 2.0.* Wakefield, MA: Author.

Conway, C., Marshall, H., & Hartz, B. (2014). Movement instruction to facilitate beat competency in instrumental music. *Music Educators Journal, 100*(3), 61–66.

Gordon, E. E. (2012). *Learning sequences in music: A contemporary learning music theory.* Chicago, IL: GIA.

Gordon, E. E. (2013). *Music learning theory for newborn and young children.* Chicago, IL: GIA.

Green, L. (2014). *Hear, listen, play! How to free your students' aural, improvisation, and performance skills*. New York, NY: Oxford University Press.

Grunow, R. F. (2005). Music learning theory: A catalyst for change in beginning instrumental music instruction. In M. Runfola & C. C. Taggart (Eds.), *The development and practical application of music learning theory* (pp. 179–200). Chicago, IL: GIA.

Grunow, R. F., Gordon, E. E., & Azzara, C. D. (2001). *Jump right in: The instrumental series*. Chicago, IL: GIA.

Hammel, A. M., & Harvey, S. A. (2009, March). *Do they hear what you hear?* Workshop presented at the Organization of American Kodály Educators National Conference, Washington, DC.

Harvey, S. A. (2010, March). *Instrumental applications of Kodály and Gordon*. Workshop presented at Manchester College, Manchester, IN.

Woody, R. H., & Lehmann, A. C. (2010). Student musicians' ear playing ability as a function of vernacular music experiences. *Journal of Research in Music Education, 58*(2), 101–115.

Teaching Students to Sing

JOY ANDERSON, *Shenandoah Valley Children's Choir*
and Eastern Mennonite School
ROBERTA Y. HICKOX, *Halifax Area School District,*
Halifax, Pennsylvania

Singing on pitch is learned behavior, just as walking, reading, driving, playing the violin, and doing algebra are learned behaviors. And just as a typical child or adult can, with varying amounts of time and effort, learn to walk, read, drive, play the violin, and do algebra, so everyone, or nearly everyone, can learn to sing on pitch. Even including the word "nearly" in that sentence is a stretch. We have witnessed highly competent pitch matchers with profound hearing impairment and have known a number of students whose continued perseverance and incremental improvement through years of work on pitch matching eventually resulted in high levels of singing expertise. The voice is a musical instrument, and part of our job as music educators is to teach our students how to "play" this instrument competently and with enjoyment and satisfaction. If pitch matching is a sequentially developed skill, the first step in the sequence is actually the teacher's—believing that all of our students can become *experts* in the skill of singing and being unwilling to let ourselves off the hook by accepting the false idea that some people are meant to be singers and others are not.

It is essential that teachers formatively assess student audiation to individualize and improve instruction. Singing is the ideal performance medium for demonstration of audiation: all students possess a singing voice and carry it with them to each class, lesson, or ensemble. Instruction in singing is crucial if singing is to be used as a tool to demonstrate understanding. Because singing is used to establish audiation before application to instruments, students in instrumental ensembles will benefit from vocal instruction as well. The information on the teaching of singing is offered here as a separate appendix because of its universal application to musicians of all age groups and settings.

FACTORS AFFECTING PITCH MATCHING

Before discussing the sequential process of developing pitch-matching skill, it may be useful to list other factors likely to affect success. It is important to foster a classroom culture that emphasizes that the skill of singing is attainable through effort and persistence. This idea suggests the following extension: that it is okay—crucial, actually—to be corrected, and that being corrected, like being corrected for an incorrect answer in math, is not a personal judgment, but feedback for continued improvement. When students are commended for effort and persistence rather than for innate singing talent, and when the teacher creates a culture in which students learn that it is respectful and helpful to correct inaccuracy, and actually disrespectful and neglectful to allow it to go unnoticed, the learning environment becomes one in which the teacher is free to correct and commend without hurt feelings. Of course, as with all teacher-learner interactions, correction of singing pitches must be done positively and sensitively.

During every step, as children learn to sing on pitch, it is critical that they hear good vocal models of singers singing well, preferably including the singing range appropriate for children. Teacher performance of appealing songs, in the context of song story books, call-and-response songs, song tales, and other opportunities for teacher singing, not only allows children to hear good singing but also conveys that singing is a pleasurable activity. Good-quality recordings of children singing well may also be used, along with instrumental recordings, for movement, beat-keeping, entering and exiting, and other activities. Again, the voices of children and women singing in a healthy children's singing range are best at this stage and for this goal. While children should not be forbidden to sing with these recordings, teachers should try to choose activities that encourage listening as a large part of the experience.

Another factor that may affect success in teaching children to sing on pitch is the use of accompaniment. When the majority of classroom singing is performed with piano accompaniment, children have more trouble hearing their own voices, and the teacher can be fooled into thinking students are singing more on pitch than they actually are. Even if the majority of students are singing on pitch with piano accompaniment, they are frequently learning to use accompaniment as a "crutch" and may have trouble singing in tune when the piano is absent. These issues can become more critical when recorded accompaniment is used, as the instrumentation and arrangements are often more complex and potentially distracting. A song's text can also be distracting, particularly if the melodic line is complex or the mode is unfamiliar: allowing students to audiate the melody without the text can increase their ability to sing on pitch as they focus more on the resting tone and melodic context. Accompaniment, when artfully composed, and especially when live, can add depth, interest, and expressiveness to singing when singers have already demonstrated competence, but should be used sparingly in early stages of singing instruction and at each introduction of a new tone set. A cappella singing is most conducive to the ability of students to hear and assess their own singing progress, and to the teacher being able to hear and make those assessments. Guitar, dulcimer, and other instruments that play softer, simpler accompaniments are good options as well.

Finally, appropriate pitching of children's singing is crucial. Children's vocal mechanisms are smaller than those of adults and, on average, are not capable of producing pitches as low as even the average adult female voice can produce. When adults sing in a pitch range that may be comfortable for them, but that includes pitches that children's voices simply cannot match, children learn to sing off-pitch habitually. Even when children can physically match the lower pitches asked of them, proximity to the speaking voice can make it difficult for them to hear and feel the voice as a "singing voice" and develop the skill of singing in tune. Opinions vary about the best pitch range to begin singing instruction with young children, but strong consensus emphasizes not asking young beginning singers to sing below the D above middle C (D4) or above the D an octave higher (D5):

We have found the most effective pitch range for young children to be the fifth from F above middle C through the C above it (F4-C5):

This higher end of the generally accepted best pitch range for young children encourages head tone singing, immediately differentiating the singing voice, aurally and physically, from the speaking voice. If possible, teachers should initially both model singing and pitch student singing in this range. This may seem high to many adult singers, but inviting children to begin singing in this range encourages accurate pitch matching and a healthy, clear tone quality.

Vocal Exploration Activities

A sequence for teaching students to use their voices would start with exploring the full range of the voice. Some activities, in addition to those ideas found in chapters 3 and 5, include the following:

- Sirens: Students imitate fire engine siren sounds.
- Draw in the air: Students "sing" what the teacher/student "draws" in the air.
- Animal sounds: Students imitate animal sounds and categorize them as "head voice" or "other" (big dog, lion—"other"; owl, wolf, little dog—"head voice").
- Students "zip up" their zippers, moving their voices from low to head voice.
- Students "sing" what the teacher's flashlight is showing.
- Students perform the rhyme or song with the vocal use indicated on a chart by the teacher: speak whisper shout sing.
- Students "sing," following the direction of the window shade as the teacher moves it up and down.
- Koosh game: Students form a standing circle. The first student looks at the person he or she is choosing, tosses the Koosh or beanbag underhand, "sings" in head voice as the Koosh/beanbag is tossed, and sits when his or her turn is completed. The next student chooses another person and performs the same tasks: look, toss, sing, sit. At the end of the round, the students review the pattern they've created, or "who tossed to whom." Subsequent rounds of the game are played with the same students tossing in the same order, with the goal of completing the round faster each time. Each round of the game can be timed if desired, with the additional

rule that each non–head voice sound (talking, whispering, etc.) will add an additional second onto the class time (see Figure A.1 and Photo A.1).

(a) The koosh game can be performed in a canon with the following changes: The first student will look, toss, and sing. After the koosh has been passed by about one-third of the class members, a second koosh or beanbag can be tossed in the same order. A flurry of head voice sounds will occur! After tossing the second object, each player will sit until the round is over. Subsequent rounds of the game are played with the same students tossing in the same order, with the goal of completing the round faster each time. Each round of the game can be timed if desired, with the additional rule that each non-head voice sound (talking, whispering, etc.) will add an additional second onto the class time.

(b)

Figure A.1 (a) Koosh canon and (b) Koosh ball.

Accessing the Head Voice

As students gain competence in expanding the range of their voices, they begin to use their head voices purposefully. From perhaps unintentional occurrences of head voice use, students will be asked to produce a head voice sound at will, as in the following activities:

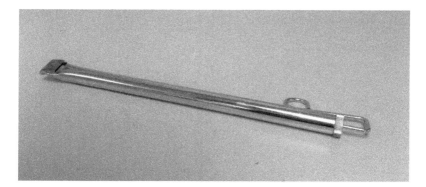

Figure A.2 Slide whistle.

- The teacher plays the slide whistle for each student to imitate individually (Photo A.2).

Figure A.3 Slinky.

- Slinky: Students "attach" their voices to the end of the slinky and use their head voices to "sing" as the teacher manipulates the slinky (Photo A.3).

Selective Use of Head Voice

Playfully using the head voice in rhymes and song material (by alternating with the teacher's singing) will expand the students' abilities, as in the examples that follow:

- "I Love My Little Rooster": Students listen to the teacher singing the song, joining in to sing "Cock-a-doodle-doo!" in their head voices (Musical Example A.1).

Musical Example A.1

My Little Rooster

Traditional

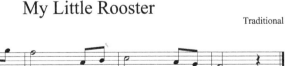

- "Cowboy Joe": The teacher speaks this story by John M. Feierabend, with the students using their head voices to perform "Yee-haw!" at the end of each verse.

- "Little Red Caboose": Students listen to the teacher singing the song, joining in to sing "toot toot!" in their head voices at the end (Musical Example A.2).

Musical Example A.2

Little Red Caboose

Traditional

Lit tle red ca-boose,   lit-tle red ca-boose,   lit-tle red ca-boose be-hind the train

smoke-stack on its back, chug-gin' on down the track,   lit-tle red ca-boose be-hind the train. Toot toot!

- "Johnny, Whoops": Students speak and demonstrate the finger play, tapping on each finger tip as they speak. On the "whoops!" students use their head voices (Musical Example A.3).

Musical Example A.3

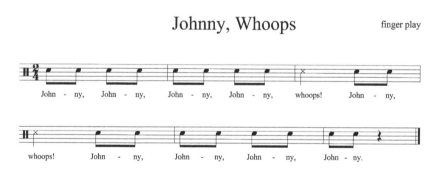

Johnny, Whoops

finger play

John - ny, John - ny, John - ny, John - ny, whoops! John - ny,

whoops! John - ny, John - ny, John - ny, John - ny.

Why Isn't My Student Matching Pitch?

When a student does not match pitch, the first determination the teacher must make is whether this inability is due to difficulty audiating pitches, such as recognizing differences in pitch between two singers (possibly one of those voices the teacher's), or whether the student can audiate the pitches but cannot match them with his or her voice. These are two entirely different issues and must be dealt with in different ways. Diagnosing this can be introduced through a variety of activities, discussed in the following sections.

Correct/Incorrect Melody Game The teacher tells students that he or she will sing a familiar song. They are to indicate when he or she is singing the melody correctly or incorrectly (in tune or not in tune) by showing thumbs up or thumbs down. The teacher begins singing well in tune but then at some point begins to sing the melody incorrectly. This game can become an assessment for individual student audiation by having students listen and give thumb signals with their eyes closed. Initially, the out-of-tune singing should be performed very obviously—extremely out of tune. In later experiences with the game, as students' audiation skills become more honed, the tuning issues can become more subtle.

Pitch-Matching Game The teacher invites a student with strong and consistent pitch-matching skills to be his or her partner. The teacher tells the class that he or she will sing a tonal pattern and then the chosen student will echo him or her, either correctly or incorrectly. The teacher may whisper to the chosen singer whether to echo correctly or not, or that student may make that choice himself or herself. Other students indicate whether the echo was correct or incorrect. The chosen student should then reveal the correct answer (which should already have been obvious to most students). Again, having students listen and indicate their opinions with their eyes closed will enable the teacher to assess which students can hear pitch inconsistencies and which cannot yet. Students may also be asked questions such as "Was the echo higher or lower than what I sang?"

Later, after the game has been played several times and emotional safety has been well established, a student who is having pitch-matching difficulty may be chosen to be the "echoer." Having that student give feedback about whether or not he or she was matching pitch and, if not matching pitch, whether he or she was higher or lower than the teacher can be very helpful. It is not uncommon for a student to be able to hear whether two other people were correctly matching pitch, but to have trouble distinguishing correct or incorrect pitch matching when one of the voices is his or her own. Frequent repetitions of these "games" will allow emerging pitch matchers opportunities to improve their audiation skills and will provide the teacher with opportunities to assess skill improvement.

If a student's inability to match pitch seems to be due to audiation issues, this usually presents a greater challenge than if pitch issues are due to not yet knowing how to "play the instrument" (the voice). However, even students who have trouble with tonal audiation can learn to sing in tune!

Music Aptitude and Pitch Matching

Music aptitude is innate but not inherent: students are born with a certain level of potential to audiate music, but this potential is not genetic. Aptitude is developmental in early childhood and with nurturing can be maintained at birth level; aptitude that is unsupported can decrease. Music aptitude stabilizes around age nine (Gordon, 2012). Administering a valid and reliable aptitude test is crucial when working with students of any age, but particularly with students whose aptitude is developmental (before age nine). We recommend the use of the Primary Measures of Music Audiation (Gordon, 1979) and Intermediate Measures of Music Audiation (Gordon, 1982) as instruments to measure music aptitude in elementary-age students, as they are standardized for kindergarten through sixth grade. Middle school students and above can be tested using the Advanced Measures of Music Audiation (Gordon, 1989) or the Music Aptitude Profile (Gordon, 1965). Scores from a music aptitude test are extremely valuable to the music teacher for use in differentiating instruction and designing curriculum for all individuals in a class or ensemble, as the score serves as a baseline of what each student audiates tonally and rhythmically. A student whose music aptitude is measured in the 80th percentile or higher tonally or rhythmically may need additional challenges in class (more difficult patterns and sight-reading, additional or fewer parameters when improvising), and a student who measures in the 80th percentile or higher tonally and rhythmically may need additional extracurricular experiences such as a dance class, participation in a children's chorus, or private lessons to remain engaged and challenged. As these aptitude tests are not standardized for students with special needs, the teacher must be particularly reflective and thoughtful about differentiating for students with special needs, as they will not have an accurately measured baseline of audiation.

The guideline of a tonal music aptitude score can aid the teacher in guiding student pitch matching. If a student has a lower tonal music aptitude score and does not match pitch, he or she may need many additional listenings to a song or pattern before he or she has fully audiated the song or pattern. Students with a lower tonal music aptitude may learn the lyrics of a song well before they have audiated the melody, and if they are encouraged to sing before audiation is complete, they will often not match pitch. By identifying students with lower tonal music aptitude, the teacher can offer more listening opportunities by singing the song many times (asking questions about the text or the form, or having the students sing a drone, patsch the beat, conduct, or tap an ostinato), singing the melody on a neutral syllable to allow the students to focus on the pitches, and perhaps asking the students with higher music aptitude (who will likely audiate the song quickly and need an additional challenge) to sing the song for the class to extend the number of listening opportunities.

If a student has an average or above-average tonal music aptitude score and does not match pitch, he or she may need additional help with vocal production: this student audiates the pattern but cannot reproduce it accurately. It can be very frustrating for students to hear the music but not be able to sing it well and, if it goes undiagnosed or unaddressed, can result in behavior problems or lack of participation. We have found that daily vocal exploration activities incorporating the head voice (like those described in this appendix) help all students warm up their voices and can especially impact those who need a frequent reminder to feel and use their head voices. When the teacher has identified several students who have an average or above-average tonal music aptitude score and struggle with pitch matching, the teacher can seat those students near others who sing well in their head registers for comparison, encourage them to use "elephant ears" (see later) to hear themselves sing, give many opportunities for those students to label others' singing as "uses head voice" or "other," and allow them to find their head voices through a quick siren or zipper sound before attempting to sing the pattern or song.

The importance of solo singing cannot be overemphasized. Students need to hear themselves sing alone to judge their use of head voice, their intonation, their ability to sing expressively, and their audiation of meter, tonality, and form. Frequent opportunities to echo tonal patterns, chain a phrase of a song, sing a motif of a song, sing the response of a song, or sing an assigned solfège syllable throughout a song increase the students' ability to assess their own singing and decreases their inhibitions. It also requires the students to audiate the entire song in their head to sing the segment of the song to which they are assigned. Feedback for all students' singing is important for growth, and it is especially important to note improvement for a student who needs many attempts to use a head voice. It is common for the class to erupt in cheering when that student succeeds in producing a head voice after many attempts!

It should never be assumed that a student won't match pitch, but rather that he or she can't match pitch yet. By determining students' tonal music aptitude scores, the teacher will have useful information to help guide the student's instruction and to facilitate pitch matching for all students. Music aptitude scores are a baseline and should never be used to discriminate against students or deny participation in classes or ensembles. Above all, the establishment of a safe singing zone, honest feedback, and teacher commitment to ALL students singing well and on pitch will ensure that your classroom remains free from the misconception that there are "singers" and "nonsingers."

Some additional thoughts about the use of head voice in the music class-room are as follows:

- Space bubble: Students may be able to better evaluate the use of their head voices if they have a "space bubble" around them. If students are sitting too close to their neighbors, they may not be able to adequately hear their own voices but will make changes based on the sound of their neighbors' voices instead.
- Elephant ears: Students can hear their own singing and the singing of their neighbors if they cup their hands around the backs of their ears to form "elephant ears" (Photo A.4).

Figure A.4 Elephant ears.

- Sing until you can't hear your own voice: Students will occasionally not match pitch so that their voices sound different from their neigh-bors' voices and ~~therefore they~~ can therefore hear themselves singing. Students need to be encouraged to "sing until you can't hear your own voice," with the understanding that when everyone sings in their head voices and matches pitch, all voices will blend until individual voices are not distinguished.

Vocal Damage

When students are unsuccessful at producing a head tone, this can be due to several possible factors. If they have not been producing head tone sounds as part of play, and particularly if their speaking voices are low or lack much inflection, the feeling of varying pitch may be completely new. In this case, continued playful opportunities to work on this skill will likely produce a successful head voice eventually. Listening to the teacher's voice (or that of another student) and indicating if the teacher or student is in his or her head voice can help these students too. A final caution is to be aware of vocal damage. Even at this young age, children can sometimes present vocal problems due to overuse, (shouting), allergies, reflux, or other factors. One indication that inability to demonstrate a head tone may be due to vocal damage is if the child successfully demonstrates a wide pitch range on a scoop, slide, or siren, in a low to medium register, and seems to be using his or her vocal mechanism in a way that should be producing a higher pitch but is only able to produce an airy sound. (Children who simply have not "found" their head voices typically continue to phonate, but at a lower register, rather than producing an "airy" sound in an attempt to reach a head tone.) The teacher who suspects vocal damage should contact the school's speech therapist for a vocal health consult, who can and suggest that the parent or guardian seek medical advice from an ear, nose, and throat specialist (a laryngologist) or vocal health specialist. Vocal damage can be diagnosed and treated, often without surgery, through vocal rest and rehabilitation with a vocal health specialist.

The voice is an instrument available to all students, and singing is a natural way to express oneself musically. It is our obligation to provide opportunity and training in vocal exploration, use of head voice, pitch matching, and healthy vocal production for our students so that singing may become a lifelong joy.

REFERENCES

Gordon, E. E. (1965). *Musical aptitude profile*. Chicago, IL: GIA.

Gordon, E. E. (1979). *Primary measures of music audiation*. Chicago, IL: GIA.

Gordon, E. E. (1982). *Intermediate measures of music audiation*. Chicago, IL: GIA.

Gordon, E. E. (1989). *Advanced measures of music audiation*. Chicago, IL: GIA.

Gordon, E. E. (2012). *Learning sequences in music: A contemporary learning theory*. Chicago, IL: GIA.

CPSIA information can be obtained
at www.ICGtesting.com
Printed in the USA
BVHW041600300822
645482BV00003B/14